Hamiltonian Monte Carlo Methods in Machine Learning

Hamiltonian Monte Carlo Methods in Machine Learning

Tshilidzi Marwala
School of Electrical and Electronic Engineering
University of Johannesburg
Auckland Park, South Africa

Wilson Tsakane Mongwe
School of Electrical and Electronic Engineering
University of Johannesburg
Auckland Park, South Africa

Rendani Mbuvha
School of Electronic Engineering and Computer Science
Queen Mary University of London
London, United Kingdom
School of Statistics and Actuarial Science
University of Witwatersrand
Braamfontein, South Africa

ELSEVIER

ACADEMIC PRESS
An imprint of Elsevier

Academic Press is an imprint of Elsevier
125 London Wall, London EC2Y 5AS, United Kingdom
525 B Street, Suite 1650, San Diego, CA 92101, United States
50 Hampshire Street, 5th Floor, Cambridge, MA 02139, United States
The Boulevard, Langford Lane, Kidlington, Oxford OX5 1GB, United Kingdom

Notices

ISBN: 978-0-443-19035-3

For information on all Academic Press publications
visit our website at https://www.elsevier.com/books-and-journals

Publisher: Mara E. Conner
Acquisitions Editor: Chris Katsaropoulos
Editorial Project Manager: Emily Thomson
Production Project Manager: Omer Mukthar
Cover Designer: Christian J. Bilbow

Typeset by VTeX

Working together
to grow libraries in
developing countries

www.elsevier.com • www.bookaid.org

We dedicate this book to all the great teachers of the world who use education to achieve peace and sustainable development.

Contents

List of figures   xiii

List of tables   xvii

Authors   xxi

Foreword   xxiii

Preface   xxv

Nomenclature   xxvii

List of symbols   xxix

1. Introduction to Hamiltonian Monte Carlo   1

    1.1. Introduction   1

    1.2. Background to Markov Chain Monte Carlo   6

    1.3. Metropolis-Hastings algorithm   8

    1.4. Metropolis Adjusted Langevin algorithm   10

    1.5. Hamiltonian Monte Carlo   11

    1.6. Magnetic Hamiltonian Monte Carlo   14

    1.7. Quantum-Inspired Hamiltonian Monte Carlo   16

    1.8. Separable Shadow Hamiltonian Hybrid Monte Carlo   18

    1.9. No-U-Turn Sampler algorithm   21

    1.10. Antithetic Hamiltonian Monte Carlo   24

    1.11. Book objectives   26

    1.12. Book contributions   27

    1.13. Conclusion   29

2. Sampling benchmarks and performance metrics   31

    2.1. Benchmark problems and datasets   31

2.1.1.   Banana shaped distribution   31

2.1.2.   Multivariate Gaussian distributions   31

2.1.3.   Neal's funnel density   32

2.1.4.   Merton jump-diffusion process model   32

2.1.5.   Bayesian logistic regression   33

2.1.6.   Bayesian neural networks   33

2.1.7.   Benchmark datasets   33

2.1.8.   Processing of the datasets   35

2.2.   Performance metrics   35

2.2.1.   Effective sample size   36

2.2.2.   Convergence analysis   37

2.2.3.   Predictive performance on unseen data   37

2.3.   Algorithm parameter tuning   38

2.4.   Conclusion   39

3.   Stochastic volatility Metropolis-Hastings   41

3.1.   Proposed methods   41

3.2.   Experiments   43

3.3.   Results and discussion   44

3.4.   Conclusion   51

4.   Quantum-inspired magnetic Hamiltonian Monte Carlo   53

4.1.   Proposed algorithm   53

4.2.   Experiment description   56

4.2.1.   Experiment settings   56

4.2.2.   Sensitivity to the vol-of-vol parameter   57

4.3.   Results and discussion   57

4.4.   Conclusion   59

5.   Generalised magnetic and shadow Hamiltonian Monte Carlo 63

5.1.   Proposed partial momentum retention algorithms   63

5.2. Experiment description 65

    5.2.1. Experiment settings 65

    5.2.2. Sensitivity to momentum refreshment parameter 66

5.3. Results and discussion 67

5.4. Conclusion 71

6. **Shadow Magnetic Hamiltonian Monte Carlo** **73**

6.1. Background 73

6.2. Shadow Hamiltonian for MHMC 74

6.3. Proposed Shadow Magnetic algorithm 75

6.4. Experiment description 77

    6.4.1. Experiment settings 77

    6.4.2. Sensitivity to momentum refreshment parameter 77

6.5. Results and discussion 78

6.6. Conclusion 81

7. **Adaptive Shadow Hamiltonian Monte Carlo** **83**

7.1. Proposed adaptive shadow algorithm 83

7.2. Experiment description 86

7.3. Results and discussion 86

7.4. Conclusion 89

8. **Adaptive noncanonical Hamiltonian Monte Carlo** **91**

8.1. Background 91

8.2. Proposed algorithm 92

8.3. Experiments 95

8.4. Results and discussion 96

8.5. Conclusions 100

9. **Antithetic Hamiltonian Monte Carlo techniques** **101**

9.1. Proposed antithetic samplers 101

9.2. Experiment description 102

9.3. Results and discussion 104

9.4. Conclusion 108

10. Bayesian neural network inference in wind speed nowcasting 109

10.1. Background 109

10.1.1. Automatic relevance determination 110

10.2. Experiment setup 113

10.2.1. WASA meteorological datasets 114

10.2.2. Relationship to wind power 115

10.2.3. Performance evaluation 116

10.2.4. Preliminary step size tuning runs 116

10.3. Results and discussion 117

10.3.1. Sampling performance 117

10.3.2. Predictive performance with ARD 120

10.3.3. ARD committees and feature importance 121

10.3.4. Re-training BNNs on relevant features 121

10.4. Conclusion 122

11. A Bayesian analysis of the efficacy of Covid-19 lockdown measures 123

11.1. Background 123

11.1.1. Review of compartment models for Covid-19 125

11.1.2. Lockdown alert levels 127

11.2. Methods 128

11.2.1. Infection data 128

11.2.2. The adjusted SIR model 129

11.2.3. Parameter inference using the No-U-Turn sampler 130

11.3. Results and discussion 130

11.3.1. Spreading rate under various lockdown alert levels 131

11.4. Conclusion   137

12. Probabilistic inference of equity option prices under
jump-diffusion processes   139
    12.1. Background   139
        12.1.1. Merton jump diffusion option pricing model   140
    12.2. Numerical experiments   141
        12.2.1. Data description   141
        12.2.2. Experiment description   142
    12.3. Results and discussions   142
    12.4. Conclusion   146

13. Bayesian inference of local government audit outcomes   149
    13.1. Background   149
    13.2. Experiment description   150
        13.2.1. Data description   150
        13.2.2. Financial ratio calculation   151
        13.2.3. Bayesian logistic regression with ARD   152
    13.3. Results and discussion   153
    13.4. Conclusion   158

14. Conclusions   159
    14.1. Summary of contributions   159
    14.2. Ongoing and future work   161

A. Separable shadow Hamiltonian   163
    A.1. Derivation of separable shadow Hamiltonian   163
    A.2. S2HMC satisfies detailed balance   164
    A.3. Derivatives from non-canonical Poisson brackets   165

B. ARD posterior variances   167

C. ARD committee feature selection   169

D. Summary of audit outcome literature survey   173

References   175

Index   185

List of figures

FIGURE 1.1   Illustration of the conservation of the Hamiltonian (i.e., total energy) through time as the skater moves from position A to C.   12

FIGURE 1.2   The algorithmic contributions of this book are highlighted as the green (gray in print version) blocks. The arrows indicate the relationship between the different algorithms and show how our proposed algorithms are derived from existing methods.   27

FIGURE 3.1   Inference results across each dataset over thirty iterations of each algorithm. The first row is the effective sample size while the second row is the time-normalised effective sample size for each dataset.   45

FIGURE 3.2   Negative log-likelihood diagnostic trace plots for various targets. These are traces plots from a single run of the MCMC chain. a) Diagnostic negative log-likelihood trace plots for the Fraud dataset and b) Diagnostic negative log-likelihood trace plots for the multivariate Gaussian with $D = 10$. The other targets produce similar convergence behaviour.   46

FIGURE 3.3   Autocorrelation plots for the first dimension across the various targets. These are autocorrelations from a single run of the MCMC chain. a) Autocorrelation plot for the first dimension on the Neal funnel for $D = 20$ and b) Autocorrelation plot for the first dimension on the multivariate Gaussian with $D = 20$.   47

FIGURE 3.4   Predictive performance for all the sampling methods on the real world classification datasets. The results were averaged over thirty runs of each algorithm. a) ROC curves for the Heart dataset and b) ROC curves for Australian credit dataset.   48

FIGURE 3.5   Predictive performance for all the sampling methods on the real world classification datasets. The results were averaged over thirty runs of each algorithm. a) ROC curves for the Fraud dataset and b) ROC curves for German dataset.   49

FIGURE 4.1   Acceptance rates, ESS and ESS/Time for ten runs of QIHMC (blue (dark gray in print version)) and QIMHMC (orange (light gray in print version)) on the a) Australian and b) German credit datasets with varying choices of the vol-of-vol β parameter. The results indicate that these metrics are a decreasing function of the vol-of-vol β parameter, with QIMHMC decreasing at a slower rate than QIHMC.   58

FIGURE 4.2   Diagnostic trace-plots of the negative log-likelihood across various targets averaged over ten runs of each method. These results show that all the MCMC methods have converged on all the targets.   59

FIGURE 4.3   Results for the datasets over ten runs of each method. For each dataset, the plots on the first row show the multivariate effective sample size and the plots on the second row show the multivariate effective sample size normalised by execution time (in seconds). For all the plots, the larger the value the better the method. The dark horizontal line in each violin plot represents the mean value over ten runs of each algorithm.   60

FIGURE 5.1   Acceptance rates, ESS and ESS/Time for ten runs of PHMC (blue (dark gray in print version)), PMHMC (orange (light gray in print version)), and PS2HMC (green (mid gray in print version)) on the a) Australian and b) German credit datasets with varying choices of the momentum refreshment parameter ρ. The results indicate that the ESS metrics are increasing functions of ρ, while the acceptance rate remains constant across all values of ρ.   67

FIGURE 5.2   Diagnostic trace-plot of the negative log-likelihood showing the convergence behaviour of the algorithms on the Bitcoin dataset. The methods which employ partial momentum refreshment converge faster than the original algorithms. This plot was produced by using $\rho = 0.7$. Two thousand samples were generated with no burn-in period. The other settings are as outlined in Section 5.2.1. The results are for a single run of each algorithm.   68

FIGURE 5.3   Results for the targets over ten runs of each method. For each dataset, the plots on the first row show the multivariate effective sample size and the plots on the second row show the multivariate effective sample size normalised by execution time (in seconds). The dark horizontal line in each violin plot represents the mean value over ten runs of each algorithm. For all the plots, the larger the value, the better the method.   69

FIGURE 6.1   Impact of the step size on the acceptance rate of SMHMC and MHMC on the Airfoil dataset. The results show that SMHMC maintains higher acceptance rates than MHMC as the step size increases. Three thousand samples were generated for each run, with the first one thousand samples being the burn-in period. The results displayed in this plot were averaged over five runs of the algorithms.   74

FIGURE 6.2   Acceptance rates, ESS and ESS/Time for ten chains of PMHMC (blue (dark gray in print version)) and SMHMC (orange (light gray in print version)) the Australian credit dataset with varying choices of ρ. The ESS metrics are an increasing function of ρ with the acceptance rate of SMHMC being larger than PMHMC for the same step size ϵ.   78

FIGURE 6.3   Diagnostic trace-plots of the negative log-likelihood across various targets averaged over ten runs of each method. These results show that all the MCMC methods have converged on all the targets.   78

FIGURE 6.4   Results for the datasets over ten runs of each method. For each dataset, the plots on the first row show the multivariate effective sample size and the plots on the second row show the multivariate effective sample size normalised by execution time (in seconds). For all the plots, the larger the value, the better the method. The dark horizontal line in each violin plot represents the mean value over ten runs of each algorithm.   79

FIGURE 7.1   Diagnostic trace-plots of the negative log-likelihood across various targets averaged over ten runs of each method. These results show that all the MCMC methods have converged on all the targets.   86

FIGURE 7.2   Results for the datasets over ten runs of each method. For each dataset, the plots on the first row show the multivariate effective sample size and the plots on the second row show the multivariate effective sample size normalised by execution time (in seconds). For all the plots, the larger the value, the better the method. The dark horizontal line in each violin plot represents the mean value over ten runs of each algorithm.   88

FIGURE 8.1   Results for the datasets over 10 runs of each method. For each dataset, the plots show the multivariate effective sample size. For all the plots, the larger the value the better the method. The dark horizontal line in each violin plot represents the mean value over 10 runs of each algorithm.   96

FIGURE 8.2   Diagnostic negative log-likelihood trace plots for various targets. Similar results are observed for targets not included in the plot. Note that HMC-NUTS is the No-U-Turn Sampler while MHMC-NUTS is the Adaptive MHMC method.   97

FIGURE 9.1   Diagnostic trace-plots of the negative log-likelihood across various targets averaged over ten runs of each method. These results show that all the MCMC methods have converged on all the targets. X is the primary chain and Y is the secondary chain for each method.   104

FIGURE 9.2   Results for the datasets over ten runs of each method across the BLR and BNN
                    datasets. For each dataset, the plots on the first row show the multivariate
                    effective sample size and the plots on the second row show the multivariate
                    effective sample size normalised by execution time (in seconds). For all the plots,
                    the larger the value, the better the method. The dark horizontal line in each
                    violin plot represents the mean value over ten runs of each algorithm.   105
FIGURE 10.1   Prior distribution for weights under various variance settings.   111
FIGURE 10.2   Map showing the locations of the locations of the weather stations included in
                    the wind datasets.   114
FIGURE 10.3   Negative log-likelihood trace plots for MH (orange (light gray in print version)),
                    HMC (blue (dark gray in print version)), S2HMC (green (mid gray in print version))
                    for weather station WM01 Alexander Bay.   117
FIGURE 10.4   Negative log-likelihood trace plots for MH (orange (light gray in print version)),
                    HMC (blue (dark gray in print version)), S2HMC (green (mid gray in print version))
                    for weather station WM05 Napier.   117
FIGURE 10.5   Negative log-likelihood trace plots for MH (orange (light gray in print version)),
                    HMC (blue (dark gray in print version)), S2HMC (green (mid gray in print version))
                    for weather station WM13 Jozini.   118
FIGURE 10.6   Boxplots showing the distribution of ESS over ten independent chains for the
                    WM01 Alexandra Bay weather station.   119
FIGURE 10.7   Boxplots showing the distribution of ESS over ten independent chains for the
                    WM05 Naiper weather station.   119
FIGURE 10.8   Boxplots showing the distribution of ESS over ten independent chains for the
                    WM13 Jozini weather station.   120
FIGURE 11.1   Diagram illustrating the three states and two transition rates of the SIR model.   129
FIGURE 11.2   Fitted model and actual new cases data (until 18 December 2021) based on the
                    adjusted SIR model with various change points.   132
FIGURE 11.3   NUTS trace plots each parameter of the time varying spreading rate adjusted SIR
                    model.   133
FIGURE 11.4   Posterior Parameter distributions for the SIR model with lockdown alert levels,
                    outlined in Table 11.1, as change points.   134
FIGURE 12.1   Calibrated jump-diffusion parameters from the MALA, HMC and NUTS algorithms.   144
FIGURE 12.2   Root mean square error distribution for the call and put option data using the
                    MALA, HMC and NUTS methods.   145
FIGURE 12.3   Averaged option price predictions for the call and put option data using the
                    MALA, HMC and NUTS algorithms.   146
FIGURE 13.1   Inference results for the BLR-ARD model across various sampling methods.
                    a) Effective sample sizes, b) Effective sample sizes normalised by execution time
                    and c) Predictive performance based on the AUC.   154
FIGURE 13.2   Average posterior standard deviations from the random walk MH and MALA
                    algorithms. The higher the value, the more important the financial ratio is to
                    modelling audit opinions.   155
FIGURE 13.3   Average posterior standard deviations from the HMC, MHMC and S2HMC
                    algorithms. The higher the value, the more important the financial ratio is to
                    modelling audit opinions.   156
FIGURE B.1   Mean posterior variances from the MH, HMC and S2HMC ARD model which
                    indicate the relevance of each attribute for each of the datasets.   167

List of tables

TABLE 1.1	This table highlights the gaps in the literature that we have identified. A NO entry means that the item is yet to be considered in the literature. A N/A entry means that the item is not applicable to the algorithm. For the items that have already been addressed in the literature, we provide an appropriate reference.	26
TABLE 2.1	Descriptive statistics for the financial markets datasets.	34
TABLE 2.2	Real-world datasets used in this book. N represents the number of observations. BJDP is Bayesian JDP, BLR is Bayesian Logistic Regression, and BNN represents Bayesian Neural Networks. D represents the number of model parameters.	35
TABLE 2.3	Common classification performance measures.	38
TABLE 2.4	Common regression performance measures.	38
TABLE 2.5	Step size and trajectory length parameters used for HMC and MHMC in this book. These methods serve as the baselines against which the novel methods presented in this book are compared. Five thousand samples were used to tune the step size for the given trajectory length using primal-dual averaging. The target acceptance rate was set to 80%.	39
TABLE 3.1	Results averaged over thirty runs of each method for the jump diffusion process datasets. Each row corresponds to the results for a specific method for each performance metric. NLL is the negative log-likelihood.	50
TABLE 3.2	Results averaged over thirty runs of each method for the logistic regression datasets. Each row corresponds to the results for a specific method for each performance metric. NLL is the negative log-likelihood.	51
TABLE 4.1	Banana shaped distribution results averaged over ten runs. The time t is in seconds. The values in **bold** indicate that the particular method outperforms the other methods on that specific metric.	59
TABLE 4.2	Multivariate Gaussian distribution results averaged over ten runs. The time t is in seconds. The values in **bold** indicate that the particular method outperforms the other methods on that specific metric.	61
TABLE 4.3	Bayesian logistic regression results averaged over ten runs. The time t is in seconds. The values in **bold** indicate that the particular method outperforms the other methods on that specific metric.	61
TABLE 5.1	JDP results averaged over ten runs. The time t is in seconds. The values in **bold** indicate that the particular method outperforms the other methods on that specific metric. AR stands for the acceptance rate of the generated samples post the burn-in period.	68
TABLE 5.2	Multivariate Gaussian distribution results averaged over ten runs. The time t is in seconds. The values in **bold** indicate that the particular method outperforms the other methods on that specific metric. AR stands for the acceptance rate of the generated samples post the burn-in period.	70
TABLE 5.3	BLR results averaged over ten runs. The time t is in seconds. The values in **bold** indicate that the particular method outperforms the other methods on that specific metric. AR stands for the acceptance rate of the generated samples post the burn-in period.	71
TABLE 6.1	Multivariate Gaussian distribution with $D = 10$ results averaged over ten runs. The time t is in seconds. The values in **bold** indicate that the particular method outperforms the other methods on that specific metric. AR stands for the acceptance rate of the generated samples post the burn-in period.	80

TABLE 6.2   Protein dataset results averaged over ten runs. The time t is in seconds. The values in **bold** indicate that the particular method outperforms the other methods on that specific metric. AR stands for the acceptance rate of the generated samples post the burn-in period.   80

TABLE 6.3   Heart dataset results averaged over ten runs. The time t is in seconds. The values in **bold** indicate that the particular method outperforms the other methods on that specific metric. AR stands for the acceptance rate of the generated samples post the burn-in period.   81

TABLE 6.4   Pima dataset results averaged over ten runs. The time t is in seconds. The values in **bold** indicate that the particular method outperforms the other methods on that specific metric. AR stands for the acceptance rate of the generated samples post the burn-in period.   81

TABLE 7.1   Banana shaped distribution results averaged over ten runs. The time t is in seconds. The values in **bold** indicate that the particular method outperforms the other methods on that specific metric. Average L represents the average trajectory length used to generate the post-burn-in samples.   87

TABLE 7.2   Multivariate Gaussian distribution with $D = 10$ results averaged over ten runs. The time t is in seconds. The values in **bold** indicate that the particular method outperforms the other methods on that specific metric. Average L represents the average trajectory length used to generate the post-burn-in samples.   87

TABLE 7.3   Neal's funnel density with $D = 25$ results averaged over ten runs. The time t is in seconds. The values in **bold** indicate that the particular method outperforms the other methods on that specific metric. Average L represents the average trajectory length used to generate the post-burn-in samples.   87

TABLE 7.4   BLR dataset results averaged over ten runs. The time t is in seconds. The values in **bold** indicate that the particular method outperforms the other methods on that specific metric. Average L represents the average trajectory length used to generate the post-burn-in samples.   89

TABLE 8.1   Jump diffusion results averaged over 10 runs. The time t is in seconds. NLL stands for negative log-likelihood. The values in **bold** indicate that the particular method outperforms the other methods on that specific metric. The relative speed up metric is with reference to the method with the lowest time normalised multivariate effective sample size. Note that A-MHMC represents Adaptive MHMC.   98

TABLE 8.2   Mean results over 10 runs of each algorithm. Each column represents the mean value for the specific method. For example, column three shows the mean results for MMHC-50. The execution time t is in seconds. The values in **bold** indicate that the particular method outperforms the other methods on that specific metric. The relative speed up metric is with reference to the method with the lowest time normalised multivariate effective sample size. AUC represents the area under the ROC curve. Note that A-MHMC represents Adaptive MHMC.   99

TABLE 9.1   Mean results over ten runs of each algorithm for the BLR datasets. Each column represents the mean value for the specific method. The execution time t is in seconds. The values in **bold** indicate that the particular method outperforms the other methods on that specific metric.   106

TABLE 9.2   Mean results over ten runs of each algorithm for the BNN datasets. Each column represents the mean value for the specific method. The execution time t is in seconds. The values in **bold** indicate that the particular method outperforms the other methods on that specific metric.   107

TABLE 10.1   An illustration of the ARD committee framework with p features and n samplers.   113

TABLE 10.2   Locations of weather stations considered for wind speed modelling.   114

TABLE 10.3   Descriptions of features utilised in the WASA data sets. All summary statistics (mean, max, etc.) are over ten minutes intervals.   115

TABLE 10.4   Experimental Settings for the BNNs and Sampling runs.   116

TABLE 10.5	Step size selections for each dataset after initial dual averaging runs.	116
TABLE 10.6	Mean ESS statistics over ten independent chains each with 5000 samples using MH, HMC and S2HMC on all datasets.	118
TABLE 10.7	Mean acceptance rates (%) over ten chains of 5000 samples for each sampler on all datasets.	119
TABLE 10.8	Mean testing RMSE (MAE) resulting from BNNs trained using ten independent chains of MH, HMC and S2HMC at each of the weather stations.	120
TABLE 10.9	Mean testing RMSE (MAE) resulting from BNNs trained using ten independent chains of MH, HMC and S2HMC at each of the weather stations.	120
TABLE 10.10	Mean Testing RMSE (MAE) resulting from BNNs re-trained using the relevant features identified in Tables C.1 to C.3 for each weather station.	121
TABLE 11.1	Date ranges corresponding to the different levels of restrictions imposed by the South African government.	127
TABLE 11.2	Table outlining the prior parameter distributions used in our approach (excluding change point estimates).	131
TABLE 11.3	Mean posterior estimates of spreading at each level of lockdown including estimates and confidence intervals of R_0.	135
TABLE 12.1	Sampling performance of the MCMC methods. A cell that is **bold** indicates that the method outperforms on that particular metric. The results are averaged over five runs of each algorithm. NLL is the negative log-likelihood.	143
TABLE 12.2	Merton jump-diffusion parameter estimates averaged over the five runs of each algorithm. This table summarises the results in Fig. 12.1. The values in the parenthesis are the standard deviations rounded to two decimal places.	143
TABLE 13.1	Five number summary of the thirteen financial ratios in the South African local government financial statement audit opinion dataset. Note that mil represents a million. Q1 and Q3 are the lower and upper quartiles.	152
TABLE 13.2	Ranking of the financial ratios by each method. For example, MHMC ranks ratio four as the most important, while MH ranks ratio seven as the third most important. The financial ratios are described in more detail in Section 13.2.2.	157
TABLE C.1	Committee table of ARD feature selections based on the top 5 features from each inference method on the WM01 Alexander Bay dataset.	169
TABLE C.2	Committee table of ARD feature selections based on the top 5 features from each inference method on the WM05 Napier dataset.	170
TABLE C.3	Committee table of ARD feature selections based on the top 5 features from each inference method on the WM13 Jozini dataset.	171
TABLE D.1	FSF definitions used through time. Each digit 1 in the table represents a study that used a given definition of FSF in the time period, where A: Investigation by authorities, Q: Qualified audit opinion, C: Combination of both definitions.	173
TABLE D.2	FSF data features used through time. Each digit 1 in the table represents a study that used a given type of data feature in the time period, where F: financial ratios, F&NF: financial and non-financial ratios, T: text, and F&T: financial variables and text.	174
TABLE D.3	The FSF detection methods through time. Each digit 2 in the table represents two studies that used the given detection method in the time period, where LR: logistic regression, ANN: artificial neural network, SVM: support vector machine, DT: decision tree, DA: discriminant analysis, and OTH: other.	174
TABLE D.4	Summary of findings from the FSF detection literature survey.	174

Authors

Tshilidzi Marwala

Dr. Tshilidzi Marwala is the Rector of the United Nations (UN) University and the UN Under-Secretary-General from 1 March 2023. He was previously the Vice-Chancellor and Principal of the University of Johannesburg, Deputy Vice-Chancellor for Research and Dean of Engineering at the University of Johannesburg. He was Associate Professor, Full Professor, and the Carl and Emily Fuchs Chair of Control Engineering at the University of the Witwatersrand. He holds a Bachelor of Science in Mechanical Engineering (magna cum laude) from Case Western Reserve University and a PhD in Artificial Intelligence (AI) from the University of Cambridge. He was a post-doctoral researcher at Imperial College (London). He is a fellow of the American Academy of Arts and Sciences, The World Academy of Sciences (TWAS), the African Academy of Sciences, and the Academy of Science of South Africa. His research interests are multi-disciplinary, including the theory and application of AI to engineering, computer science, finance, social science and medicine. He has supervised 37 Doctoral students, published 25 books in AI (one translated into Chinese), over 300 papers in journals, proceedings, book chapters and magazines, and holds five patents. He has been a visiting scholar at Harvard University, the University of California at Berkeley, the University of Cambridge, Nanjing Tech University and the Silesian University of Technology in Poland. His opinions have appeared in the New Scientist, The Economist, Time Magazine, BBC, CNN and the Oxford Union. Dr. Marwala is the author of Rational Machines and Artificial Intelligence from Elsevier Academic Press.

Wilson Tsakane Mongwe

Wilson Tsakane Mongwe was born in Tembisa (Gauteng, South Africa) and matriculated from Bankuna High School in 2008 where he was the overall second best-preforming learner in the Limpopo Province. He holds a BSc in Computing from the University of South Africa (cum laude), BBusSci in Actuarial Science from the University of Cape Town (with a distinction in Statistics) and a Masters in Mathematical Finance from the University of Cape Town (with distinction). He was a recipient of the Google Ph.D. fellowship in machine learning which supported his Ph.D. research at the University of Johannesburg. He is a recipient of the Mail and Guardian Top 200 young South Africans for 2020, and was recognised as one of 30 Young Mandelas by News 24 for 2022. Wilson is currently employed as a Senior Quantitative Analyst at Absa Capital, and is a machine learning research fellow at the University of Johannesburg.

Rendani Mbuvha

Rendani Mbuvha is the DeepMind Academic Fellow in Machine Learning at Queen Mary University of London and Associate Professor of Actuarial Science at the University of Witwatersrand. He is a qualified Actuary and a holder of the Chartered Enterprise Risk Actuary designation. He holds a BSc with Honours in Actuarial Science and Statistics from the University of Cape Town and an MSc in Machine Learning from KTH, Royal Institute of Technology in Sweden. He is a recipient of the Google Ph.D. fellowship in machine learning which supported his Ph.D. research at the University of Johannesburg. Rendani is an Honorary Senior Research Associate in Computer Science at University College London.

Foreword

The 4th Industrial Revolution is evolving with its great technological and social impacts. It is fuelled by rapid advances in Internets, wireless device and communication, big data, cloud computing, artificial intelligence (AI) and robotics. Machine learning (ML) is a core branch of AI. It produces useful models from data, which lead to wide applications such as speech recognition, medical diagnosis and autonomous driving. One fundamental task in ML as well as optimisation and statistics is to sample from a probability distribution. These samples can be used to infer models such as deep neural networks, to ensure robustness to optimisation methods by allowing them to escape local minima/saddle points, and to prevent them from overfilling.

Sampling methods are often the key to solve integration, counting, and volume computation problems that are rampant in various applications at the intersection of sciences and ML. In modern programming languages there are functions to sample from simple distributions such as uniform, normal and Poisson. But for a general or Gibbs distribution, Markov chain Monte Carlo (MCMC) methods are commonly employed in Bayesian machine learning, where a Markov chain is constructed as a sample of the desired distribution. There are two basic MCMC techniques. In Gibbs sampling, typically one parameter is drawn from the distribution at a time, holding all others fixed. In the Metropolis algorithm, all the parameters can be varied at once. The parameter vector is perturbed from the current sequence point by adding a trial step and the trial position is either accepted or rejected on the basis of the probability at the trial position relative to the current one. However, there are the problems of low acceptance rates of proposals for Metropolis techniques and the low performance of the Gibbs algorithm in multidimensional problems.

This led to the emergence of a new MCMC technique using Hamiltonian dynamics, that is, Hamiltonian Monte Carlo – HMC. The HMC is an adaptation of the Metropolis technique and employs a guided scheme for generating new proposals: this improves the proposals acceptance rate and, consequently, efficiency. More specifically, the HMC uses the posterior log gradient to direct the Markov chain to regions of higher posterior density, where most samples are collected. As a result, a Markov chain with HMC algorithm will accept proposals at a much higher rate than the traditional Metropolis algorithm. HMC was first discovered by physicists and was adopted with much success in ML. It is currently the main algorithm of MCMC methods used in practice.

In view of great importance of HMC, three scholars at University of Johannesburg have timely prepared a book solely focused on HMC, "Hamiltonian Monte Carlo Methods in Machine Learning". The lead author is Prof. Tshilidzi Marwala who is one of best known African scientists in the AI field. Many of us can recall his popular comment on the efficient market hypothesis, in which he stated[1] "artificial intelligence (AI) influences the applicability of the efficient market hypothesis in that the greater amount of AI-based market participants, the more efficient the markets become". Despite his busy daily schedule as vice-chancellor of the University of Johannesburg, Prof. Marwala is very active in research with 25 books published before. In this new book, he with his collaborators gives a comprehensive coverage of HMC based on their latest extensive research findings. The book is first of its kind solely focused on HMC. After a concise introduction to HMC and performance measures, the book details branches of HMC in several chapters, namely, Stochastic Volatility Metropolis-Hastings, Quantum-Inspired Magnetic Hamiltonian Monte Carlo, Generalised Magnetic And Shadow Hamiltonian Monte Carlo, Shadow Magnetic Hamiltonian Monte Carlo, Adaptive Shadow Hamiltonian Monte Carlo, Adaptive Noncanonical Hamiltonian Monte Carlo, and Antithetic Hamiltonian Monte Carlo Techniques. The book also shows various applications of HMC in Bayesian Neural Network Inference in Wind Speed Forecasting, A Bayesian Analysis of Lockdown Alert Level framework for Combating COVID-19, Probabilistic Inference of Equity Option Prices Under Jump-Diffusion Processes, and Bayesian Inference of Local Government Audit Outcomes.

The book is well written. The structure is solid and the materials are easy to follow. The book is highly recommended to AI researchers, graduate students and engineers. In conclusion, my overall opinion on the book is that it constitutes a valuable contribution to HMC. Congratulations to the authors!

Prof. Qing-Guo Wang
United International College (UIC),
Beijing Normal University–Hong Kong Baptist University,
Zhuhai, Guangdong, China
April 2022

---

[1] https://en.wikipedia.org/wiki/Efficient-market_hypothesis.

Preface

Complex non-linear systems, in particular machine learning models, have become highly prevalent in numerous aspects of modern-day life. Applications driven by machine learning models include *inter alia* health care, financial services, transportation and energy [12,131,138,142,143].

Applications that utilise machine learning models rely on training a learning machine that encodes the relationship between the inputs and outputs of the specific phenomenon being modelled. These input-output relationships are extracted from data generated by the phenomenon [125]. Such learning machines leverage non-linear relationships that were typically considered computationally prohibitive [139]. Recent advances in microprocessor, graphical processor, and data storage technology have increased computational efficiency that allows for both offline training and prediction as well as real-time-online training and prediction.

Learning machines can be parameterised to encode relationships exhibited within the data generated by a specific phenomena being modelled. Popular learning machines in literature and practice include artificial neural networks, decision trees, support vector machines and ensembles or weighted committees of each of the respective models such as random forests, bagged and boosted models [27,94].

In the past, the predictive performance of such learning machines significantly relied on domain-specific expertise to design inputs or features that represent the signals emanating from the phenomenon that is being modelled [125]. This has significantly changed with the development of deep learning models that can learn representations, such as convolutional neural networks. A direct result of the advancements in representation learning is the increased application of learning machines in many critical domains such as X-ray analysis and autonomous driving without a domain expert's presence or supervision.

The process of training these learning machines has thus become a focal area due to the critical nature of the tasks where learning machines are deployed [74]. The training process is the process through which we obtain model parameters that are used for future predictions. In statistical literature, this process is referred to as inference. In essence, model parameters and the data used to train or infer them encapsulate both the model's predictive potential and the risk associated with incorrect predictions. The societal cost of incorrect predictions can be as high as resulting in automotive or aviation accidents, incorrect forecasts of pandemic trajectories, clinical misdiagnosis and unfair bias or prejudice [74]. Thus ideal parameter inference methods for critical applications should adequately reflect the level of uncertainty around such parameters and their associated predictions.

This book presents Hamiltonian Monte Carlo (HMC) and its derivatives that not only provide uncertainty estimates but also yield asymptotic guarantees for convergence to the true parameter posterior distributions. The book further presents methods that address sampling efficiency pathologies in HMC through sampling from a perturbed 'Shadow' Hamiltonian, introducing non-canonical dynamics and automatically tuning sampler hyperparameters. We conclude the book by showcasing applications of HMC and its derivatives in epidemiology, renewable energy, financial engineering and auditing.

We are grateful to Google for their financial support. The work of Wilson Tsakane Mongwe and Rendani Mbuvha is partly funded by the Google Africa PhD Fellowships in machine learning. We also thank the Centre For High-Performance Computing at the Council for Scientific and Industrial Research South Africa for providing the computational resources that make the work in this book possible.

The views expressed in this book are not the views of the United Nations University, the Queen Mary University of London, the University of the Witwatersrand or the University of Johannesburg.

Tshilidzi Marwala
Wilson Tsakane Mongwe
Rendani Mbuvha
Johannesburg
August 2022

Nomenclature

A-MHMC Antithetic Magnetic Hamiltonian Monte Carlo.
A-S2HMC Antithetic Separable Shadow Hamiltonian Hybrid Monte Carlo.
AG-SA Auditor General of South Africa.
A-HMC Antithetic Hamiltonian Monte Carlo.
ARD Automatic Relevance Determination.
AUC Area Under The Receiver Operating Curve.
BCH Baker-Campbell-Hausdorff.
BLR Bayesian Logistic Regression.
BNN Bayesian Neural Network.
ESS Effective Sample Size.
FSF Financial Statement Fraud.
HMC Hamiltonian Monte Carlo.
JDP Jump-Diffusion Process.
JS2HMC Jittered S2HMC.
JSE Johannesburg Stock Exchange.
MALA Metropolis Adjusted Langevin Algorithm.
MCMC Markov Chain Monte Carlo.
MH Metropolis-Hastings.
MHMC Magnetic Hamiltonian Monte Carlo.
MLP Multilayer Perceptron.
MSE Mean Square Error.
NUTS No-U-Turn Sampler.
PHMC Hamiltonian Monte Carlo With Partial Momentum Refreshment.
PMHMC Magnetic Hamiltonian Monte Carlo With Partial Momentum Refreshment.
PS2HMC Separable Shadow Hamiltonian Hybrid Monte Carlo With Partial Momentum Refreshment.
QIHMC Quantum-Inspired Hamiltonian Monte Carlo.
QIMHMC Quantum-Inspired Magnetic Hamiltonian Monte Carlo.
RMHMC Riemannian Manifold Hamiltonian Monte Carlo.
ROC Receiver Operating Curve.
S2HMC Separable Shadow Hamiltonian Hybrid Monte Carlo.
SHMC Shadow Hamiltonian Monte Carlo.
SMHMC Shadow Magnetic Hamiltonian Monte Carlo.

List of symbols

N	Total number of samples generated
L	Trajectory length parameter in Hamiltonian samplers
ϵ	Step size parameter in Hamiltonian samplers
$\mathbf{w}$	Model parameters
D	Dimension of the model parameters $\mathbf{w}$
$\mathbf{p}$	Auxiliary momentum variable that is independent of $\mathbf{w}$
$U(\mathbf{w})$	Potential energy evaluated at $\mathbf{w}$
$K(\mathbf{p})$	Kinetic energy evaluated at $\mathbf{p}$
$H(\mathbf{w}, \mathbf{p})$	Hamiltonian evaluated at $\mathbf{w}$ and $\mathbf{p}$
$\mathbf{M}$	Mass matrix for the momentum auxiliary variable $\mathbf{p}$
$\mathcal{N}(a, b)$	Normal distribution with mean a and variance b
$\mathbf{P_M(M)}$	Probability distribution of the mass matrix $\mathbf{M}$
$\mathbf{G}$	Magnetic field in **MHMC**
β	Volatility of volatility parameter in **QIHMC**
ρ	Momentum refreshment parameter
$\hat{R}$	Potential scale reduction factor

1

Introduction to Hamiltonian Monte Carlo

1.1 Introduction

Machine learning technologies have been successfully deployed in various industries including self-driving cars, health, and weather forecasting among others [17,66,123,156, 196]. Deep learning is a class of machine learning models that has fostered the growth of artificial intelligence in industry and is a crucial enabler of the fourth industrial revolution [195]. These machine learning models are typically trained within a frequentist paradigm using gradient and evolutionary-based optimisation techniques, key of which is gradient descent and its extensions [30].

A disadvantage of the frequentist approach to training machine learning models is the inability of the trained models to naturally produce uncertainties in the parameters of the model and their resultant predictions [62,75]. There has been recent progress in addressing this limitation, with the majority of the approaches typically being model specific [7,124] or already having Bayesian equivalents [75]. Forming uncertainties around model predictions is particularly important for complex and mission-critical systems such as self-driving cars, medical diagnosis of patients, and a bank deciding whether or not to grant credit to a customer [1,62]. In all these instances, various stakeholders would be interested in establishing the extent to which the model is certain about its forecasts [152].

The Bayesian framework offers a probabilistically robust approach to training machine learning models [1,75,124,134]. This approach provides confidence levels in the model parameters and the resultant model predictions. It also allows one to perform comparisons between different models using the Bayesian evidence metric [134]. The Bayesian approach incorporates already existing knowledge before the data is observed through the prior distribution. The observations are then incorporated via the likelihood function, which generates the posterior distribution when combined with our prior beliefs. The posterior distribution is thus a refinement of our prior convictions in light of the newly observed data [192]. A fundamental limitation of training machine learning models within the Bayesian paradigm is that Bayesian approaches tend to be computationally expensive, and are thus difficult to scale to larger and more complex models [78,156,222].

The Bayesian framework of inference is founded on Bayes theorem, which states that for a given model M with parameters $\mathbf{w}$ and data D, we have:

Hamiltonian Monte Carlo Methods in Machine Learning. https://doi.org/10.1016/B978-0-44-319035-3.00013-6

$$\underbrace{\mathbb{P}(\mathbf{w}|D, M)}_{\text{posterior}} = \frac{\overbrace{\mathbb{P}(D|\mathbf{w}, M)}^{\text{likelihood}} \overbrace{\mathbb{P}(\mathbf{w}|M)}^{\text{prior}}}{\underbrace{\mathbb{P}(D|M)}_{\text{evidence}}} \tag{1.1}$$

where $\mathbb{P}(\mathbf{w}|D, M)$ is the posterior of the parameters given the model M and data D, $\mathbb{P}(D|\mathbf{w}, M)$ is the likelihood of the data, $\mathbb{P}(\mathbf{w}|M)$ is the prior distribution for the parameters and $\mathbb{P}(D|M)$ is the Bayesian evidence for model M and can be utilised for model selection [152]. In this book, we aim to infer the posterior distribution of the parameters $\mathbb{P}(\mathbf{w}|M)$ for a given model so we can perform predictions using the model. The posterior distribution is typically not available in closed form, and thus, numerical techniques are often required to determine the posterior [134]. The common approaches for training models, that is, determining the posterior distribution, within the Bayesian framework are variational inference techniques and Markov Chain Monte Carlo (MCMC) algorithms.

Variational inference [101] and its extensions [103] are approximate inference techniques in that the posterior distribution is assumed to come from a particular family of simpler distributions, with the commonly used family being that of Gaussian distributions [78]. This allows the sampling problem to be converted into an optimisation problem in which the Kullback-Leibler divergence between the target posterior and the approximating distribution is minimised [78]. This attribute makes variational methods typically much faster than MCMC methods [78,101].

MCMC algorithms are preferable to variational techniques as they are guaranteed to converge to the correct target distribution if the sample size is sufficiently large [203,205]. These methods are premised on building a Markov chain of samples that asymptotically, as the number of samples $n \to \infty$, converge to the desired equilibrium distribution. By definition, the samples generated by MCMC algorithms are auto-correlated, which means that they will have higher variance than classical Monte Carlo techniques. This branch of inference techniques was initially developed by physicists, with famous examples being the Metropolis-Hastings (MH) [95] algorithm of Metropolis and Hastings and Hamiltonian Monte Carlo (HMC) of Duane et al. [60]. These MCMC methods then later entered the field of computational statistics, where they are used today to sample from various complex probabilistic models [83]. This book focuses primarily on HMC and its variants with the aim of developing improved versions of HMC and its descendants.

The random walk MH algorithm forms the foundation of more complicated algorithms such as HMC and the Metropolis Adjusted Langevin Algorithm (MALA) [79,95,175]. The simplicity and robustness of this algorithm have resulted in it still being extensively used in various applications [228]. This method generates proposed samples from a Gaussian distribution whose mean is the last accepted state [95,144]. This proposal exhibits random walk behaviour, which usually results in low sample acceptance rates and generates strongly correlated samples [144,175]. In practice, the scale matrix of the Gaussian proposal distribution is typically treated as being diagonal, with all the dimensions having the same standard deviation $\sigma \geq 0$ [198]. Extending random walk MH by treating the scale matrix as being stochastic and allowing it to depend on the local geometry of the target is still an open area of research.

HMC is the most popular MCMC algorithm within machine learning literature and is used in a wide range of applications including health, finance and cosmology [79,98,144, 161–163,172,175,178,192,214]. Its popularity is largely based on its ability to use first-order gradient information of the posterior distribution to guide its exploration, thus suppressing the random walk behaviour observed with the random walk MH algorithm [25,175]. This approach can be easily applied to sample from any differentiable target on Euclidean spaces [37,175]. Betancourt [25] provides the geometrical foundations of HMC, as well as the conditions under which HMC is geometrically ergodic – that is, the algorithm will eventually visit all parts of the parameter space.

Although HMC serves as an improvement on the MH algorithm, it still results in relatively high auto-correlations between the generated samples. This has prompted further development of MCMC algorithms that extend HMC to incorporate second-order gradient information of the posterior [24,79], techniques that utilise random mass matrices [128] for the auxiliary momentum variable, methods that automatically tune the parameters of HMC [3,105], algorithms that utilise non-canonical Hamiltonian dynamics [38,165,213], approaches that couple HMC chains so as to reduce the variance of the resultant HMC based estimators [161,162,189], as well as methods that use modified or shadow Hamiltonians to sample from high dimensional targets [98,145,161,192,212].

The seminal work of Girolami and Caldehad [79] introduced Riemannian Manifold Hamiltonian Monte Carlo (RMHMC) which improves on HMC by taking into account the local geometry of the target through the use of second-order gradient information. Making use of second-order gradient information is particularly important for ill-conditioned target distributions such as Neal's [174] funnel. The incorporation of local curvature information results in more efficient exploration of the target compared to HMC. A key disadvantage of RMHMC is that the Hamiltonian is not separable, which necessitates the use of an implicit integration scheme that is computationally expensive [50,79]. Cobb et al. [50] introduced an explicit scheme for RMHMC which alleviates the computational burden of using the implicit generalised leapfrog integration scheme without a decrease in sampling performance.

Quantum-Inspired Hamiltonian Monte Carlo (QIHMC) uses a random mass matrix to mimic the behaviour of quantum particles as opposed to the fixed mass of classical particles. This results in better sampling than HMC and RMHMC on spiky and multi-modal distributions [128,162,166]. QIHMC achieves the outperformance over HMC without any noticeable increase in the execution time. The main drawback of QIHMC is the requirement for the user to specify the distribution of the mass matrix and the likely tuning of the parameters of the chosen distribution [128]. Determining the optimal distribution to use for the mass matrix is still an open area of research.

The No-U-Turn Sampler (NUTS) of Hoffman and Gelman [105] automates the tuning of the step size and trajectory length parameters for HMC. The step size parameter is tuned during the burn-in phase using the primal-dual averaging methodology [11] by targeting a user-specified level of acceptance rate in the generated samples [3,105]. The trajectory length is set by iteratively doubling the trajectory length until specific criteria are met [3,105,159,160]. Empirical results show that NUTS performs at least as efficiently as and sometimes more efficiently than a well-tuned standard HMC method, without requiring user intervention or costly tuning runs [105]. NUTS has also been generalised to Riemannian manifolds [24] and thus allowing the automatic tuning of the parameters of RMHMC. Wang et al. [223,224] introduce a Bayesian optimisation framework for tuning the parameters of HMC and RMHMC samplers. The authors show that their approach is ergodic and, in some instances, precludes the need for more complex samplers. The empirical results show that this approach has a higher effective number of samples per unit of computation used than NUTS. Hoffman et al. [102] propose an adaptive MCMC scheme for tuning the trajectory length parameter in HMC and show that this new technique typically yields higher effective samples sizes normalised by the number of gradient evaluation when compared to NUTS. This approach can also be easily run in parallel and use GPUs, unlike NUTS.

Magnetic Hamiltonian Monte Carlo (MHMC) utilises non-canonical dynamics to better explore the posterior [38,161,213]. MHMC introduces a magnetic field to HMC in addition to the force field already present HMC. This magnetic field results in faster convergence and lower auto-correlations in the generated samples [85,157,213]. When the magnetic component is removed, MHMC has the same performance as HMC. This implies that the magnetic component adds a degree of freedom to improve the performance of HMC. MHMC has been extended to manifolds by Brofos and Lederman [37] and shows good improvement over MHMC. However, MHMC has the disadvantage that the magnetic component has to be specified by the user. In the existing literature on MHMC, there are no automated means of tuning the magnetic component [38,161,213]. In addition, the use of a random mass matrix for the momentum variable in MHMC as well as the automatic tuning of the step size and trajectory length parameters in MHMC is yet to be explored in the literature.

Since the seminal work of Izaguirre and Hampton [110] on integrator dependent shadow Hamiltonians, there has been a proliferation of shadow HMC methods in the literature. The shadow Hamiltonian methods are premised on the fact that shadow Hamiltonians are better conserved when compared to the true Hamiltonians [110]. This allows one to use larger step sizes or perform sampling on problems with larger dimensions, without a significant decrease in the acceptance rates when compared to HMC methods [6,98,192]. To control the momentum generation, the authors introduce a parameter c, which determines how close the true and the shadow Hamiltonians are. The momentum generation increases the overall computational time of the method. In addition, the algorithm requires the user to tune the parameter c to attain optimal results.

Sweet et al. [212] improve on the work of Izaguirre and Hampton [110] by using a canonical transformation on the parameters and momentum. This canonical transformation is substituted into the non-separable Hamiltonian introduced in Izaguirre and Hampton [110] so that it now becomes separable. The canonical transformation results in a processed leapfrog integration scheme which is more computationally efficient when compared to the original shadow HMC method of Izaguirre and Hampton [110]. This is because computationally expensive momentum generation for the non-separable Hamiltonian is no longer required. Furthermore, no new hyperparameters are introduced, with the method having the same parameters as traditional HMC. The authors refer to this new method as the Separable Shadow Hamiltonian Hybrid Monte Carlo (S2HMC) algorithm. The tuning of the parameters of S2HMC, and shadow Hamiltonian methods in general, is yet to be explored in the literature.

Partial momentum refreshment has been successfully utilised by Radivojevic and Akhmatskay [192] and Akhmatskaya and Reich [6] to generate momenta in the context of non-separable Hamiltonians. Radivojevic and Akhmatskay [192] also consider higher-order integrators and their corresponding shadow Hamiltonians and propose the Mix and Match Hamiltonian Monte Carlo algorithm, which provides better sampling properties to HMC. Heide et al. [98] derive a non-separable shadow Hamiltonian for the generalised leapfrog integrator used in RMHMC, which results in improved performance relative to sampling from the true Hamiltonian. The authors employed partial momentum refreshment to generate the momenta but do not offer an approach for tuning the partial momentum refreshment parameter that they introduce.

The use of partial momentum refreshment in MHMC and S2HMC is yet to be considered in the literature. Horowitz [107] employed a partial momentum update to HMC and found that it significantly improved the performance of HMC. That is, keeping some of the dynamics of the chain improved performance without harming the legitimacy of the Monte Carlo method [61,106,107,165,167]. Given that MHMC is closely related to HMC, one would expect that employing partial momentum refreshment to MHMC would result in the same or better sampling properties as observed by Horowitz [107] on HMC. Similarly, one would expect that incorporating partial momentum refreshment within the processed leapfrog integrator in S2HMC could potentially improve the performance of S2HMC.

Although HMC and its variants discussed above serve as an improvement to other MCMC methods, like other MCMC methods, it still suffers from the presence of autocorrelations in the generated samples [79,126]. This results in the high variance of HMC based estimators. One approach of tackling the high variance of MCMC estimators is by using results from MCMC coupling theory [99,111]. The coupling of MCMC methods has been used as a theoretical tool to prove convergence behaviour of Markov chains [31,111,113,114,201]. More recently, MCMC couplings have been studied for HMC with good results [176,189]. Markov chain coupling has also been used to provide unbiased HMC estimators [81,99,111]. Piponi et al. [189] use approximate coupling theory to construct the Antithetic Hamiltonian Monte Carlo (A-HMC) algorithm. These anti-correlated chains are created by running the second chain with the auxiliary momentum variable having the opposite sign of the momentum of the first chain [161,189]. Their results show that adding antithetic sampling to HMC increases the effective sample size rates. Incorporating antithetic sampling in MHMC and S2HMC to reduce their variance is yet to be explored in the literature.

In the next section, we provide a brief background to MCMC.

1.2 Background to Markov Chain Monte Carlo

Suppose that we are interested in estimating the expectation of some arbitrary function $f(x)$ with $x \in \mathbb{R}^D$ having a well specified probability distribution. Mathematically, this is written as:

$$\mathbb{E}_\mu[f] = \int_{\mathbb{R}^D} f(x)d\mu(x) \tag{1.2}$$

where $f \in L^1(\mu)^1$ with respect to a probability measure μ, and D is the dimensionality of x. If f and the probability measure μ result in a simple tractable product as an intergrand, one could calculate this expectation analytically. If however, the product of these two functions is not simple, one would have to consider numerical approximations to the integral in Eq. (1.2). These techniques could be deterministic quadrature (e.g. Trapezoidal rule [193] and various forms of Gaussian quadrature [132]), Monte Carlo [95], Sparse grids [41] and Bayesian quadrature [86,183], amongst others.

Deterministic quadrature methods perform poorly as the dimension D of the problem increases. This is due to the convergence rate being bounded as outlined in Bakhalov's theorem [19]. The bulk of quadrature methods were created for integrals with a single dimension. One would then obtain multi-dimensional integrals by employing the tensor product rule from Fubini's theorem [219], which repeats the integrals in each dimension. Multiple one-dimensional integrals result in the function evaluations growing exponentially with the number of dimensions D. The other three methods being Monte Carlo, Sparse grids, and Bayesian quadrature, can (to some extent) overcome this curse of dimensionality.

Sparse grids were developed by Russian mathematician Sergey A. Smolyak and have various applications, including multi-dimensional interpolation and numerical integration [20,41,120,232]. Sparse grids were constructed with a focus on extending full grids methods to higher dimensions, and come at the cost of a slight increase in error [120,231]. Full-grid approaches are only feasible for small dimensions. For $D > 4$, full grids become computationally expensive as the complexity of full grids grows exponentially with D [20,156,231].

Bayesian quadrature is a class of numerical algorithms for solving multi-dimensional integrals in a probabilistic fashion [36,183]. It has the advantage of providing uncertainty over the solution of the integral. This technique has been successfully utilised to calculate the Bayesian evidence metric [86,183], which can be used for model comparison and selection. This approach uses a small number of observations of the likelihood to infer a distribution of the integrals akin to those in Eq. (1.2) using Gaussian processes [86,183].

---

[1]That is: $\int_{\mathbb{R}^D} |f(x)|d\mu(x) < \infty$.

Bayesian quadrature offers improved sample efficiency, which is essential for samples drawn from complex and computationally expensive models. This technique has, however, displayed high variance around the integral estimate and convergence diagnostics due to variations in the sample observations selected [86].

Monte Carlo methods utilise repeated random sampling instead of deterministic points as used in deterministic quadrature, and are easier to extend to multidimensional integrals. For this approach, the estimator of the integral in Eq. (1.2) using n samples has a standard deviation that is proportional to $\frac{1}{\sqrt{n}}$, and importantly does not rely on the dimension D [217]. At the same time, the worst-case error for quadrature is $\propto n^{-\frac{r}{D}}$ where r is the number of quadrature points, with the error depending on D [217]. This suggests that the Monte Carlo approach may perform better when D is large. However, it is not straightforward to directly compare quadrature with Monte Carlo as the former is a frequentist notion while the latter is Bayesian [217].

The Monte Carlo estimate of the integral in Eq. (1.2) is given as the average of the observations of $x_i \sim \mu$ as [25]:

$$\mathbb{E}_\mu[f] \approx \frac{1}{n} \sum_{i=1}^{n} f(x_i) \tag{1.3}$$

The difficulty in deploying Monte Carlo integration in practice is generating representative samples x_i of the distribution μ.

MCMC techniques, such as the MH algorithm [95] and Slice sampling [174], are a significant subset of Monte Carlo algorithms which can be used to generate $x_i \sim \mu$. In this work, we focus on Monte Carlo based, particularly MCMC, methods for solving the integral in Eq. (1.2) via the generation of draws from target posterior distributions. MCMC algorithms produce observations of the distribution of interest using a Markov chain [145]. This Markov chain is created so that the equilibrium density is equal to the distribution of interest.

Before delving further into MCMC methods, we recall the following ideas from the theory of Markov Chains taken from [96].

Definition 1. A Markov chain is a set of stochastic variables $\{a_1, a_2, ..., a_n\}$ that satisfy:

$$\mathbb{P}(a_n|a_1, a_2, ..., a_{n-1}) = \mathbb{P}(a_n|a_{n-1}) \tag{1.4}$$

That is, the density of the current position is independent of the past when given the previous position [96]. This construction implies that one only requires the initial density and a transition density, governing movements between states, to completely specify a Markov chain [96,145].

Definition 2. π is the stationary distribution for a Markov chain $\iff$

$$\pi(b) = \int_a \mathbb{P}(b|a)\pi(a)da \quad \forall b, a \tag{1.5}$$

This definition means that the transitions of the chain from one state to the other leave such a distribution invariant [96]. This equation is often called the fixed point equation [96,210].

Definition 3. A Markov chain is irreducible and aperiodic $\iff$ it is ergodic.

Irreducibility refers to the chain being able to traverse to any state from any other state [96]. Aperiodic means that the chain eventually returns to the current state after a finite number of steps.

Definition 4. If $\exists \pi$ such that:

$$\mathbb{P}(k|w)\pi(w) = \mathbb{P}(w|k)\pi(k) \quad \forall k, w \tag{1.6}$$

then the Markov chain is reversible.

Note that Eq. (1.6) implies that the transitions from-and-to two different states occur at the same rate when in *equilibrium* [96]. A chain that satisfies Eq. (1.6) is said to satisfy detailed balance, which is a concept we consistently revisit in this book. To guarantee that π is indeed the stationary distribution, we need the chain to be ergodic as defined in Definition 3 [96]. Detailed balance is a more stringent condition than ergodicity, and is not necessary (although it is sufficient) for a chain to converge to the desired equilibrium distribution [96].

In the section, we discuss the MCMC method that forms the basis for more complicated MCMC methods being MH.

1.3 Metropolis-Hastings algorithm

MCMC methods were originally developed by physicists such as Ulam, Von Neumann, Fermi, and Metropolis, amongst others in the 1940s [197]. MCMC approaches have since been successfully employed *inter alia* in cosmology, health, energy and finance [144,145]. The MH method is one of the oldest and foundational MCMC algorithms and forms the core of more complex MCMC techniques which use advanced proposal distributions. Suppose we are interested in determining the posterior distribution of parameters $\mathbf{w}$ from some model M. This posterior distribution could then be used to determine expectations of the form in Eq. (1.2). The MH method produces recommended samples using a proposal distribution $T(\mathbf{w}^*|\mathbf{w})$. The next state $\mathbf{w}^*$ is rejected or accepted using the ratio of likelihoods [39,145]:

$$\mathbb{P}(\text{accept } \mathbf{w}^*) = \min\left(1, \frac{\pi(\mathbf{w}^*)T(\mathbf{w}|\mathbf{w}^*)}{\pi(\mathbf{w})T(\mathbf{w}^*|\mathbf{w})}\right) \tag{1.7}$$

where $\pi(\mathbf{w})$ is the stationary target density evaluated at $\mathbf{w}$, for some arbitrary $\mathbf{w}$.

Random walk Metropolis is a version of MH that utilises a Gaussian distribution whose mean is the current state as the proposal distribution [145]. The transition density in random walk Metropolis is $\mathcal{N}(\mathbf{w}, \epsilon\mathbf{\Sigma})$, where $\epsilon\mathbf{\Sigma}$ is the covariance matrix of the proposal distribution [145]. Note that $\mathbf{\Sigma}$ is typically set to be the identity matrix in practice, leaving only ϵ to be specified and tuned by the user. When the proposal distribution is symmetric (e.g. when it is Gaussian), it results in $T(\mathbf{w}|\mathbf{w}^*) = T(\mathbf{w}^*|\mathbf{w})$ and leads to Eq. (1.7) becoming [145]:

$$\mathbb{P}(\text{accept } \mathbf{w}^*) = \min\left(1, \frac{\pi(\mathbf{w}^*)}{\pi(\mathbf{w})}\right) \tag{1.8}$$

The proposal density in random walk MH usually results in random walk behaviour, which leads to high auto-correlations between the generated samples as well as slow convergence [145]. Algorithm 1.1 provides the pseudo-code for the MH algorithm, and Theorem 1.3.1 shows why this algorithm converges to the correct stationary distribution.

Algorithm 1.1 The Metropolis-Hastings algorithm.

    Input: w_{init}, ϵ, N and unnormalised target $\pi(\mathbf{w})$
    Output: $(w)_{m=0}^N$
1: $w_0 \leftarrow w_{\text{init}}$
2: **for** $m \to 1$ to N **do**
3:     $\mathbf{\Sigma} = \mathbf{I}$
4:     $\mathbf{w}^* \sim T$ with $T = \mathcal{N}(\mathbf{w}, \epsilon\mathbf{\Sigma})$
5:     $\mathbf{w}_n \leftarrow \mathbf{w}^*$ with probability: $\alpha(\mathbf{w}^*|\mathbf{w}) = \min(1, \frac{\pi(\mathbf{w}^*)T(\mathbf{w}|\mathbf{w}^*)}{\pi(\mathbf{w})T(\mathbf{w}^*|\mathbf{w})})$
6: **end for**

Theorem 1.3.1. *The MH algorithm in Algorithm 1.1 leaves the target distribution invariant.*

Proof.

$$\underbrace{\alpha(\mathbf{w}^*|\mathbf{w})T(\mathbf{w}^*|\mathbf{w})}_{\mathbb{P}(\mathbf{w}^*|\mathbf{w})}\pi(\mathbf{w}) = \min\left(1, \frac{\pi(\mathbf{w}^*)T(\mathbf{w}|\mathbf{w}^*)}{\pi(\mathbf{w})T(\mathbf{w}^*|\mathbf{w})}\right)T(\mathbf{w}^*|\mathbf{w})\pi(\mathbf{w})$$

$$= \min(T(\mathbf{w}|\mathbf{w}^*)\pi(\mathbf{w}^*), T(\mathbf{w}^*|\mathbf{w})\pi(\mathbf{w}))$$

$$= \min\left(1, \frac{\pi(\mathbf{w})T(\mathbf{w}^*|\mathbf{w})}{\pi(\mathbf{w}^*)T(\mathbf{w}|\mathbf{w}^*)}\right)T(\mathbf{w}|\mathbf{w}^*)\pi(\mathbf{w}^*) \tag{1.9}$$

$$= \underbrace{\alpha(\mathbf{w}|\mathbf{w}^*)T(\mathbf{w}|\mathbf{w}^*)}_{\mathbb{P}(\mathbf{w}|\mathbf{w}^*)}\pi(\mathbf{w}^*)$$

$$\implies \mathbb{P}(\mathbf{w}^*|\mathbf{w})\pi(\mathbf{w}) = \mathbb{P}(\mathbf{w}|\mathbf{w}^*)\pi(\mathbf{w}^*)$$

which is the required result.   □

    A significant drawback of the MH seminal method is the relatively high auto-correlations between the generated samples. The high auto-correlations lead to slow convergence in the Monte Carlo estimates and consequently the necessity to generate large sample sizes.

Approaches that reduce the random walk behaviour are those that enhance the classical MH algorithm and utilise more information about the target posterior distributions [79]. The most common extension is to incorporate first-order gradient information to guide the exploration of the target, as well as second-order gradient information to consider the local curvature of the posterior [79]. Methods that use first-order gradient information include methods that utilise Langevin and Hamiltonian dynamics on a Euclidean manifold, while approaches that use second-order gradient information are methods on Riemannian and other manifolds [37,60,79,213]. Methods that use Hamiltonian dynamics on Euclidean spaces have shown great success in practice, and are a focus of this book. We assess different aspects of Hamiltonian dynamics-based samplers with a focus on identifying the gaps in the literature.

In the next section, we outline the methods that form the basis of the new algorithms presented in this book. The chapter proceeds as follows: we first review MALA, HMC, MHMC and QIHMC, we then proceed to discuss in Section 1.8 how to improve these samplers via modified or shadow Hamiltonians, we then discuss how one can automatically tune the parameters of these samplers in Section 1.9, and finally in Section 1.10, we conduct a review of coupling theory which will be employed when reducing the variance of Hamiltonian chains using antithetic sampling.

1.4 Metropolis Adjusted Langevin algorithm

The MALA is a MCMC method that incorporates first-order gradient information of the target posterior to enhance the sampling behaviour of the MH algorithm [79,85]. MALA reduces the random walk behaviour of MH via the use of Langevin dynamics which are given as follows [79,85]:

$$d\mathbf{w}_t = \frac{1}{2}\nabla_\mathbf{w}\ln\pi(\mathbf{w})dt + dZ_t \tag{1.10}$$

where $\pi(\mathbf{w})$ represents the unnormalised target distribution (which is the negative log-likelihood), $\mathbf{w}$ is the position vector and Z_t is a Brownian motion process at time t. As the Langevin dynamics are in the form of a stochastic differential equation, we typically will not be able to solve it analytically, and we need to use a numerical integration scheme. The first-order Euler-Maruyama integration scheme is the commonly used integration scheme for solving Langevin dynamics and the update equation is given as: [79,85]:

$$\mathbf{w}_{t+1} = \mathbf{w}_t + \frac{\epsilon^2}{2}\nabla_\mathbf{w}\ln\pi(\mathbf{w}) + \epsilon z_t \tag{1.11}$$

where ϵ is the integration step size and $z_t \sim \mathcal{N}(0, \mathbf{I})$.

The Euler-Maruyama integration scheme does not provide an exact solution to the Langevin dynamics, and hence produces numerical integration errors. These errors result in detailed balance being broken, and one ends up not sampling from the correct distribution. In order to ensure detailed balance, an MH acceptance step is required. The transition probability density function of MALA is given as [85]:

$$
\begin{aligned}
K\left(\mathbf{w}'|\mathbf{w}\right) &= \mathcal{N}\left(\gamma\left(\mathbf{w}\right), \epsilon^2\mathbf{I}\right), \\
K\left(\mathbf{w}|\mathbf{w}'\right) &= \mathcal{N}\left(\gamma\left(\mathbf{w}'\right), \epsilon^2\mathbf{I}\right), \\
\gamma\left(\mathbf{w}'\right) &= \mathbf{w} + \frac{\epsilon^2}{2}\nabla_\mathbf{w}\ln\pi\left(\mathbf{w}\right), \\
\gamma\left(\mathbf{w}\right) &= \mathbf{w}' + \frac{\epsilon^2}{2}\nabla_\mathbf{w}\ln\pi\left(\mathbf{w}'\right),
\end{aligned}
\tag{1.12}
$$

where $K\left(\mathbf{w}'|\mathbf{w}\right)$ and $K\left(\mathbf{w}|\mathbf{w}'\right)$ are transition probability distributions, $\mathbf{w}$ is the current state and $\mathbf{w}'$ is the new proposed state. The acceptance rate of the MALA takes the form:

$$
\min\left[1, \frac{\pi\left(\mathbf{w}'\right)K\left(\mathbf{w}'|\mathbf{w}\right)}{\pi\left(\mathbf{w}\right)K\left(\mathbf{w}|\mathbf{w}'\right)}\right]
\tag{1.13}
$$

It can be shown that MALA converges in the correct stationary by showing that it satisfies the Fokker–Planck equation as in [79], or by following a similar approach to the proof for MH in Theorem 1.3.1.

Unlike the MH algorithm, the MALA considers the first-order gradient data of the density, which results in the algorithm converging to the stationary distribution at an accelerated rate [79,85]. However, the generated samples are still highly correlated. Girolami and Caldehad [79] extend MALA from being on a Euclidean manifold to a Riemannian manifold, and hence incorporating second-order gradient information of the target. This approach showed considerable improvements on MALA, with an associated increase in compute time.

In the following sections, we present Hamiltonian dynamics-based methods that explore the posterior distribution more efficiently than MALA.

1.5 Hamiltonian Monte Carlo

Hamiltonian Monte Carlo is composed of two steps: 1) the molecular dynamics step and 2) the Monte Carlo step. The molecular dynamics step involves integrating Hamiltonian dynamics, while the Monte Carlo step employs the MH algorithm to account for any errors introduced by the numerical integrator used in the molecular dynamics step [6,60,95,110, 172,173,178]. Note that if we could exactly solve the molecular dynamics step, we would not need the Monte Carlo step.

HMC improves upon the MH [95] algorithm by utilising first-order gradient information of the unnormalised target posterior. This gradient information is used to guide HMC's exploration of the parameter space [60,178]. These necessities that the target posterior function is differentiable and has support almost everywhere on $\mathbb{R}^D$, which is the case for the majority of machine learning models of interest. In HMC, the position vector $\mathbf{w}$ is augmented with auxiliary momentum variable $\mathbf{p}$, which is typically chosen to be independent

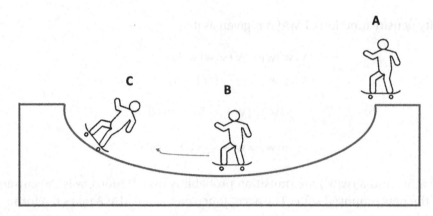

FIGURE 1.1 Illustration of the conservation of the Hamiltonian (i.e., total energy) through time as the skater moves from position A to C.

of **w**. The Hamiltonian H(**w**, **p**), which represents the total energy, from this system is written as follows:

$$H(\mathbf{w}, \mathbf{p}) = U(\mathbf{w}) + K(\mathbf{p}) \tag{1.14}$$

where U(**w**) is potential energy or the negative log-likelihood of the target posterior distribution and K(**p**) is the kinetic energy defined by the kernel of a Gaussian with a covariance matrix **M** [175]:

$$K(\mathbf{p}) = \frac{1}{2}\log\big((2\pi)^D |\mathbf{M}|\big) + \frac{\mathbf{p}^\mathrm{T}\mathbf{M}^{-1}\mathbf{p}}{2}. \tag{1.15}$$

Within this framework, the evolution of the physical system is governed by Hamiltonian dynamics [175,210]. As the particle moves through time using Hamiltonian dynamics, the total energy is conserved over the entire trajectory of the particle, with kinetic energy being exchanged for potential energy and vice versa to ensure that the Hamiltonian or total energy is conserved [175,210]. As an illustration, consider a person skating from position A to C as displayed in Fig. 1.1. At position A, the person only has potential energy and no kinetic energy, and they only have kinetic energy at point B. At position C, they have both kinetic and potential energy. Throughout the movement from A to C, the total energy will be conserved if the individual traverses the space using Hamiltonian dynamics. This allows the individual to traverse long distances. This energy conservation property of Hamiltonian dynamics is key to the efficiency of HMC in exploring the target posterior.

The equations governing the Hamiltonian dynamics are defined by Hamilton's equations in a fictitious time t as follows [172]:

$$\frac{d\mathbf{w}}{\partial t} = \frac{\partial H(\mathbf{w}, \mathbf{p})}{\partial \mathbf{p}}; \quad \frac{d\mathbf{p}}{\partial t} = -\frac{\partial H(\mathbf{w}, \mathbf{p})}{\partial \mathbf{w}}. \tag{1.16}$$

which can also be re-expressed as:

$$\frac{d}{\partial t}\begin{bmatrix} \mathbf{w} \\ \mathbf{p} \end{bmatrix} = \begin{bmatrix} \mathbf{0} & \mathbf{I} \\ -\mathbf{I} & \mathbf{0} \end{bmatrix}\begin{bmatrix} \nabla_w H(\mathbf{w}, \mathbf{p}) \\ \nabla_p H(\mathbf{w}, \mathbf{p}) \end{bmatrix} \tag{1.17}$$

The Hamiltonian dynamics satisfy the following important properties, which make it ideal for efficiently generating distant proposals [25,173]:

1. **Conservation of energy:** That is, the change of the Hamiltonian through time is zero as illustrated in Fig. 1.1. Mathematically:

$$\begin{aligned} \frac{\partial H(\mathbf{w}, \mathbf{p})}{\partial t} &= \frac{\partial H(\mathbf{w}, \mathbf{p})}{\partial \mathbf{w}}\frac{\partial \mathbf{w}}{\partial t} + \frac{\partial H(\mathbf{w}, \mathbf{p})}{\partial \mathbf{p}}\frac{\partial \mathbf{p}}{\partial t} \\ &= \frac{\partial H(\mathbf{w}, \mathbf{p})}{\partial \mathbf{w}}\left(\frac{\partial H(\mathbf{w}, \mathbf{p})}{\partial \mathbf{p}}\right) + \frac{\partial H(\mathbf{w}, \mathbf{p})}{\partial \mathbf{p}}\left(-\frac{\partial H(\mathbf{w}, \mathbf{p})}{\partial \mathbf{w}}\right) \\ \implies \frac{\partial H(\mathbf{w}, \mathbf{p})}{\partial t} &= 0 \end{aligned} \tag{1.18}$$

2. **Reversibility:** That is, the dynamics can be moved forward in time by a certain amount and backwards in time by the same amount to get back to the original position. Mathematically: Let $\Phi_{t,H}\begin{bmatrix} \mathbf{w_0} \\ \mathbf{p_0} \end{bmatrix}$ be the unique solution at time t of Eq. (1.16) with initial position $\begin{bmatrix} \mathbf{w_0} \\ \mathbf{p_0} \end{bmatrix}$. As the Hamiltonian in Eq. (1.14) is time-homogeneous, we have that:

$$\begin{aligned} \Phi_{t,H} \circ \Phi_{s,H}\begin{bmatrix} \mathbf{w_0} \\ \mathbf{p_0} \end{bmatrix} &= \Phi_{t+s,H}\begin{bmatrix} \mathbf{w_0} \\ \mathbf{p_0} \end{bmatrix} \\ \implies \Phi_{-t,H} \circ \Phi_{t,H}\begin{bmatrix} \mathbf{w_0} \\ \mathbf{p_0} \end{bmatrix} &= \begin{bmatrix} \mathbf{w_0} \\ \mathbf{p_0} \end{bmatrix} \end{aligned} \tag{1.19}$$

3. **Volume preservation:** This property serves to simplify the MH step in HMC so that it does not require a Jacobian term, as volume preservation means that the Jacobian term is equal to one [3,175]. There have also been extensions of HMC that do no not preserve volume [210].

These three properties are significant in that conservation of energy allows one to determine if the approximated trajectory is diverging from the expected dynamics, reversibility of the Hamiltonian dynamics ensures reversibility of the sampler, and volume preservation simplifies the MH acceptance step [98,175].

The differential equation in Eq. (1.16) and (1.17) cannot be solved analytically in most instances. This necessitates the use of a numerical integration scheme. As the Hamiltonian in Eq. (1.14) is separable, to traverse the space, we can employ the leapfrog integrator [60, 172]. The position and momentum update equations for the leapfrog integration scheme are:

$$\mathbf{p}_{t+\frac{\epsilon}{2}} = \mathbf{p}_t + \frac{\epsilon}{2} \frac{\partial H(\mathbf{w}_t, \mathbf{p}_t)}{\partial \mathbf{w}}$$
$$\mathbf{w}_{t+\epsilon} = \mathbf{w}_t + \epsilon \mathbf{M}^{-1} \mathbf{p}_{t+\frac{\epsilon}{2}} \qquad (1.20)$$
$$\mathbf{p}_{t+\epsilon} = \mathbf{p}_{t+\frac{\epsilon}{2}} + \frac{\epsilon}{2} \frac{\partial H(\mathbf{w}_{t+\epsilon}, \mathbf{p}_{t+\frac{\epsilon}{2}})}{\partial \mathbf{w}}.$$

Algorithm 1.2 Hamiltonian Monte Carlo algorithm.

Input: N, ϵ, L, w_{init}, $H(w, p)$
Output: $(w)_{m=0}^{N}$

1: $w_0 \leftarrow w_{\text{init}}$
2: **for** $m \rightarrow 1$ to N **do**
3:      $p_{m-1} \sim \mathcal{N}(0, \mathbf{M})$ $\leftarrow$ **momentum refreshment**
4:      $p_m, w_m = \textbf{Leapfrog}(p_{m-1}, w_{m-1}, \epsilon, L, H)$ in Eq. (1.20)
5:      $\delta H = H(w_{m-1}, p_{m-1}) - H(w_m, p_m)$
6:      $\alpha_m = \min(1, \exp(\delta H))$
7:      $u_m \sim \text{Unif}(0, 1)$
8:      $w_m = \textbf{Metropolis}(\alpha_m, u_m, w_m, w_{m-1})$ in Eq. (1.21)
9: **end for**

Due to the discretisation errors arising from the numerical integration, the Monte Carlo step in HMC utilises the MH algorithm in which the parameters $\mathbf{w}^*$ proposed by the molecular dynamics step are accepted with probability:

$$P(\text{accept } \mathbf{w}^*) = \min\left(1, \frac{\exp(-H(\mathbf{w}^*, \mathbf{p}^*))}{\exp(-H(\mathbf{w}, \mathbf{p}))}\right). \qquad (1.21)$$

Algorithm 1.2 shows the pseudo-code for the HMC where ϵ is the discretisation step size and L is the trajectory length. The overall HMC sampling process follows a Gibbs sampling scheme, where we *fully* sample the momentum (see line 3 in Algorithm 1.2) and then sample a new set of parameters given the drawn momentum.

It can be shown that MALA is a special case of HMC with $L = 1$ [79]. Although HMC improves on MH and MALA, it still produces relatively high correlated samples [110,213]. In the following sections we consider methods that improve on the sampling efficiency of HMC in various ways.

1.6 Magnetic Hamiltonian Monte Carlo

MHMC is a special case of non-canonical HMC using a symplectic structure corresponding to motion of a particle in a magnetic field [38,213]. MHMC extends HMC by endowing it with a magnetic field, which results in non-canonical Hamiltonian dynamics [213]. This magnetic field offers a significant amount of flexibility over HMC and encourages more efficient exploration of the posterior, which results in faster convergence and lower auto-correlations in the generated samples [85,161,213]. MHMC uses the same Hamiltonian as in HMC, but exploits non-canonical Hamiltonian dynamics where the canonical matrix now has a non-zero element on the diagonal. The MHMC dynamics are given as:

$$\frac{d}{\partial t}\begin{bmatrix}\mathbf{w}\\\mathbf{p}\end{bmatrix}=\begin{bmatrix}\mathbf{0}&\mathbf{I}\\-\mathbf{I}&\mathbf{G}\end{bmatrix}\begin{bmatrix}\nabla_w\mathrm{H}(\mathbf{w},\mathbf{p})\\\nabla_p\mathrm{H}(\mathbf{w},\mathbf{p})\end{bmatrix} \tag{1.22}$$

where $\mathbf{G}$ is a skew-symmetric[2] (or antisymmetric) matrix and is the term that represents the magnetic field. This also shows that MHMC only differs from HMC dynamics in Eq. (1.17) by $\mathbf{G}$ being non-zero. When $\mathbf{G}=\mathbf{0}$, MHMC and HMC have the same dynamics. Tripuraneni et al. [213] prove that in three dimensions, these dynamics are Newtonian mechanics of a charged particle in a magnetic field. How this magnetic field relates to the force field (e.g. are they orthogonal?) will determine the extent of the sampling efficiency of MHMC over HMC [85].

As with HMC, these non-canonical dynamics cannot be integrated exactly, and we resort to a numerical integration scheme with a MH acceptance step to ensure detailed balance. The update equations for the leapfrog-like integration scheme for MHMC, for the case where $\mathbf{M}=\mathbf{I}$, are given as [213]:

$$\begin{aligned}
\mathbf{p}_{t+\frac{\epsilon}{2}}&=\mathbf{p}_t+\frac{\epsilon}{2}\frac{\partial H(\mathbf{w}_t,\mathbf{p}_t)}{\partial\mathbf{w}}\\
\mathbf{w}_{t+\epsilon}&=\mathbf{w}_t+\mathbf{G}^{-1}\big(\exp{(\mathbf{G}\epsilon)}-\mathbf{I}\big)\mathbf{p}_{t+\frac{\epsilon}{2}}\\
\mathbf{p}_{t+\frac{\epsilon}{2}}&=\exp{(\mathbf{G}\epsilon)}\mathbf{p}_{t+\frac{\epsilon}{2}}\\
\mathbf{p}_{t+\epsilon}&=\mathbf{p}_{t+\frac{\epsilon}{2}}+\frac{\epsilon}{2}\frac{\partial H(\mathbf{w}_{t+\epsilon},\mathbf{p}_{t+\frac{\epsilon}{2}})}{\partial\mathbf{w}}.
\end{aligned} \tag{1.23}$$

The above equations show that we can retrieve the update equations of traditional HMC by first performing a Taylor matrix expansion for the exponential and then substituting $\mathbf{G}=0$. The pseudo-code for the MHMC algorithm is shown in Algorithm 1.3. It is important to note that we need to flip the sign of $\mathbf{G}$ (see lines 8–15 in Algorithm 1.3), as we do the sign of $\mathbf{p}$ in HMC, so as to render the MHMC algorithm reversible. In this sense, we treat $\mathbf{G}$ as being an auxiliary variable in the same fashion as $\mathbf{p}$ [213]. In this setup, $\mathbf{p}$ would be Gaussian while $\mathbf{G}$ would have a binary distribution [213] and only taking on the values $\pm\mathbf{G_0}$, with $\mathbf{G_0}$ being specified by the user. Exploring more complex distributions for $\mathbf{G}$ is still an open area of research.

Although MHMC requires matrix exponentiation and inversion as shown in Eq. (1.23), this only needs to be computed once upfront and stored [213]. Following this approach results in computation time that is comparable to HMC, which becomes more important in models that have many parameters such as neural networks.

---

[2] That is: $\mathbf{G}^T=-\mathbf{G}$.

As **G** only needs to be antisymmetric, there is no guarantee that it will be invertible. In this case, we need first to diagonalise **G** and separate its invertible or singular components [213]. As **G** is strictly antisymmetric, we can express it as $i\mathbf{H}$ where **H** is a Hermitian matrix, and can thus be diagonilised over the space of complex numbers $\mathbb{C}$ as [213]:

$$\mathbf{G} = [W_\Lambda \quad W_0] \begin{bmatrix} \Lambda & \mathbf{0} \\ \mathbf{0} & \mathbf{0} \end{bmatrix} \begin{bmatrix} W_\Lambda^T \\ W_0^T \end{bmatrix} \qquad (1.24)$$

where Λ is a diagonal submatrix consisting of the nonzero eigenvalues of **G**, columns of W_Λ, and W_0 are the eigenvectors of **G** corresponding to its nonzero and zero eigenvalues, respectively. This leads to the following update for **w** in Eq. (1.23) [213]:

$$\mathbf{w}_{t+\epsilon} = \mathbf{w}_t + [W_\Lambda \quad W_0] \begin{bmatrix} \Lambda^{-1}(\exp(\Lambda t) - \mathbf{I}) & \mathbf{0} \\ \mathbf{0} & \mathbf{I} \end{bmatrix} \begin{bmatrix} W_\Lambda^T \\ W_0^T \end{bmatrix} \mathbf{p}_{t+\frac{\epsilon}{2}} \qquad (1.25)$$

It is worthwhile noting that when $\mathbf{G} = 0$ in Eq. (1.25) then the flow map will reduce to an Euler translation as in traditional HMC [213].

1.7 Quantum-Inspired Hamiltonian Monte Carlo

Inspired by the energy-time uncertainty relation from quantum mechanics, Liu and Zhang [128] developed the QIHMC algorithm which sets **M** to be random with a probability distribution rather than a fixed mass as is the case in HMC [178]. That is, QIHMC sets the covariance mass matrix **M** in HMC in Eq. (1.15) to be a stochastic process [128]. The authors show that QIHMC outperforms HMC, RMHMC and the NUTS [105] on a variety of spiky and multi-modal distributions which occur in sparse modelling via bridge regression, image denoising and Bayesian Neural Network (BNN) pruning, and furthermore leaves the target distribution invariant. The proof that QIHMC leaves the target distribution invariant utilises Bayes theorem to marginalise out the random mass matrix, and can be found in Liu and Zhang [128].

A key feature of QIHMC is that it requires very little modification to existing HMC implementations, which makes it straightforward to incorporate into already existing HMC code. HMC is typically inefficient in sampling from spiky and multi-modal distributions [128]. Setting the mass matrix **M** to be random alleviates this drawback of HMC.

Suppose it is straightforward to generate samples from the distribution of the mass matrix $\mathbf{M} \sim \mathcal{P}_\mathbf{M}$. In that case, there will be very little additional computational overhead in QIHMC, but with potentially significant improvements in target exploration [128]. It is worth noting that HMC is a special case of QIHMC when the probability distribution over the mass matrix is the Dirac delta function [128]. This feature illustrates how closely related these two algorithms are.

As the Hamiltonian in QIHMC is the same as in HMC, we integrate the dynamics using the leapfrog scheme outline in Eq. (1.20). The only difference with HMC is that the mass matrix of the auxilary momentum variable is chosen from a user-specified distribution for

---

Algorithm 1.3 Magnetic Hamiltonian Monte Carlo algorithm.

Input: $N, \epsilon, L, w_{\text{init}}, H(w, p), G$

Output: $(w)_{m=0}^{N}$

1:   $w_0 \leftarrow w_{\text{init}}$
2:   **for** $m \rightarrow 1$ to N **do**
3:     $p_{m-1} \sim \mathcal{N}(0, \mathbf{M})$ $\leftarrow$ **momentum refreshment**
4:     $p_m, w_m = \textbf{Integrator}(p_{m-1}, w_{m-1}, \epsilon, L, G, H)$ in Eq. (1.23)
5:     $\delta H = H(w_{m-1}, p_{m-1}) - H(w_m, p_m)$
6:     $\alpha_m = \min(1, \exp(\delta H))$
7:     $u_m \sim \text{Unif}(0, 1)$
8:     **if** $\alpha_m > u_m$ **then**
9:       $w_m = w_m$
10:      $G = -G, p_m = -p_m$
11:    **else**
12:      $w_m = w_{m-1}$
13:    **end if**
14:    $p_m = -p_m \leftarrow$ **flip momentum**
15:    $G = -G \leftarrow$ **flip magnetic field**
16: **end for**

Algorithm 1.4 Quantum-Inspired Hamiltonian Monte Carlo algorithm.

Input: $N, \epsilon, L, w_{\text{init}}, H(w, p)$

Output: $(w)_{m=0}^{N}$

1:   $w_0 \leftarrow w_{\text{init}}$
2:   **for** $m \rightarrow 1$ to N **do**
3:     $\mathbf{M} \sim \mathcal{P}_{\mathbf{M}}(\mathbf{M})$ $\leftarrow$ **only difference with HMC** in Algorithm 1.2
4:     $p_{m-1} \sim \mathcal{N}(0, \mathbf{M})$ $\leftarrow$ **momentum refreshment**
5:     $p_m, w_m = \textbf{Leapfrog}(p_{m-1}, w_{m-1}, \epsilon, L, H)$ in Eq. (1.20)
6:     $\delta H = H(w_{m-1}, p_{m-1}) - H(w_m, p_m)$
7:     $\alpha_m = \min(1, \exp(\delta H))$
8:     $u_m \sim \text{Unif}(0, 1)$
9:     $w_m = \textbf{Metropolis}(\alpha_m, u_m, w_m, w_{m-1})$ in Eq. (1.21)
10: **end for**

---

each generation of a new sample. The pseudo-code for the QIHMC algorithm is shown in Algorithm 1.4. Line 3 in Algorithm 1.4 is the only difference between QIHMC and HMC.

A fundamental limitation of QIHMC is what probability distribution $\mathcal{P}_{\mathbf{M}}$ over $\mathbf{M}$ to use, as well as the potential tuning of the parameters of the chosen probability distribution. An improperly chosen distribution could result in wasted computation without any significant improvements to sampling performance. Liu and Zhang [128] employ a log-normal distribution for the diagonal elements of the mass matrix, but do not provide a mechanism or a heuristic to tune the parameters to obtain optimal results. The selection of the optimal $\mathcal{P}_\mathbf{M}$ is still an open research problem.

1.8 Separable Shadow Hamiltonian Hybrid Monte Carlo

The leapfrog integrator for HMC only preserves the Hamiltonian, that is, the total energy of the system, up to second order $\mathcal{O}(\epsilon^2)$ [110,212]. This leads to a larger than expected value for δH in line 5 of Algorithm 1.2 for long trajectories, which results in more rejections in the MH step in line 8 of Algorithm 1.2. To increase the accuracy of the preservation of the total energy to higher orders, and consequently maintain high acceptance rates, one could: 1) decrease the step size and thus only consider short trajectories, or 2) utilise numerical integration schemes which preserve the Hamiltonian to a higher order, 3) or a combination of 1) and 2). These three approaches typically lead to a high computational burden, which is not ideal [98,192].

An alternative strategy is to assess the error produced by feeding the solution backward through [90,145] the leapfrog integration scheme in Eq. (1.20), to derive a modified Hamiltonian whose energy is preserved to a higher-order by the integration scheme than the true Hamiltonian [145]. This modified Hamiltonian is also referred to as the shadow Hamiltonian. We then sample from the shadow density and correct for the induced bias via importance sampling as is done in [98,110,192,212], among others.

Shadow Hamiltonians are perturbations of the Hamiltonian that are by design exactly conserved by the numerical integrator [110,145,161,192]. In the case of shadow Hamiltonian Hybrid Monte Carlo, we sample from the importance distribution defined by the shadow Hamiltonian [145]:

$$\hat{\pi} \propto \exp\left(-\tilde{H}^{[k]}(\mathbf{w}, \mathbf{p})\right) \tag{1.26}$$

where $\tilde{H}^{[k]}$ is the shadow Hamiltonian defined using backward error analysis of the numerical integrator up to the kth order [145]. These modified densities can be proved to be Hamiltonian for symplectic integrators such as the leapfrog integrator [110,145,161,212]. In this book, we focus on a fourth-order truncation of the shadow Hamiltonian under the leapfrog integrator. Since the leapfrog is second-order accurate ($\mathcal{O}^2$), the fourth-order truncation is conserved with higher accuracy ($\mathcal{O}^4$) than the true Hamiltonian, which should improve the acceptance rate. In Theorem 1.8.1, we derive the fourth-order shadow Hamiltonian corresponding to the leapfrog integrator.

Theorem 1.8.1. *Let $H : R^d \times R^d = R$ be a smooth Hamiltonian function. The fourth–order shadow Hamiltonian function $\hat{H} : R^d \times R^d = R$ corresponding to the leapfrog integrator of HMC is given by:*

$$\hat{H}(\mathbf{w}, \mathbf{p}) = H(\mathbf{w}, \mathbf{p}) + \frac{\epsilon^2}{12}[K_\mathbf{p} U_{\mathbf{ww}} K_\mathbf{p}] - \frac{\epsilon^2}{24}[U_\mathbf{w} K_{\mathbf{pp}} U_\mathbf{w}] + \mathcal{O}(\epsilon^4) \tag{1.27}$$

Proof. The Hamiltonian vector field: $\vec{H} = \vec{A} + \vec{B}$ will generate the exact flow corresponding to exactly simulating the HMC dynamics [213]. We obtain the shadow density by making use of the separability of the Hamiltonian in Eq. (1.14). The leapfrog integration scheme in Eq. (1.20) splits the Hamiltonian as:

$$H(\mathbf{w}, \mathbf{p}) = H_1(\mathbf{w}) + H_2(\mathbf{p}) + H_1(\mathbf{w}) \tag{1.28}$$

and exactly integrates each sub-Hamiltonian. Through the BCH formula, we obtain [91]:

$$\begin{aligned}
\Phi_{\epsilon,H} &= \Phi_{\epsilon,H_1(\mathbf{w})} \circ \Phi_{\epsilon,H_2(\mathbf{p})} \circ \Phi_{\epsilon,H_1(\mathbf{w})} \\
&= \exp\left(\frac{\epsilon}{2}\vec{B}\right) \circ \exp\left(\epsilon\,\vec{A}\right) \circ \exp\left(\frac{\epsilon}{2}\vec{B}\right) \\
&= \mathrm{H}(\mathbf{w}, \mathbf{p}) + \frac{\epsilon^2}{12}\{K, \{K, U\}\} - \frac{\epsilon^2}{24}\{U, \{U, K\}\} + \mathcal{O}(\epsilon^4)
\end{aligned} \tag{1.29}$$

where the canonical Poisson brackets are defined as:

$$\begin{aligned}
\{f, g\} &= [\nabla_{\mathbf{w}} f, \nabla_{\mathbf{p}} f] \begin{bmatrix} \mathbf{0} & \mathbf{I} \\ -\mathbf{I} & \mathbf{0} \end{bmatrix} [\nabla_{\mathbf{w}} g, \nabla_{\mathbf{p}} g]^T \\
&= -\nabla_{\mathbf{p}} f \nabla_{\mathbf{w}} g + \nabla_{\mathbf{w}} f \nabla_{\mathbf{p}} g
\end{aligned} \tag{1.30}$$

The shadow Hamiltonian for the leapfrog integrator is then:

$$\hat{\mathrm{H}}(\mathbf{w}, \mathbf{p}) = \mathrm{H}(\mathbf{w}, \mathbf{p}) + \frac{\epsilon^2}{12}[K_{\mathbf{p}} U_{\mathbf{ww}} K_{\mathbf{p}}] - \frac{\epsilon^2}{24}[U_{\mathbf{w}} K_{\mathbf{pp}} U_{\mathbf{w}}] + \mathcal{O}(\epsilon^4) \tag{1.31}$$

It is worth noting that the shadow Hamiltonian in (1.31) is conserved to fourth-order [98, 192,212]. □

Izaguirre and Hampton [110] utilised the shadow Hamiltonian in Theorem 1.8.1 to derive the Shadow Hamiltonian Monte Carlo (SHMC) algorithm, which produce better efficiency and acceptance rates when compared to HMC. It is worth noting that the shadow Hamiltonian in Theorem 1.8.1 is not separable, i.e., the terms that depend on $\mathbf{w}$ and $\mathbf{p}$ can not be separated. The non-separable shadow Hamiltonian is not ideal as it requires computationally expensive methods for generating the momenta. Sweet et al. improve on the SHMC method by introducing the S2HMC algorithm which utilises a processed leapfrog integrator to create a separable Hamiltonian [145,161,212]. The separable Hamiltonian in S2HMC is as follows:

$$\tilde{\mathrm{H}}(\mathbf{w}, \mathbf{p}) = \mathrm{U}(\mathbf{w}) + \mathrm{K}(\mathbf{p}) + \frac{\epsilon^2}{24} U_{\mathbf{w}}^T \mathrm{M}^{-1} U_{\mathbf{w}} + \mathcal{O}(\epsilon^4) \tag{1.32}$$

which is obtained by substituting a canonical transformation $(\hat{\mathbf{w}}, \hat{\mathbf{p}}) = \mathcal{X}(\mathbf{w}, \mathbf{p})$ into (1.31). We provide a detailed derivation of the separable Hamiltonian in Eq. (1.32) in Appendix A.1.

The canonical transformation required to generate the separable Hamiltonian in S2HMC is a transformation of both the position $\mathbf{w}$ and the momenta $\mathbf{p}$ variables so as to remove the mixed terms in the shadow Hamiltonian in Theorem 1.8.1. This transformation or map should commute with reversal of momenta and should preserve phase space volume so that the resulting S2HMC algorithm satisfies detailed balance [145,161,212]. Propagation of positions and momenta on this shadow Hamiltonian is performed after performing this reversible mapping $(\hat{\mathbf{w}}, \hat{\mathbf{p}}) = \mathcal{X}(\mathbf{w}, \mathbf{p})$. The canonical transformation $\mathcal{X}(\mathbf{w}, \mathbf{p})$ is given as [145,161,212]:

$$\hat{\mathbf{p}} = \mathbf{p} - \frac{\epsilon^2}{12} U_{\mathbf{ww}} K_{\mathbf{p}} + \mathcal{O}(\epsilon^4)$$

$$\hat{\mathbf{w}} = \mathbf{w} + \frac{\epsilon^2}{12} K_{\mathbf{pp}} U_{\mathbf{w}} + \mathcal{O}(\epsilon^4)$$

(1.33)

where $(\hat{\mathbf{w}}, \hat{\mathbf{p}})$ is found through fixed point[3] iterations as:

$$\hat{\mathbf{p}} = \mathbf{p} - \frac{\epsilon}{24} \left[U_{\mathbf{w}}(\mathbf{w} + \epsilon \mathbf{M}^{-1} \hat{\mathbf{p}}) - U_{\mathbf{w}}(\mathbf{w} - \epsilon \mathbf{M}^{-1} \hat{\mathbf{p}}) \right]$$

$$\hat{\mathbf{w}} = \mathbf{w} + \frac{\epsilon^2}{24} \mathbf{M}^{-1} \left[U_{\mathbf{w}}(\mathbf{w} + \epsilon \mathbf{M}^{-1} \hat{\mathbf{p}}) + U_{\mathbf{w}}(\mathbf{w} - \epsilon \mathbf{M}^{-1} \hat{\mathbf{p}}) \right]$$

(1.34)

After the leapfrog is performed, this mapping is reversed using post-processing via following fixed point iterations:

$$\mathbf{w} = \hat{\mathbf{w}} - \frac{\epsilon^2}{24} \mathbf{M}^{-1} \left[U_{\mathbf{w}}(\mathbf{w} + \epsilon \mathbf{M}^{-1} \hat{\mathbf{p}}) + U_{\mathbf{w}}(\mathbf{w} - \epsilon \mathbf{M}^{-1} \hat{\mathbf{p}}) \right]$$

$$\mathbf{p} = \hat{\mathbf{p}} + \frac{\epsilon}{24} \left[U_{\mathbf{w}}(\mathbf{w} + \epsilon \mathbf{M}^{-1} \hat{\mathbf{p}}) - U_{\mathbf{w}}(\mathbf{w} - \epsilon \mathbf{M}^{-1} \hat{\mathbf{p}}) \right]$$

(1.35)

Theorem 1.8.2 guarantees that S2HMC, which uses the processed leapfrog integrator, satisfies detailed balance and thus leaves the target density invariant.

Theorem 1.8.2. *S2HMC satisfies detailed balance.*

Proof. To prove that S2HMC satisfies detailed balance, we need to show that the processing map $(\hat{\mathbf{w}}, \hat{\mathbf{p}}) = \mathcal{X}(\mathbf{w}, \mathbf{p})$ commutes with reversal of momenta and preserves phase space volume. This will ensure that the resulting processed leapfrog integrator used in S2HMC is both sympletic and reversible. The detailed proof of this is provided in Sweet et al. [212], and we present this in Appendix A.2 for ease of reference.   □

Once the samples are obtained from S2HMC as depicted in Algorithm 1.5, importance weights are calculated to allow for the use of the shadow canonical density rather than the true density. These weights are based on the differences between the true and shadow Hamiltonians as:

---

[3] Hessian approximated as: $U_{\mathbf{ww}} K_{\mathbf{p}} = \frac{1}{2\epsilon} [U_{\mathbf{w}}(\mathbf{w} + \epsilon \mathbf{M}^{-1} \hat{\mathbf{p}}) - U_{\mathbf{w}}(\mathbf{w} - \epsilon \mathbf{M}^{-1} \hat{\mathbf{p}})]$.

Algorithm 1.5 Separable Shadow Hamiltonian Hybrid Monte Carlo algorithm.

Input: $N, \epsilon, L, w_{\text{init}}, H(w, p), \tilde{H}(w, p)$
Output: $(w)_{m=0}^N$, importance weights $= (b)_{m=0}^N$

1:   $w_0 \leftarrow w_{\text{init}}$
2: **for** $m \rightarrow 1$ to N **do**
3:     $p_{m-1} \sim \mathcal{N}(0, \mathbf{M})$ ← **momentum refreshment**
4:     Apply the pre-processing mapping $(\hat{\mathbf{w}}, \hat{\mathbf{p}}) = \mathcal{X}(\mathbf{w}, \mathbf{p})$ in Eq. (1.34)
5:     $p_m, w_m = \textbf{Leapfrog}(p_{m-1}, w_{m-1}, \epsilon, L, \tilde{H})$ in Eq. (1.20)
6:     Apply the post-processing mapping $(\mathbf{w}, \mathbf{p}) = \mathcal{X}^{-1}(\hat{\mathbf{w}}, \hat{\mathbf{p}})$ in Eq. (1.35)
7:     $\delta H = \tilde{H}(w_{m-1}, p_{m-1}) - \tilde{H}(w_m, p_m)$
8:     $\alpha_m = \min(1, \exp(\delta H))$
9:     $u_m \sim \text{Unif}(0, 1)$
10:    $w_m = \textbf{Metropolis}(\alpha, u_m, w_m, w_{m-1})$
11:    $b_m = \exp(-(H(w_m, p_m) - \tilde{H}(w_m, p_m)))$
12: **end for**

$$b_m = \exp\left[-\left(\mathrm{H}(\mathbf{w}, \mathbf{p}) - \hat{\mathrm{H}}(\mathbf{w}, \mathbf{p})\right)\right]. \tag{1.36}$$

Expectations of $f(\mathbf{w})$ are then computed as a weighted average. It is important to note that the weights in Eq. (1.36) should always be taken into account in every performance measure utilised to assess the performance of S2HMC. This is because non-uniform weights impact the overall utility of importance samplers.

Lines 4 to 6 in Algorithm 1.5 represent the processed leapfrog integrator. This scheme degenerates to the traditional leapfrog integration scheme when the shadow Hamiltonian is equal to the true Hamiltonian.

1.9 No-U-Turn Sampler algorithm

We have yet to address how one selects the step size ϵ and trajectory length L parameters of samplers based on Hamiltonian dynamics such as HMC, MHMC and S2HMC. These parameters significantly influence the sampling performance of the algorithms [105]. A significant step size typically results in most of the produced samples being rejected, while a small step size results in slow convergence and mixing of the chain [105]. When the trajectory length is too small, then the method displays random walk behaviour, and when the trajectory length is considerable, the algorithm wastes computational resources [105]. The NUTS algorithm of Hoffman and Gelman [105] automates the tuning of the HMC step size and trajectory length parameters.

In NUTS, the step size parameter is tuned through primal-dual averaging during an initial burn-in phase. A user specified MH acceptance rate δ is targeted via primal-dual averaging given as [11,141]:

$$\epsilon_{t+1} \leftarrow \mu - \frac{\sqrt{t}}{\gamma} \frac{1}{t+t_0} \sum_{i=1}^{t} H_i$$

(1.37)

$$\bar{\epsilon}_{t+1} \leftarrow \eta_t \epsilon_{t+1} + (1 - \eta_t)\bar{\epsilon}_t$$

where μ is a free parameter that ϵ_t gravitates to, γ controls the convergence towards μ, η_t is a decaying rate of adaptation in line with [11], and H_t is the difference between the target acceptance rate and the actual acceptance rate [105,145]. The primal-dual averaging updates are such that [145]:

$$\mathbb{E}[H_t] = \mathbb{E}[\delta - \alpha_t] = 0.$$

(1.38)

This has the effect of updating the step size towards the target acceptance rate δ. Hoffman and Gelman [105] found that setting $\mu = \log(10\epsilon_0)$, $\bar{\epsilon}_0 = 1$, $\bar{H}_0 = 0$, $\gamma = 0.05$, $t_0 = 10$, $\kappa = 0.75$ with ϵ_0 being the initial step size results in good performance across various target posterior distributions. These are the settings that we utilise in this book with $\epsilon_0 = 0.0001$.

In the NUTS methodology, the trajectory length parameter is automatically tuned by iteratively doubling the trajectory length until the Hamiltonian becomes infinite or the chain starts to trace back [3,144]. That is, when the last proposed position state $\mathbf{w}^*$ starts becoming closer to the initial position $\mathbf{w}$. This happens if: $(\mathbf{w}^* - \mathbf{w}) \times \mathbf{p} \leq 0$. This approach, however, violates the detailed balance condition. To overcome the violation of detailed balance in NUTS, a path of states $\mathcal{B}$ is generated such that its size is determined by the termination criterion [3,105]. The set $\mathcal{B}$ has the following property, which is required for detailed balance [3,105]:

$$P(\mathcal{B}|\mathbf{z}) = P(\mathcal{B}|\mathbf{z}') \quad \forall \mathbf{z}, \mathbf{z}' \in \mathcal{B}.$$

(1.39)

where $\mathbf{z} = (\mathbf{w}, \mathbf{p})$ is the current state. That is, the probability of generating $\mathcal{B}$, starting from any of its members is the same [3,105]. Having $\mathcal{B}$, the current state $\mathbf{z}$ and a slice variable u that is uniformly drawn from the interval $[0, \pi_Z(\mathbf{z})]$, a set of chosen states $\mathcal{C}$ [3,105]:

$$\mathcal{C} := \left\{ \mathbf{z}' \in \mathcal{B} \quad s.t \quad \pi_Z(\mathbf{z}) \geq u \right\}$$

(1.40)

is constructed from which the next state is drawn uniformly.

Algorithm 1.6 shows the pseudo-code for NUTS with dual averaging, showing how the trajectory length L and the step size ϵ are set automatically. The NUTS algorithm has a main *while* loop that contains the termination criterion and is presented in Algorithm 1.6, as well as an algorithm for iteratively doubling the trajectory length which is shown in Algorithm 1.7. The overall methodology of generating a single sample from NUTS can be summarised as follows, with the reader being referred to Hoffman and Gelman [105] for more information on the NUTS algorithm:

1. Set the initial states – which is the **Input** step in Algorithm 1.6
2. Generate the auxiliary momentum and slice variables as shown in line 2 of Algorithm 1.6

3. Generate the set of chosen states $\mathcal{C}$ via the doubling procedure in Algorithm 1.7. Note the use of the leapfrog integration scheme in line 2 in Algorithm 1.7

4. Each proposal is accepted or rejected in line 12 of Algorithm 1.6. Note that this is not the typical Metropolis acceptance probability as the proposal is chosen from multiple candidates in $\mathcal{C}$

5. Update the step size via dual averaging in lines 17 – 21 in Algorithm 1.6. Note that this step size is no longer updated post the burn-in period which is indicated by M^{adapt}.

One then repeats steps 2 through 5 to generate the required number of samples N.

Algorithm 1.6 No-U-Turn Sampler with Primal-Dual Averaging algorithm.

Input: M, M^{adapt}, ϵ_0, w^0, $\mu = \log(10\epsilon_0)$, $\bar{\epsilon}_0 = 1$, $\bar{H}_0 = 0$, $\gamma = 0.05$, $t_0 = 10$, $\kappa = 0.75$ and $\epsilon_0 = 0.0001$

Output: $(w)_{m=0}^N$

1: **for** $m \to 1$ to M **do**

2: $\quad p^{m-1} \sim \mathcal{N}(0, \mathbf{I})$, $u \sim \mathrm{Unif}[0, \exp(-H(w^{m-1}, p^{m-1}))]$

3: $\quad w^- = w^{m-1}, w^+ = w^{m-1}, w^- = w^{m-1}, p^- = p^{m-1}, p^+ = p^{m-1}, j = 0, n = 1, s = 1.$

4: $\quad$ **while** $s = 1$ **do**

5: $\qquad v \sim \mathrm{Unif}[-1, 1]$

6: $\qquad$ **if** $v = -1$ **then**

7: $\qquad\quad w^-, p^-, -, -, w', p', n', s', \alpha, n_\alpha = \mathbf{BuildTree}(w^-, p^-, u, v, j, \epsilon_{m-1}, w^{m-1}, p^{m-1})$ in Algorithm 1.7

8: $\qquad$ **else**

9: $\qquad\quad -, -, w^+, p^+, w', p', n', s', \alpha, n_\alpha = \mathbf{BuildTree}(w^+, p^+, u, v, j, \epsilon_{m-1}, w^{m-1}, p^{m-1})$ in Algorithm 1.7

10: $\qquad$ **end if**

11: $\qquad$ **if** $s' = 1$ **then**

12: $\qquad\quad$ With prob. $\min(1, \frac{n'}{n})$, set $w^m = w', p^m = p'$

13: $\qquad$ **end if**

14: $\qquad n = n + n', j = j + 1$

15: $\qquad s = s' \mathbf{I}[(w^+ - w^-)p^- \geq 0]\mathbf{I}[(w^+ - w^-)p^+ \geq 0]$

16: $\quad$ **end while**

17: $\quad$ **if** $m < M^{adapt}$ **then**

18: $\qquad \bar{H}_m = (1 - \frac{1}{m+t_0})\bar{H}_{m-1} + \frac{1}{m+t_0}(\delta - \alpha_m)$

19: $\qquad \log \epsilon_m = \mu - \frac{\sqrt{m}}{\gamma}\bar{H}_m, \log \bar{\epsilon}_m = m^{-\kappa} \log \epsilon_m + (1 - m^{-\kappa}) \log \bar{\epsilon}_{m-1}$

20: $\quad$ **else**

21: $\qquad \epsilon_m = \bar{\epsilon}_{M^{adapt}}$

22: $\quad$ **end if**

23: **end for**

Algorithm 1.7 Algorithm for iteratively doubling the trajectory length.

    function BuildTree($w, p, u, v, j, \epsilon, w^0, p^0$)
    Output: $w^-, p^-, w^+, p^+, w', p', n', s', \alpha', n'_\alpha$

1: **if** $j = 0$ **then**
2:    $w', p' = $ **Leapfrog**$(p, w, \epsilon v)$
3:    $n' = \mathbf{I}[u < \exp(-H(w', p'))], s' = \mathbf{I}[u < \exp(\Delta_{max} - H(w', p'))]$
4:    $n_\alpha = 1, \alpha = \min(1, \exp(H(w^0, p^0) - H(w', p')))$
5:    **return** $w', p', w', p', w', p', n', s', \alpha, n_\alpha$
6: **else**
7:    $w^-, {}^-, w^+, {}^+, w', p', n', s', \alpha', n'_\alpha = $ BuildTree$(w, p, u, v, j - 1, \epsilon, w^0, p^0)$
8:    **if** s'=1 **then**
9:      **if** $v = -1$ **then**
10:        $w^-, p^-, -, -, w'', p'', n'', s'', \alpha'', n''_\alpha = $ BuildTree$(w^-, p^-, u, v, j - 1, \epsilon, w^0, p^0)$
11:      **else**
12:        $-, -, w^+, p^+, w'', p'', n'', s'', \alpha'', n''_\alpha = $ BuildTree$(w^+, p^+, u, v, j - 1, \epsilon, w^0, p^0)$
13:      **end if**
14:      With prob. $\frac{n'}{n'+n''}$, set $w' = w'', p' = p''$
15:      $\alpha' = \alpha' + \alpha'', n' = n' + n'', n'_\alpha = n'_\alpha + n''_\alpha$
16:      $s' = s''\mathbf{I}[(w^+ - w^-)p^- \geq 0]\mathbf{I}[(w^+ - w^-)p^+ \geq 0]$
17:    **end if**
18:    **return** $w^-, p^-, w^+, p^+, w', p', n', s', \alpha', n'_\alpha$
19: **end if**

1.10 Antithetic Hamiltonian Monte Carlo

The coupling of MCMC chains has been used as a theoretical tool to prove convergence behaviour of Markov chains [31,111,113,114,201]. Johnson [114] presents a convergence diagnostic for MCMC methods that is based on coupling a Markov chain with another chain that is periodically restarted from fixed parameter values. The diagnostic provides an informal lower bound on the Effective Sample Size (ESS) rates of the MCMC chain. Jacob et al. [111] remove the bias in MCMC chains by using couplings of Markov chains using a telescopic sum argument. The resulting unbiased estimators can then be computed independently in parallel. More recently, MCMC couplings have been studied for HMC with Heng and Jacob [99] proposing an approach that constructs a pair of HMC chains that are coupled in such a way that they meet after some random number of iterations. These chains can then be combined to create unbiased chains. Unlike the approach of Heng and Jacob [99] and other authors [111,189], Bou-Rabee et al. [31] present a new coupling algorithm where the momentum variable is not shared between the coupled chains.

    In this book, we explore methods that use the results from coupling theory to create anti-correlated HMC based chains where the momentum variable is shared between the chains. We create these anti-correlated chains by running the second chain with the auxiliary momentum variable having the opposite sign of the momentum of the first chain. These chains also share the random uniform variable in the MH acceptance step. When these two chains anti-couple strongly, taking the average of the two chains results in estimators that have lower variance, or equivalently, these chains produce samples that have higher ESSs than their non-antithetic counterparts.

The work that is closely related to ours is the recent article by Piponi et al. [189], where the authors introduce the antithetic HMC variance reduction technique. The antithetic HMC samplers have an advantage over antithetic Gibbs samplers. Antithetic HMC methods apply to problems where conditional distributions are intractable and where Gibbs sampling may mix slowly [189]. The pseudo-code for the antithetic HMC method of Piponi et al. is shown in Algorithm 1.8. The difference between the antithetic HMC algorithm and the original HMC method is that the momentum variable (see line 3 and 4 in Algorithm 1.8) and the uniform random variable in the MH acceptance step (see line 13 and 14 in Algorithm 1.8) are shared between the two chains.

Algorithm 1.8 Antithetic Hamiltonian Monte Carlo algorithm.

Input: $N, \epsilon, L, w^x_{\text{init}}, w^y_{\text{init}}, H(w, p)$
Output: $(w^x)^N_{m=0}, (w^y)^N_{m=0}$

1: $w^x_0 \leftarrow w^x_{\text{init}}$
2: $w^y_0 \leftarrow w^y_{\text{init}}$
3: **for** $m \to 1$ to N **do**
4:　　$p^x_{m-1} \sim \mathcal{N}(0, \mathbf{M})$
5:　　$p^y_{m-1} = -p^x_{m-1}$ ← **momentum shared between the two chains**
6:　　$p^x_m, w^x_m = \textbf{Leapfrog}(p^x_{m-1}, w^x_{m-1}, \epsilon, L, H)$
7:　　$p^y_m, w^y_m = \textbf{Leapfrog}(p^y_{m-1}, w^y_{m-1}, \epsilon, L, H)$

8:　　$\delta H^x = H(w^x_{m-1}, p^x_{m-1}) - H(w^x_m, p^x_m)$
9:　　$\delta H^y = H(w^y_{m-1}, p^y_{m-1}) - H(w^y_m, p^y_m)$

10:　$\alpha^x_m = \min(1, \exp(\delta H^x))$
11:　$\alpha^y_m = \min(1, \exp(\delta H^y))$

12:　$u_m \sim \text{Unif}(0, 1)$ ← **uniform random variable shared in line 13 and 14 below**
13:　$w^x_m = \textbf{Metropolis}(\alpha^x_m, u_m, w^x_m, w^x_{m-1})$
14:　$w^y_m = \textbf{Metropolis}(\alpha^y_m, u_m, w^y_m, w^y_{m-1})$
15: **end for**

Suppose we have two random variables X and Y, that are not necessarily independent, with the same marginal distribution U, we have that:

$$\text{Var}\left[\frac{f(X) + f(Y)}{2}\right] = \frac{1}{4}[\text{Var}f(X) + \text{Var}f(Y)] + \frac{1}{2} \times \text{Cov}[f(X), f(Y)]. \qquad (1.41)$$

When $f(X)$ and $f(Y)$ are negatively correlated, the average of the two random variables will produce a lower variance than the average of two independent variables. This equation forms the basis for the antithetic sampling algorithms that we introduce in this book.

The full benefit of antithetic sampling is most significant when the target distribution $\mathbf{U}(\mathbf{w})$ is symmetrical about some vector [70,189]. For the majority of target distribution of interest to machine learning researchers, the symmetry holds only approximately [189]. The approximate symmetry results in approximate anti-coupling; that is, we will not observe perfect anti-correlation in practice as would be the case if $\mathbf{U}(\mathbf{w})$ was symmetric. However, the approximate anti-coupling nonetheless still provides decent variance reduction in practice [189]. We rely on these results to propose new antithetic versions of MHMC and S2HMC later in this book.

1.11 Book objectives

Our primary objective in this book is to improve MHMC and S2HMC by developing more efficient and alternative methodologies to enhance their performance in sampling from various probabilistic machine learning models. We aim to do this by combining ideas of utilising random mass matrices for the auxiliary momentum variable, employing partial momentum refreshment, deriving shadow Hamiltonians, automatically tuning the parameters of the methods as well as using antithetic sampling to reduce the variance of MHMC and S2HMC. This combination of ideas is based on addressing the gaps we identified in the literature as summarised in Table 1.1. A secondary aim of this book is to apply MCMC methods in various real world scenarios. Thus, we apply Bayesian inference to wind speed forecasting, Covid-19 lockdown analysis, option pricing and analysing South African municipal financial statement audit outcomes. In Section 1.12 below, we outline the contributions to knowledge provided by this book in more detail.

Table 1.1 This table highlights the gaps in the literature that we have identified. A NO entry means that the item is yet to be considered in the literature. A N/A entry means that the item is not applicable to the algorithm. For the items that have already been addressed in the literature, we provide an appropriate reference.

Algorithm	Partial Momentum Retention	Shadow Density	Random Mass Matrix	Adaptive Approaches	Antithetic Sampling
MH	[177]	N/A	NO	[88,151]	[189]
MALA	[177]	N/A	NO	[14]	[189]
HMC	[107]	[110,212]	[128]	[3,105]	[189]
MHMC	NO	NO	NO	NO	NO
RMHMC	[98]	[98]	NO	[24,105]	NO
S2HMC	NO	N/A	NO	NO	NO

1.12 Book contributions

The contributions of this book are both of a theoretical nature in terms of new or improved methods and novel application areas using the Bayesian framework. The contributions of this book are summarised in Fig. 1.2 and presented in detail below:

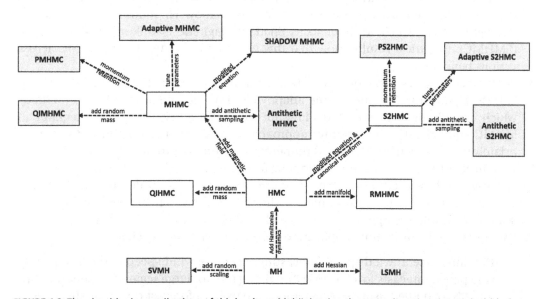

FIGURE 1.2 The algorithmic contributions of this book are highlighted as the green (gray in print version) blocks. The arrows indicate the relationship between the different algorithms and show how our proposed algorithms are derived from existing methods.

1. We begin the book by introducing the Stochastic Volatility Metropolis-Hastings (SVMH) and Locally Scaled Metropolis-Hastings (LSMH) methods. These algorithms extend random walk MH by treating the scale matrix as being stochastic and allowing it to depend on the local geometry of the target respectively. These approaches provide improved sampling behaviour when compared to MH, with SVMH provided a better time-normalised ESS performance over NUTS as the dimensionality of the problem increases.

2. We then present a new technique which we refer to as the Quantum-Inspired Magnetic Hamiltonian Monte Carlo (QIMHMC) algorithm. This method uses a random mass matrix instead of a fixed mass for the auxiliary momentum variable in MHMC. This approach mimics the behaviour of quantum particles and leads to better results when compared to HMC, MHMC and QIHMC.

3. We proceed to present novel sampling techniques that employ partial momentum refreshments in the generation of each sample. These are the Magnetic Hamiltonian Monte Carlo With Partial Momentum Refreshment (PMHMC) and Separable Shadow Hamiltonian Hybrid Monte Carlo With Partial Momentum Refreshment (PS2HMC). These two new algorithms illustrate the sampling benefits of not fully refreshing the

auxiliary momentum variable in MHMC and S2HMC respectively. Numerical experiments on numerous targets show that PMHMC outperforms HMC, MHMC and Hamiltonian Monte Carlo With Partial Momentum Refreshment (PHMC) while PS2HMC outperforms S2HMC and PMHMC on an ESS basis.

4. We further derive the fourth-order modified Hamiltonian associated with the numerical integrator employed in MHMC. From this shadow Hamiltonian, we construct a novel sampler which we refer to as Shadow Magnetic Hamiltonian Monte Carlo (SMHMC). Empirical results show that this new method outperforms MHMC across various benchmarks.

5. We then address the issue of automatically tuning the parameters of the MHMC and S2HMC algorithms. We present the adaptive MHMC and adaptive S2HMC methods which extends the NUTS methodology to use the processed leapfrog integrator in MHMC and S2HMC. This adaptive approaches are shown to outperform the appropriately tuned base methods across numerous benchmark problems.

6. We consider the use of antithetic sampling for MHMC and S2HMC to reduce the overall variance of the estimators based on these samplers, or equivalently to increase the effective sample size of these samplers. The results show that the new methods with antithetic sampling outperform the original methods without antithetic sampling.

7. We present first-in-literature applications of the Bayesian approach in:

   - BNN inference in wind speed forecasting. Accurate wind speed and consequently wind power forecasts form a critical enabling tool for large scale wind energy adoption. BNNs trained using HMC methods are used to forecast one hour ahead wind speeds on the Wind Atlas for South Africa datasets. A generalisable Automatic Relevance Determination (ARD) committee framework is introduced to synthesise the various sampler ARD outputs into robust feature selections.

   - Analysing South Africa's efforts in combating the spread of the Severe Acute Respiratory Syndrome Coronavirus 2 (SARS-CoV-2) using lockdown levels. We utilise the NUTS algorithm in sampling posterior distributions of parameters induced by a Susceptible Infected Recovered (SIR) model configured change points corresponding to the different levels of lockdown put in place by the South African Government in terms of the Disaster Management Act. We utilise these results to analyse the effectiveness of the distinct lockdown alert levels entailed by South Africa's regulations to the Disaster Management Act.

   - Infer South African equity option prices. We calibrate the one-dimensional Merton jump-diffusion model to European put and call option data on the All-Share price index using MCMC methods. Our approach produces a distribution of the jump-diffusion model parameters, which can be used to build economic scenario generators and price exotic options such as those embedded in life insurance contracts.

   - Modelling audit outcomes of South African local government entities. Furthermore, we perform ARD using MCMC methods to identify which financial ratios are essential for modelling audit outcomes of municipalities. Stakeholders could use these

results in understanding what drives the audit outcomes of South African municipalities.

1.13 Conclusion

In this chapter, we presented a review of the MCMC methods that form the core of the algorithms that we propose in this book. We also provided an outline of the contributions of
the book, which span both theoretical developments as well as novel real world applications.

In the next chapter, we outline the benchmark test suite and performance metrics that
we utilise to assess the performance of the MCMC methods that we propose in this book.

2

Sampling benchmarks and performance metrics

2.1 Benchmark problems and datasets

In this section, we present the benchmark posterior distributions that we consider in this book. These benchmark target posterior densities have been extensively used in the Bayesian literature [79,98,161,162,165,192,213], including in the seminal work of Girolami and Caldehead [79]. We also present the benchmark datasets that we model using Jump-Diffusion Process (JDP)s, Bayesian Logistic Regression (BLR) and BNNs respectively.

2.1.1 Banana shaped distribution

The Banana shaped density of Haario et al. [88] is a 2-dimensional non-linear target and provides an illustration of a distribution with significant ridge-like structural features that commonly occur in non-identifiable models [88,98,192]. The likelihood and prior distributions are as follows:

$$y|\mathbf{w} \sim \mathcal{N}\left(w_1 + w_2^2 = 1, \sigma_y^2\right), \quad w_1, w_2 \sim \mathcal{N}\left(0, \sigma_\mathbf{w}^2\right) \tag{2.1}$$

We generated one hundred data points for y with $\sigma_y^2 = 4$ and $\sigma_\mathbf{w}^2 = 1$. Due to independence of the data and parameters, the posterior distribution is proportional to:

$$\prod_{i=1}^{i=N} p(y_k|\mathbf{w})p(w_1)p(w_2), \tag{2.2}$$

where $N = 100$ is the number of observations.

2.1.2 Multivariate Gaussian distributions

The task is to sample from D-dimensional Gaussian distributions $\mathcal{N}(0, \boldsymbol{\Sigma})$ with mean zero and covariance matrix $\boldsymbol{\Sigma}$. The covariance matrix $\boldsymbol{\Sigma}$ is diagonal, with the standard deviations simulated from a log-normal distribution with mean zero and unit standard deviation. For the simulation study, we consider the number of dimensions D to be in the set $\{10, 50\}$.

Hamiltonian Monte Carlo Methods in Machine Learning. https://doi.org/10.1016/B978-0-44-319035-3.00014-8

2.1.3 Neal's funnel density

Neal [174] introduced the funnel distribution as an example of a density that illustrated the issues that arise in Bayesian hierarchical and hidden variable models [26,98]. The variance of the parameters is treated as a latent variable with a log-normal distribution [26,98]. In this book, we consider the number of dimensions $D = 25$. The target density of interest is:

$$P(v, \mathbf{x}) = \mathcal{N}(v|\mu, \sigma^2) \prod_{i=1}^{D} \mathcal{N}(x_i|0, \exp(v)), \qquad (2.3)$$

where $\mu = 0, \sigma = 3, v \sim \mathcal{N}(\mu, \sigma^2)$ and $\mathbf{x_i} \in \mathbb{R}$. Note that v and $\mathbf{x}$ are the parameters of interest.

2.1.4 Merton jump-diffusion process model

It is well documented that financial asset returns do not have a Gaussian distribution, but instead have fat tails [51,155]. Stochastic volatility models, Levy models, and combinations of these models have been utilised to capture the leptokurtic nature of asset return distributions [5,8,149,216]. JDPs were introduced into the financial markets literature by Merton and Press in the 1970s [149,155,191]. In this book, we study the JDP model of Merton [149], which is a one-dimensional Markov process $\{X_t, t \geq 0\}$ with the following dynamics as described in Mongwe [155]:

$$d \ln X_t = \left(a - \frac{1}{2}b^2\right)dt + bd Z_t + d\left(\sum_{i=1}^{K_t} J_i\right) \qquad (2.4)$$

where a and b are drift and diffusion terms, Z_t and K_t are the Brownian motion process and Poisson process with intensity λ respectively, and $J_i \sim \mathcal{N}(a_{jump}, b^2_{jump})$ is the size of the ith jump. As shown in Mongwe [155], the density implied by the dynamics in Eq. (2.4) is:

$$\mathbb{P}\big(\ln X(t + \tau) = x_2| \ln X(t) = x_1\big) = \sum_{n=0}^{\infty} \frac{e^{-\lambda\tau}(\lambda\tau)^n}{n!} \frac{\phi\left(\frac{x_2 - x_1 - (a\tau + na_{jump})}{\sqrt{b^2\tau + nb^2_{jump}}}\right)}{\sqrt{b^2\tau + nb^2_{jump}}} \qquad (2.5)$$

with x_2 and x_1 being realisations of $\ln X(t)$ at times $t + \tau$ and t, and ϕ is a Gaussian probability density function. The resultant likelihood is multi-modal as it is an infinite combination of Gaussian random variables, where the Poisson distribution produces the mixing weights [155]. In this book, we truncate the infinite summation in Eq. (2.5) to the first 10 terms as done in [155]. Furthermore, the JDP model is calibrated to historical financial market returns data as outlined in Table 2.2.

2.1.5 Bayesian logistic regression

We utilise BLR to model the real world binary classification datasets in Table 2.2. The negative log-likelihood $l(\text{D}|w)$ function for logistic regression is given as:

$$l(\text{D}|\mathbf{w}) = \sum_{i}^{N} y_i \log(\mathbf{w}^T x_i) + (1 - y_i)\log(1 - \mathbf{w}^T x_i) \qquad (2.6)$$

where D is the data and N is the number of observations. The log of the unnormalised target posterior distribution is given as:

$$\ln p(\mathbf{w}|\text{D}) = l(\text{D}|\mathbf{w}) + \ln p(\mathbf{w}|\alpha) \qquad (2.7)$$

where $\ln p(\mathbf{w}|\alpha)$ is the log of the prior distribution on the parameters given the hyperparameters α. The parameters $\mathbf{w}$ are modelled as having Gaussian prior distributions with zero mean and standard deviation $\alpha = 10$ as in Girolami and Caldehead [79].

2.1.6 Bayesian neural networks

Artificial neural networks are learning machines that have been extensively employed as universal approximators of complex systems with great success [145,161]. This book focuses on Multilayer Perceptron (MLP)s with one hidden layer, five hidden units, and a single output neuron. The MLPs are used to model the real-world benchmark datasets outlined in Table 2.2. These datasets are regression datasets, with the negative log-likelihood being the sum of squared errors.

The outputs of a network with a single output are defined as:

$$f_k(x) = b_k + \sum_{j} v_{jk} h_j(x)$$

$$h_j(x) = \Psi\left(a_j + \sum_{i} w_{ij} x_i\right) \qquad (2.8)$$

where w_{ij} is the weight connection for the ith input to the jth hidden neuron and v_{jk} is the weight connection between the jth hidden neuron to the kth output neuron [145]. In this book we only consider single output MLPs so that $k = 1$. Note that Ψ is the activation function which produces the required non-linearity [145], and we set Ψ to be the hyperbolic tangent activation function in this book.

2.1.7 Benchmark datasets

We present the details of the financial and real-world benchmark datasets used in this book in Table 2.2. The datasets are subdivided based on the type of model utilised to model the datasets. The datasets consist of historical financial market data that we use to calibrate the jump-diffusion process model, as well as real-world benchmark classification datasets,

Table 2.1   Descriptive statistics for the financial markets datasets.

Dataset	mean	standard deviation	skew	kurtosis
S&P 500 Index	0.00043	0.01317	−1.159	21.839
Bitcoin	0.00187	0.04447	−0.925	13.586
USDZAR	0.00019	0.00854	0.117	1.673

which we model using BLR, and real-world benchmark regression datasets modelled using BNNs.

Jump-diffusion process datasets: We calibrate the JDP to three datasets. These are real-world datasets across different financial markets. The real-world financial market datasets consist of daily prices, which we convert into log-returns, that were obtained from Google Finance[1] [82]. The specifics of the datasets are as follows:

- *Bitcoin dataset*: 1461 daily data points for the cryptocurrency (in USD) from 1 Jan. 2017 to 31 Dec. 2020.
- *S&P 500 dataset*: 1007 daily data points for the stock index from 1 Jan. 2017 to 31 Dec. 2020.
- *USDZAR dataset*: 1425 daily data points for the currency from 1 Jan. 2017 to 31 Dec. 2020.

Note that the formula used to calculate the log-returns is given as:

$$r_i = \log(S_i / S_{i-1}) \tag{2.9}$$

where r_i is the log-return on day i and S_i is the stock or currency level on day i. The descriptive statistics of the dataset are shown in Table 2.1. This table shows that the USDZAR dataset has a very low kurtosis, suggesting that it has very few (if any) jumps when compared to the other two datasets.

Bayesian logistic regression datasets: There are four datasets that we modelled using BLR. All the datasets have two classes and thus present a binary classification problem. These datasets are available on the UCI machine learning repository.[2] The specifics of the datasets are:

- *Pima Indian Diabetes dataset* – This dataset has seven features and a total of 532 observations. The aim of this dataset is to predict if a patient has diabetes based on diagnostic measurements made on the patient [150].
- *Heart dataset* – This dataset has 13 features and 270 data points. The purpose of the dataset is to predict the presence of heart disease based on medical tests performed on a patient [150].

---

[1] https://www.google.com/finance/.

[2] https://archive.ics.uci.edu/ml/index.php.

Table 2.2   Real-world datasets used in this book. N represents the number of observations. BJDP is Bayesian JDP, BLR is Bayesian Logistic Regression, and BNN represents Bayesian Neural Networks. D represents the number of model parameters.

Dataset	Features	N	Model	D
S&P 500	1	1007	BJDP	5
Bitcoin	1	1461	BJDP	5
USDZAR	1	1425	BJDP	5
Pima	7	532	BLR	8
Heart	13	270	BLR	14
Australian	14	690	BLR	15
German	24	1000	BLR	25
Power	4	9568	BNN	31
Airfoil	5	1503	BNN	36
Concrete	8	1030	BNN	51
Protein	9	45 730	BNN	56

- *Australian credit dataset* – This dataset has 14 features and 690 data points. The objective for this dataset is to assess applications for credit cards [150].
- *German credit dataset* – This dataset has 25 features and 1 000 data points. The aim for this datatset was to classify a customer as either good or bad credit [150].

Bayesian Neural Network Datasets: There are four datasets that we model using BNNs. All the datasets are regression datasets and as with the BLR datasets, are also available on the UCI machine learning repository. The specifics of the datasets is as follows:

- *Power dataset* – This data set has 9568 observations and 4 features.
- *Airfoil dataset* – This dataset has 5 features and 1503 observations.
- *Concrete dataset* – This dataset has 1030 observations and 8 features [229].
- *Power dataset* – This dataset has 9 features and 45 730 observations.

2.1.8 Processing of the datasets

The JDP datasets used a time series of log returns as the input. The features for the BLR and BNN datasets were normalised. A random 90-10 train-test split was used for all the datasets. The train-test split is based on a cutoff date that confines 90% of the data into the training set for the time series datasets.

2.2 Performance metrics

We now present the performance metrics used to measure the performance of the algorithms proposed in this book. The performance metrics used are the acceptance rate, the multivariate ESS, the multivariate ESS normalised by the execution time, as well predictive performance on unseen data. We also assess the convergence of the proposed MCMC methods using the potential scale reduction factor metric. The acceptance rate metric measures the number of generated samples that are accepted in the MH acceptance step of the algorithm. The higher the number of accepted samples for the same step size, the more preferable the method. We discuss the remaining metrics in more detail in the following sections.

2.2.1 Effective sample size

The ESS metric is a commonly used metric for assessing the sampling efficiency of an MCMC algorithm. It indicates the number of effectively uncorrelated samples out of the total number of generated samples [192]. The larger the ESS, the better the performance of the MCMC method. The ESS normalised by execution time metric takes into account the computational resources required to generate the samples and penalises MCMC methods that require more computational resources to generate the same number of uncorrelated samples. The larger this metric, the better the efficiency of the algorithm.

This book employs the multivariate ESS metric developed by Vats et al. [218] instead of the minimum univariate ESS metric typically used in analysing MCMC results. The minimum univariate ESS measure is not able to capture the correlations between the different parameter dimensions, while the multivariate ESS metric can incorporate this information [79,161,162,218]. The minimum univariate ESS calculation results in the estimate of the ESS being dominated by the parameter dimensions that mix the slowest and ignore all other dimensions [161,218]. The multivariate ESS is calculated as:

$$\text{mESS} = N \times \left(\frac{|\Lambda|}{|\Sigma|} \right)^{\frac{1}{D}} \tag{2.10}$$

where N is the number of generated samples, D is the number of parameters, $|\Lambda|$ is the determinant of the sample covariance matrix and $|\Sigma|$ is the determinant of the estimate of the Markov chain standard error. When $D = 1$, mESS is equivalent to the univariate ESS measure [218]. Note that when there are no correlations in the chain, we have that $|\Lambda| = |\Sigma|$ and mESS $= N$.

We now address the ESS calculation for Markov chains that have been re-weighted via importance sampling, such is the case for the shadow HMC algorithms considered in this book [98,145,161,192]. For N samples re-weighted by importance sampling, the common approach is to use the approximation by Kish [98,119] given by

$$\text{ESS}_{IMP} = \frac{1}{(\sum_{j=1}^{N} \bar{b}_j^2)} \tag{2.11}$$

where $\bar{b}_j = b_j / \sum_{k=1}^{N} b_k$. This accounts for the possible non-uniformity in the importance sampling weights. In order to account for both the effects of sample auto-correlation and re-weighting via importance sampling, we approximate ESS under importance sampling by taking directions from Heide et al. [98] and using:

$$\text{ESS} := \frac{\text{ESS}_{IMP}}{N} \times \text{mESS} = \frac{1}{(\sum_{j=1}^{N} \bar{b}_j^2)} \times \left(\frac{|\Lambda|}{|\Sigma|} \right)^{\frac{1}{D}} \tag{2.12}$$

2.2.2 Convergence analysis

The $\hat{R}$ diagnostic of Gelman and Rubin [77] is a popular method for establishing the convergence of MCMC chains [202]. This diagnostic relies on running multiple chains $\{X_{i0}, X_{i1}, ..., X_{i(N-1)}\}$ for $i \in \{1, 2, 3, ..., m\}$ staring at various initial states with m being the number of chains and N being the sample size. Using these parallel chains, two estimators of the variance can be constructed. The estimators are the between-the-chain variance estimate and the within-the-chain variance. When the chain has converged, the ratio of these two estimators should be one. The $\hat{R}$ metric, which is formally known as the potential scale reduction factor, is defined as:

$$\hat{R} = \frac{\hat{V}}{W} \tag{2.13}$$

where

$$W = \sum_{i=1}^{m} \sum_{j=0}^{N-1} \frac{(X_{ij} - \bar{X}_{i.})^2}{m(N-1)} \tag{2.14}$$

is the within-chain variance estimate and $\hat{V} = \frac{N-1}{N} W + \frac{B}{N}$ is the pooled variance estimate which incorporates the between-chains

$$B = \sum_{j=0}^{N-1} \frac{(\bar{X}_{i.} - \bar{X}_{..})^2}{m-1} \tag{2.15}$$

and within-chain W variance estimates, with $\bar{X}_{i.}$ and $\bar{X}_{..}$ being the ith chain mean and overall mean respectively for $i \in \{1, 2, 3, ..., m\}$. Values larger than the convergence threshold of 1.05 for the $\hat{R}$ metric indicate divergence of the chain [38,77]. In this book, we assess the convergence of the chains by computing the *maximum* $\hat{R}$ metric over each of the parameter dimensions for the given target.

2.2.3 Predictive performance on unseen data

Examples of performance measures used for classification problems are shown in Table 2.4 where TP is the true positive, FN is the false negative, FP is the false positive and TN is the true negative. Other examples of performance measures include Receiver Operating Curve (ROC) as well as Area Under The Receiver Operating Curve (AUC). ROC plots the true positives from the model on the y-axis against the false positives on the x-axis [158]. AUC is the area under the ROC, and represents the average miss-classifications rate. AUC is useful as a performance measure when the costs of classification are unknown [34,73,158], such as when modelling Financial Statement Fraud (FSF).

Table 2.3   Common classification performance measures.

accuracy $= \frac{TP+TN}{TP+FP+FN+TN}$	sensitivity $= \frac{TP}{TN+FN}$	specificity $= \frac{TN}{TN+FP}$
precision $= \frac{TP}{TP+FP}$	recall $= \frac{TP}{TP+FN}$	F-Measure $= \frac{2 \times \text{precision} \times \text{recall}}{\text{precision} + \text{recall}}$

Examples of performance metrics used in regression problems are the coefficient of determination (R^2), Mean Absolute Error (MAE), and the Mean Square Error (MSE) and are shown in Table 2.3 [145]. In this table, we have that K_i are the observations with average $\bar{K}$, M is the number of observations and P_i are the predictions. MSE and MAE are similar in that they measure the difference between the observations and the predictions, while the R^2 measures the percentage of the variability in the target variable that is explained by the model. Models that have low values for MSE and MAE are preferable, while models that have a high R^2 measure are preferable.

Table 2.4   Common regression performance measures.

MSE $= \frac{1}{M} \sum_{i=1}^{M}(K_i - P_i)^2$	MAE $= \frac{1}{M} \sum_{i=1}^{M} |K_i - P_i|$	$R^2 = 1 - \frac{\sum_{i=1}^{M}(K_i - P_i)^2}{\sum_{i=1}^{M}(K_i - \bar{K})^2}$

2.3 Algorithm parameter tuning

As mentioned in Section 1.6, the matrix $\mathbf{G}$ in the MHMC method provides an extra degree of freedom which typically results in better sampling behaviour than HMC [37,161,213]. It is not immediately clear how this matrix should be set – this is still an open area of research [38,161,213]. In this book, we take direction from the inventors [213] of the method and select only a few dimensions to be influenced by the magnetic field. In particular, $\mathbf{G}$ was set such that $\mathbf{G_{1i}} = g$, $\mathbf{G_{i1}} = -g$ and zero elsewhere where $g = 0.2$ for the BLR datasets, and $g = 0.1$ for all the other targets.

These settings mean that the choice of $\mathbf{G}$ is not necessarily the optimal choice for all the target distributions considered, but was sufficient for our purposes as this basic setting still leads to good performance on the algorithms that we propose in this book. Tuning $\mathbf{G}$ for each target posterior should result in improved performance compared to the results presented in this manuscript. An alternative approach to the selection of $\mathbf{G}$ would have been to follow [38] and selecting $\mathbf{G}$ to be a random antisymmetric matrix. It is not immediately clear if the approach of [38] is necessary optimal, and we plan to explore this approach in future work.

In this book, unless otherwise stated, we tune the step size ϵ parameter for each problem for a given fixed trajectory length L parameter for the HMC and MHMC methods, with $\mathbf{G}$ being as described above. The methods we construct on top of these two algorithms then

Table 2.5 Step size and trajectory length parameters used for HMC and MHMC in this book. These methods serve as the baselines against which the novel methods presented in this book are compared. Five thousand samples were used to tune the step size for the given trajectory length using primal-dual averaging. The target acceptance rate was set to 80%.

Problem	L	HMC	MHMC
Banana	15	0.1209	0.1179
Neal with $D = 25$	50	0.3823	0.0507
Gaussian with $D = 10$	15	0.3491	0.1414
Gaussian with $D = 50$	15	0.1491	0.1219
Bitcoin	15	0.0021	0.0021
S&P 500	15	0.0028	0.0027
USDZAR	15	0.0003	0.0003
Pima	50	0.1062	0.0300
Heart	50	0.1595	0.0241
Australian	50	0.1060	0.0300
German	50	0.0572	0.0413
Power	25	0.0281	0.0275
Airfoil	25	0.0547	0.0497
Concrete	25	0.0761	0.0634
Protein	25	0.0793	0.0691

use the same step size as these two base methods. The step size is tuned to target an acceptance rate of **80%** using the primal-dual averaging methodology [105]. The trajectory lengths used vary across the different targets, with the final step sizes and trajectory lengths used for the various problems presented in Table 2.5.

All the experiments in this book were conducted on a machine with a 64bit CPU using PyTorch. We are in the process of making the PyTorch code used in this book open source.

2.4 Conclusion

This chapter outlined the target distributions considered in this book. Various combinations of these target distributions will be used throughout the book. This chapter also discussed the performance metrics that will be employed to assess the performance of the MCMC methods.

In the next chapter, we present the novel LSMH and SVMH algorithms, which utilise a Hessian and employ a random mass matrix as the scaling matrix in MH respectively. These minor modifications to MH lead to significant improvements in the time-normalised performance over MH.

3

Stochastic volatility Metropolis-Hastings

3.1 Proposed methods

The MH method uses a Gaussian distribution whose mean is the current state to prose the next state [95,144]. This proposal distribution produces random walk behaviour, which generates highly correlated samples and low sample acceptance rates [144,175]. The MALA, HMC, and MHMC methods all employ first-order gradient information of the posterior. Although this leads to a better exploration of the target, it also results in the algorithms having a higher computational time when compared to the MH algorithm. The MH algorithm is still heavily used in practice due to its robustness and simplicity [228].

In this chapter, we strive to address some of the deficiencies of the MH method by designing algorithms that reduce correlations in the generated samples without a significant increase in computational cost. These new methods are based on different formulations of the scale matrix in the MH algorithm, with the proposal Gaussian distribution still having the mean being the current state. In practice, typically, the scale matrix is treated as being diagonal, with all the dimensions having the same standard deviation σ [198]. The MH algorithm can be made arbitrarily poor by making σ either very small or very large [198,220]. Roberts and Rosenthal [198] attempt to find the optimal σ based on assuming a specific form for the distribution [220], and targeting specific acceptance rates – which are related to the efficiency of the algorithm. Yang et al. [228] extend this to more general target distributions.

Within MH sampling, the use of gradient and Hessian information has been successfully employed to construct intelligent proposal distributions [54,79]. In the MALA [54,199], a drift term that includes first-order gradient data is used to control the exploration of the parameter space. In the manifold MALA [79], the local structure of the target distribution is acknowledged through the use of the Hessian or different metric tensor [54,79]. One typically has to conduct pilot runs in order to tune the parameters of MH and MALA respectively [54]. Scaling the proposal distribution with a metric tensor that takes into account the curvature of the posterior distribution can simplify the tuning of the method such that expensive pilot runs are no longer needed [54].

Dahlin et al. [54] introduce the particle MH algorithm, which uses gradient and Hessian information of the approximated target posterior using a Laplace approximation. In this chapter, we propose Locally Scaled Metropolis-Hastings (LSMH), which uses the local geometry of the target to scale MH, and Stochastic Volatility Metropolis-Hastings (SVMH), which randomly scales MH. These two algorithms deviate from the particle MH algorithm

Hamiltonian Monte Carlo Methods in Machine Learning. https://doi.org/10.1016/B978-0-44-319035-3.00015-X

in that we focus solely on designing the scale matrix, so we do not consider first-order gradient information. Secondly, for the LSMH algorithm – the Hessian is based on the exact unnomalised posterior and not on the approximated target posterior. Both the LSMH and SVMH algorithms are easier to implement, needing only minor adjustments to MH, when compared to the particle MH algorithm of Dahlin et al. [54]. The particle MH algorithm is more complex when compared to the vanilla MH algorithm as the method was specifically developed to perform Bayesian parameter deduction in nonlinear state-space models, which typically have intractable likelihoods [54]. Thus, the particle MH method allows for both intractable likelihoods and posteriors, while the MH algorithm and the proposed methods use tractable likelihoods.

The LSMH algorithm extends the MH method by designing the scale matrix so that it depends on the local geometry of the target distribution in the same way as in manifold MALA and Riemannian Manifold Hamiltonian Monte Carlo [79]. The use of the local curvature of the target reduces the correlations in the samples generated by MH. However, this comes at a cost of a substantial increase in the computation cost due to the calculation of the Hessian matrix of the posterior distribution.

The SVMH method sets the scaling matrix in MH to be random with a user-specified distribution, similarly to setting the mass matrix in Quantum-Inspired Hamiltonian Monte Carlo [128,166] to be random to mimic the behaviour of quantum particles. This approach has the benefit of improving the exploration of MH without any noticeable increase in computational cost. This strategy has been shown in the QIHMC [128] Carlo to improve sampling of multi-modal distributions. The weakness of this approach is that it requires the user to specify the distribution of the scale matrix and possibly tune the parameters of the chosen distribution.

We compare the novel LSMH and SVMH methods to MH, the NUTS method, and MALA. The performance is measured using the effective sample size, effective sample size normalised by execution time, and predictive performance on unseen data using the negative log-likelihood using test data and the area under the receiver operating curve (AUC). Techniques that produce higher effective sample sizes and AUC are preferable to those that do not, and methods that produce lower negative log-likelihood (NLL) on test data are preferable.

The experimental results show that LSMH and SVMH significantly enhance the MH algorithm's effective sample sizes and predictive performance in both the simulation study and real-world applications – that is, across all the target posteriors considered. In addition, SVMH does this with essentially no increase in the execution time in comparison to MH. Given that only minor changes are required to create SVMH from MH, there seems to be relatively little impediment to employing it in practice instead of MH.

The results show that although both MALA and NUTS exceed the proposed algorithms on an effective sample size basis, the SVMH algorithm has similar or better predictive performance (AUC and NLL) than MALA and NUTS on most of the targets densities considered. Furthermore, the SVMH algorithm outperforms MALA and NUTS on the majority of the jump diffusion datasets on time normalised effective sample size basis. These results illustrate the overall benefits that can be derived by using a well-chosen random scaling matrix in MH.

As highlighted previously, the MH algorithm experiences random walk behaviour, which causes the generated samples to have high autocorrelations. We attempt to address this by designing the scaling matrix in two distinct ways.

Firstly, we set Σ so that it depends on the neighbourhood curvature of the distribution, similarly to manifold MALA and Riemannian Manifold Monte Carlo [79,162]. We call this algorithm the LSMH algorithm. In this algorithm, we set the Σ to be equal to the Hessian of the target posterior evaluated at the current state. In this chapter, for the instances where the negative log-density is highly non-convex such as Neal's funnel, we employed the SoftAbs metric to approximate the Hessian [24]. The SoftAbs metric needs an eigen decomposition and all second-order derivatives of the target distribution, which leads to higher execution times [23,24]. However, the SoftAbs metric is more generally suitable as it eliminates the boundaries of the Riemannian metric, which limits the use to models that are analytically available [23].

Secondly, we consider Σ to be random and assume that it has distribution $\Sigma \sim \mathcal{P}_{\Sigma}(\Sigma)$, with $\mathcal{P}_{\Sigma}(\Sigma)$ being a user-specified distribution in a related fashion to Quantum-Inspired Hamiltonian Monte Carlo [128,162]. We refer to this proposed algorithm the SVMH algorithm. In this chapter, we set the covariance matrix to be diagonal, with the diagonal components sampled from a log-normal distribution with mean zero and variance 1.

The pseudo-code for the LSMH and SVMH algorithms is the same as that of the MH algorithm in Algorithm 1.1, with the only exception being how Σ is treated. In particular:

- For LSMH: $\Sigma(\mathbf{w}) = -\frac{d^2 \ln \pi(\mathbf{w})}{d\mathbf{w}^2}$ and $\alpha(\mathbf{w}^*|\mathbf{w}) = \min\left(1, \frac{\pi(\mathbf{w}^*)\mathcal{N}(\mathbf{w}^*,\epsilon\Sigma(\mathbf{w}))}{\pi(\mathbf{w})\mathcal{N}(\mathbf{w},\epsilon\Sigma(\mathbf{w}))}\right)$

- For SVMH: $\Sigma \sim \mathcal{P}_{\Sigma}(\Sigma)$ and $\alpha(\mathbf{w}^*|\mathbf{w}) = \min\left(1, \frac{\pi(\mathbf{w}^*)\mathcal{N}(\mathbf{w}^*,\epsilon\Sigma)}{\pi(\mathbf{w})\mathcal{N}(\mathbf{w},\epsilon\Sigma)}\right)$

We tune ϵ via primal-dual averaging [105] targeting a sample approval rate of 70%. Our pilot runs indicated that targeting various acceptance rates (e.g., 25% as with MH) did not materially change the overall results.

It becomes apparent that LSMH will require the most computational resources out of all the algorithms due to the requirement to calculate the Hessian of the target at each state. SVMH should have a similar execution time to MH because only one extra step is added to the MH algorithm. If the assumed distribution for the scale matrix is not too difficult to sample from, MH and SVMH should have almost indistinguishable computational requirements.

3.2 Experiments

This section describes the performance metrics, the dual averaging methodology used to tune the parameters of the MCMC methods, the simulation study undertaken, and the tests performed on real world datasets. The investigation in this chapter is performed using a simulation study based on Neal's funnel of varying dimensions, multivariate Gaussian distributions of different dimensions, and using real world data modelled using jump diffusion processes and Bayesian logistic regression, respectively.

3.3 Results and discussion

The sampling performance of the algorithms for the simulation study and real world benchmark datasets is shown in Fig. 3.1. The detailed results for the financial market data and real world classification datasets across different metrics is shown in Tables 3.1 and 3.2 respectively. Note that the execution time t in Tables 3.1 and 3.2 is in seconds.

Fig. 3.2 shows the diagnostic negative log-likelihood trace plots for each sampler across various targets. Fig. 3.3 shows the autocorrelations produced by each MCMC method for the first dimension across various targets. Fig. 3.4 shows the predictive performance of each of the sampling methods on the real world classification datasets modelled using BLR.

The first two rows in Fig. 3.1 show the mESS and mESS normalised by execution time for the multivariate Gaussian distributions and Neal's funnel used in the simulation study with increasing dimensionality D. The third and fourth row in Fig. 3.1 show the mESS and mESS normalised by execution time for the financial market datasets modelled using jump diffusion processes, while rows five and six show the results for real world classification datasets modelled using Bayesian logistic regression. The results in Tables 3.1 and 3.2 are the mean results over the thirty iterations for each algorithm.

The first couple rows of Fig. 3.1 show that in all the values of D on both targets, SVMH and LSMH outperform MH in terms of effective sample sizes with SVMH and LSMH having similar effective sample sizes. When execution time is taken into consideration, SVMH outperforms LSMH and MH. The results also show that the NUTS algorithm outperforms all the MCMC methods on an effective sample size basis, while the MALA outperforms all the other MCMC methods on a normalised effective sample size basis.

Rows three to six in Fig. 3.1 show that across all the real world datasets, SVMH and LSMH have similar effective sample sizes, with MH producing the smallest effective sample size. NUTS outperforms all the algorithms on an effective sample size basis. On a normalised effective sample size basis, SVMH outperforms all the algorithms on the jump diffusion datasets except for the USDZAR dataset. NUTS outperforms on the USDZAR dataset due to the lower kurtosis on this dataset as seen in Table 2.2. NUTS appears to perform poorly on the datasets that have a high kurtosis.

Fig. 3.2 shows that the SVMH algorithm converges to the same level as NUTS on the majority of the datasets. On the other hand, the MH and LSMH algorithms converge to higher (i.e., less optimal) negative log-likelihoods. Fig. 3.3 shows that NUTS produces the lowest autocorrelations on all the targets except on the jump-diffusion datasets. MH produces the highest autocorrelations on the majority of the targets. The autocorrelations on the SVMH algorithm are higher than NUTS and MALA but approach zero quicker than for

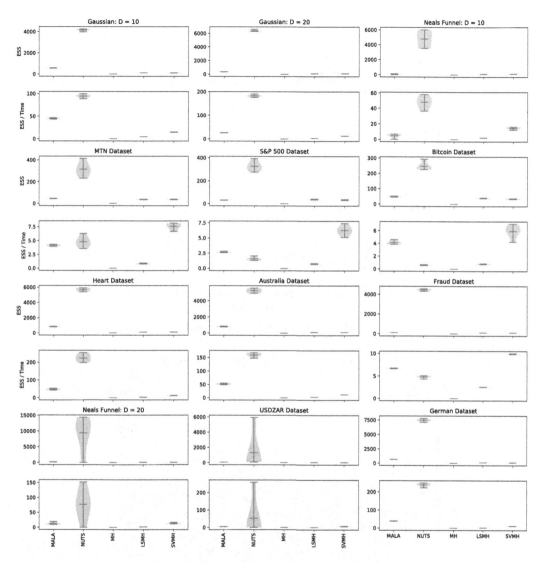

FIGURE 3.1 Inference results across each dataset over thirty iterations of each algorithm. The first row is the effective sample size while the second row is the time-normalised effective sample size for each dataset.

MH across the targets considered. Note that these are auto correlations after the burn-in period.

Table 3.1 and 3.2 show that, as expected, MH produces the lowest execution time with SVMH being a close second. LSMH is slower than SVMH due to the computation of the Hessian matrix at each state. The NUTS algorithm has the highest execution time on the jump diffusion datasets.

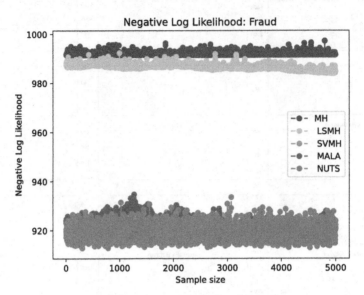

(a) Diagnostics trace plot for Fraud dataset.

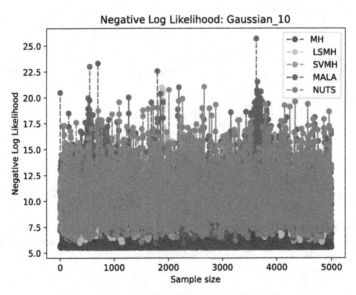

(b) Diagnostics trace plot for multivariate Gaussian with $D = 10$.

FIGURE 3.2 Negative log-likelihood diagnostic trace plots for various targets. These are traces plots from a single run of the MCMC chain. a) Diagnostic negative log-likelihood trace plots for the Fraud dataset and b) Diagnostic negative log-likelihood trace plots for the multivariate Gaussian with $D = 10$. The other targets produce similar convergence behaviour.

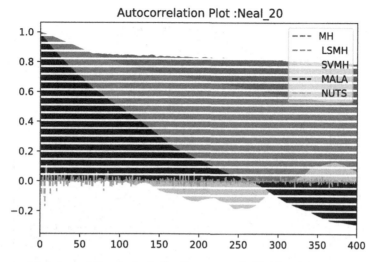

(a) Autocorrelation plot for the first dimension on the Neal funnel for $D = 20$.

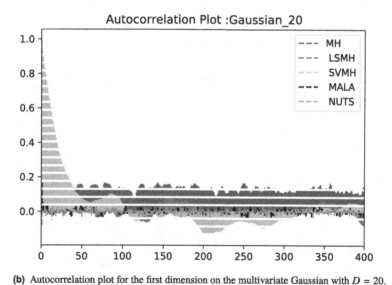

(b) Autocorrelation plot for the first dimension on the multivariate Gaussian with $D = 20$.

FIGURE 3.3 Autocorrelation plots for the first dimension across the various targets. These are autocorrelations from a single run of the MCMC chain. a) Autocorrelation plot for the first dimension on the Neal funnel for $D = 20$ and b) Autocorrelation plot for the first dimension on the multivariate Gaussian with $D = 20$.

Tables 3.1 and 3.2 as well as Figs. 3.4 and 3.5 show that, in terms of predictive performance using the negative log-likelihood on test data and AUC, the SVMH algorithm outperforms all the algorithms on the bulk of the real world datasets. Note that the SVMH method outperforms all the methods or has similar performance on a test negative log-likelihood basis on the logistic regression datasets. The results also show that the MH

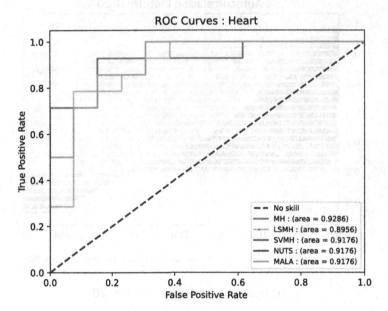

(a) ROC curves for the Heart dataset.

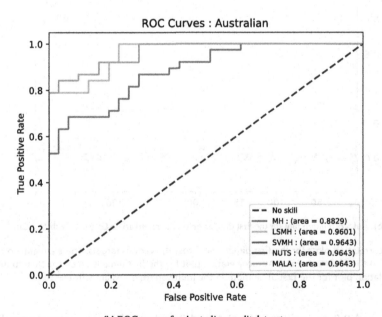

(b) ROC curves for Australian credit dataset.

FIGURE 3.4 Predictive performance for all the sampling methods on the real world classification datasets. The results were averaged over thirty runs of each algorithm. a) ROC curves for the Heart dataset and b) ROC curves for Australian credit dataset.

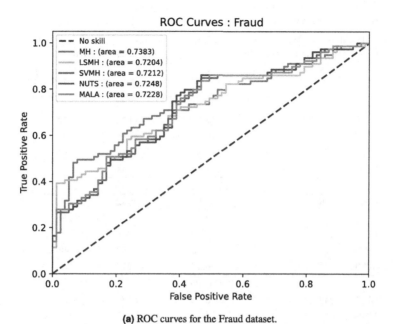

(a) ROC curves for the Fraud dataset.

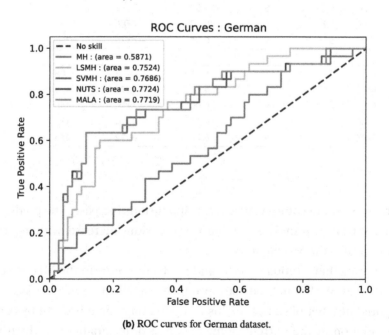

(b) ROC curves for German dataset.

FIGURE 3.5 Predictive performance for all the sampling methods on the real world classification datasets. The results were averaged over thirty runs of each algorithm. a) ROC curves for the Fraud dataset and b) ROC curves for German dataset.

Table 3.1 Results averaged over thirty runs of each method for the jump diffusion process datasets. Each row corresponds to the results for a specific method for each performance metric. NLL is the negative log-likelihood.

	mESS	t (in secs)	mESS/t	NLL (train)	NLL (test)
		MTN dataset			
NUTS	**314**	65	4.77	**−2153**	−174
MALA	45	11	4.14	**−2153**	−174
MH	0	**5**	0.00	−1981	−173
LSMH	36	45	0.82	−2056	**−180**
SVMH	37	**5**	**7.56**	−2144	−174
		S&P 500 dataset			
NUTS	**326**	209	1.56	**−2942**	−278
MALA	30	11	2.64	−2910	−286
MH	0	**5**	0.73	−2544	−283
LSMH	37	51	0.00	−2782	**−300**
SVMH	35	6	**6.27**	−2911	−286
		Bitcoin dataset			
NUTS	**247**	426	0.58	−2387	−286
MALA	47	11	4.11	−2315	**−291**
MH	0	**5**	0.00	−2282	−286
LSMH	39	50	0.78	−2286	−289
SVMH	34	6	**5.94**	−2325	**−291**
		USDZAR dataset			
NUTS	**1302**	118	**52.76**	−4457	**−489**
MALA	54	11	4.61	**−4272**	−475
MH	0	**5**	0.00	−3978	−446
LSMH	37	52	0.72	**−4272**	−475
SVMH	36	6	6.48	**−4272**	−474

algorithm progressively becomes worse as the dimensions increase. The predictive performance of the LSMH algorithm is not stable as dimensions increase, with its performance at times being close to the MH algorithm.

It is worth noting that although LSMH and SVMH outperform the MH on several metrics, the LSMH and SVMH methods still produce low effective sample sizes compared with the required number of samples. This can potentially be improved by centering the proposal distribution at the current point plus first-order gradient – which should assist in guiding the exploration (and decrease the autocorrelations in the generated samples) as in Metropolis Adjusted Langevin Algorithm [79], and Hamiltonian Monte Carlo [60,175].

Table 3.2 Results averaged over thirty runs of each method for the logistic regression datasets. Each row corresponds to the results for a specific method for each performance metric. NLL is the negative log-likelihood.

	mESS	t (in secs)	mESS$/t$	NLL (train)	NLL (test)
		Heart dataset			
NUTS	**5656**	25	**223.34**	**132**	**56**
MALA	848	18	47.14	**132**	**56**
MH	0.29	**9**	0.04	298	67
LSMH	97	41	2.38	352	82
SVMH	114	9	12.01	**132**	**56**
		Australian credit dataset			
NUTS	**5272**	33	**159.40**	248	**70**
MALA	787	15	51.43	248	**70**
MH	0	**7**	0.00	750	112
LSMH	109	37	2.89	407	88
SVMH	115	9	12.35	**247**	**70**
		Fraud dataset			
NUTS	**4449**	921	4.84	**919**	144
MALA	110	16	6.69	921	**143**
MH	0	**8**	0.00	993	150
LSMH	98	38	2.54	983	146
SVMH	96	10	**9.88**	**919**	**143**
		German credit dataset			
NUTS	**7493**	31	**239.57**	510	134
MALA	654	16	38.65	510	134
MH	0.0	**8**	0.00	1662	267
LSMH	110	62	1.76	745	174
SVMH	107	10	10.58	**510**	**134**

3.4 Conclusion

This chapter introduced the Stochastic Volatility Metropolis-Hastings and Locally Scaled Metropolis-Hastings Markov Chain Monte Carlo algorithms. We compare these methods with the vanilla Metropolis-Hastings algorithm using a simulation study on multivariate Gaussian distributions and Neal's funnel and real-world datasets modelled using jump diffusion processes and Bayesian logistic regression. The proposed methods are compared against the Metropolis-Hastings method, the Metropolis Adjusted Langevin Algorithm, and the No-U-Turn Sampler.

Overall, the No-U-Turn Sampler outperforms all the MCMC methods on an effective sample size basis. Stochastic Volatility Metropolis-Hastings (SVMH) and Locally Scaled Metropolis-Hastings produce higher effective sample sizes than Metropolis-Hastings, even after accounting for the execution time. In addition, SVMH outperforms all the methods in terms of predictive performance on the majority of the real world datasets. Furthermore, the SVMH method outperforms NUTS and MALA on the majority of the jump diffusion datasets on time normalised effective sample size basis. Given that SVMH does not add notable computational complexity to the Metropolis-Hastings algorithm, there seem to be trivial impediments to its use in place of Metropolis-Hastings in practice.

The work in this chapter can be improved by examining the case where the scaling matrix in Stochastic Volatility Metropolis-Hastings is sampled from a Wishart distribution so that correlations between the different parameter dimensions are taken into account. An analysis to determine the optimal distribution for the scaling matrix could improve this chapter. Constructing the stochastic volatility version of the Metropolis Adjusted Langevin Algorithm could also be of interest, significantly since Metropolis Adjusted Langevin Algorithm can use first-order gradient information to improve exploration of the target. Furthermore, we plan on including the calibration of jump diffusion with stochastic volatility characteristics using MCMC techniques in future work.

In the next chapter, we present the novel QIMHMC algorithm, which employs a random mass matrix $\mathbf{M}$ for the auxiliary momentum variable $\mathbf{p}$ in MHMC to enhance the performance of MHMC.

Quantum-inspired magnetic Hamiltonian Monte Carlo

4.1 Proposed algorithm

One of the parameters of HMC and MHMC that needs to be set by the user is the mass matrix $\mathbf{M}$ of the auxiliary momentum variable. This mass matrix is typically set to equal the identity matrix $\mathbf{I}$ [79,173,178,213]. Although this typically produces good results in practice, it is not necessarily the optimal choice across all possible target distributions. An approach to address this drawback would be to set the mass matrix to depend on the target distribution's local geometry or make the mass matrix a stochastic process with a user-specified distribution.

In RMHMC, the mass matrix is the Hessian of the negative log-density, which is the fisher information metric [24,79]. This allows the method to take into account the local curvature of the target and has been shown to enhance the sampling performance of HMC, especially for ill-conditioned target distributions [50,79,98]. On the other hand, QIHMC [128] sets the mass matrix to be a stochastic process and varies for each sample generated. This is motivated by the energy-time uncertainty relation from quantum mechanics, which allows a particle's mass to be stochastic rather than fixed, as is the case with classical particles [128].

QIHMC has been shown to improve the sampling performance when sampling from a broad class of distributions which occur in sparse modelling via bridge regression, image denoising, and BNN pruning [128,162]. This is particularly important for spiky and multimodal distributions where HMC is inefficient [128,162]. The use of a random mass matrix is yet to be considered for MHMC in the literature. Given that MHMC is closely related to HMC and outperforms HMC for a well-chosen magnetic field, one would expect that making the mass matrix random in MHMC would result in improved sampling performance when compared to MHMC with a fixed mass.

In this chapter, we set the mass matrix $\mathbf{M}$ in MHMC in Algorithm 1.3 to be random with distribution $\mathbf{P_M}(\mathbf{M})$ to create the novel QIMHMC method. This proposed algorithm has similar dynamics to MHMC in Eq. (1.23), with the exception that the mass matrix is random and is re-sampled before generating the auxiliary momentum variable. The algorithmic description of QIMHMC is presented in Algorithm 4.1. QIMHMC only differs from MHMC by the addition of line 3 in Algorithm 4.1 and a modified integrator in line 5, with every other step of the algorithm being the same as that of MHMC in Algorithm 1.3.

Note that the algorithm for QIHMC used in this chapter is the one outlined in Algorithm 1.4.

Hamiltonian Monte Carlo Methods in Machine Learning. https://doi.org/10.1016/B978-0-44-319035-3.00016-1

Algorithm 4.1 Quantum-inspired magnetic Hamiltonian Monte Carlo algorithm.

Input: N, ϵ, L, w_{init}, $H(w, p)$, $\mathbf{G}$, $\mathbf{P_M(M)}$
Output: $(w)_{m=0}^N$

1: $w_0 \leftarrow w_{\text{init}}$
2: **for** $m \rightarrow 1$ to N **do**
3:    $\mathbf{M} \sim \mathbf{P_M(M)}$ $\leftarrow$ **re-sample mass matrix.**
4:    $p_{m-1} \sim \mathcal{N}(0, \mathbf{M})$
5:    $p_m, w_m = $ **Integrator**$(p_{m-1}, w_{m-1}, \epsilon, L, H, \mathbf{G}, \mathbf{M})$ in Eq. (4.1)
      Remaining steps proceed as in MHMC in Algorithm 1.3
6: **end for**

It is worth noting that we refer to the proposed algorithm as Quantum-Inspired Magnetic Hamiltonian Monte Carlo as it utilises a random mass matrix, which is consistent with the behaviour of quantum particles. A particle can have a random mass with a distribution in quantum mechanics, while in classical mechanics, a particle has a fixed mass. The classical version of the proposed algorithm is the Magnetic Hamiltonian Monte Carlo method. When a random mass is utilised as inspired by quantum particles, the result is Quantum-Inspired Magnetic Hamiltonian Monte Carlo. Furthermore, this naming convention is consistent with that used by Liu and Zhang [128] for Hamiltonian Monte Carlo. Their work differs from ours in that the quantum particle is now subjected to a magnetic field.

In Theorem 4.1.1, we extend Eq. (1.23) of Tripuraneni et al. [213] to allow for the presence of a mass matrix that is not equal to the identity, that is for the case $\mathbf{M} \neq \mathbf{I}$. This extension is required for the implementation of the new QIMHMC method that we are proposing. This is because the mass matrix $\mathbf{M}$ will be changing for each new position sample generated, and this new $\mathbf{M}$ must be incorporated in the integration scheme.

Theorem 4.1.1. *The leapfrog-like numerical integration scheme for MHMC in the presence of a mass matrix* $\mathbf{M}$ *that is not equal to the identity matrix* $\mathbf{I}$ *is:*

$$
\begin{aligned}
\mathbf{p}_{t+\frac{\epsilon}{2}} &= \mathbf{p}_t + \frac{\epsilon}{2} \frac{\partial H(\mathbf{w}_t, \mathbf{p}_t)}{\partial \mathbf{w}} \\
\mathbf{w}_{t+\epsilon} &= \mathbf{w}_t + \mathbf{G}^{-1} \left(\exp\left(\mathbf{G}\mathbf{M}^{-1}\epsilon\right) - \mathbf{I} \right) \mathbf{p}_{t+\frac{\epsilon}{2}} \\
\mathbf{p}_{t+\frac{\epsilon}{2}} &= \exp\left(\mathbf{G}\mathbf{M}^{-1}\epsilon\right) \mathbf{p}_{t+\frac{\epsilon}{2}} \\
\mathbf{p}_{t+\epsilon} &= \mathbf{p}_{t+\frac{\epsilon}{2}} + \frac{\epsilon}{2} \frac{\partial H\left(\mathbf{w}_{t+\epsilon}, \mathbf{p}_{t+\frac{\epsilon}{2}}\right)}{\partial \mathbf{w}}.
\end{aligned} \tag{4.1}
$$

Proof. The Hamiltonian in Eq. (1.14) can be re-expressed as:

$$H(\mathbf{w}, \mathbf{p}) = \frac{U(\mathbf{w})}{2} + K(\mathbf{p}) + \frac{U(\mathbf{w})}{2}$$

$$= \underbrace{\frac{U(\mathbf{w})}{2}}_{H_1(\mathbf{w})} + \underbrace{\frac{1}{2}\log\left((2\pi)^D |\mathbf{M}|\right) + \frac{\mathbf{p}^\mathsf{T} \mathbf{M}^{-1} \mathbf{p}}{2}}_{H_2(\mathbf{p})} + \underbrace{\frac{U(\mathbf{w})}{2}}_{H_1(\mathbf{w})} \qquad (4.2)$$

$$H(\mathbf{w}, \mathbf{p}) = H_1(\mathbf{w}) + H_2(\mathbf{p}) + H_1(\mathbf{w})$$

where each of the sub flows $H_1(\mathbf{w})$ and $H_2(\mathbf{p})$ can be integrated exactly as follows:

$$\frac{d}{dt}\begin{bmatrix}\mathbf{w}\\\mathbf{p}\end{bmatrix} = \begin{bmatrix}\mathbf{0} & \mathbf{I}\\-\mathbf{I} & \mathbf{G}\end{bmatrix}\begin{bmatrix}\nabla_w H_1(\mathbf{w})\\\nabla_p H_1(\mathbf{w})\end{bmatrix} = \begin{bmatrix}\mathbf{0} & \mathbf{I}\\-\mathbf{I} & \mathbf{G}\end{bmatrix}\begin{bmatrix}\frac{U(\mathbf{w})}{2}\\\mathbf{0}\end{bmatrix} = \begin{bmatrix}\mathbf{0}\\-\frac{U(\mathbf{w})}{2}\end{bmatrix}$$

$$\implies d\mathbf{p} = -\frac{dt}{2}U(\mathbf{w})$$

$$\mathbf{p} = \mathbf{p} - \frac{\epsilon}{2}U(\mathbf{w}) \qquad (4.3)$$

$$\implies \Phi_{\epsilon, H_1(\mathbf{w})}\begin{bmatrix}\mathbf{w}\\\mathbf{p}\end{bmatrix} = \begin{bmatrix}\mathbf{w}\\\mathbf{p} - \frac{\epsilon}{2}U(\mathbf{w})\end{bmatrix}$$

and

$$\frac{d}{dt}\begin{bmatrix}\mathbf{w}\\\mathbf{p}\end{bmatrix} = \begin{bmatrix}\mathbf{0} & \mathbf{I}\\-\mathbf{I} & \mathbf{G}\end{bmatrix}\begin{bmatrix}\nabla_w H_2(\mathbf{p})\\\nabla_p H_2(\mathbf{p})\end{bmatrix} = \begin{bmatrix}\mathbf{0} & \mathbf{I}\\-\mathbf{I} & \mathbf{G}\end{bmatrix}\begin{bmatrix}\mathbf{0}\\\mathbf{M}^{-1}\mathbf{p}\end{bmatrix} = \begin{bmatrix}\mathbf{M}^{-1}\mathbf{p}\\\mathbf{G}\mathbf{M}^{-1}\mathbf{p}\end{bmatrix}$$

$$\implies d\mathbf{p} = \mathbf{G}\mathbf{M}^{-1}\mathbf{p}\,dt$$

$$\mathbf{p} = \exp\left(\mathbf{G}\mathbf{M}^{-1}t\right)\mathbf{p}$$

$$d\mathbf{w} = \mathbf{M}^{-1}\exp\left(\mathbf{G}\mathbf{M}^{-1}t\right)\mathbf{p}\,dt \qquad (4.4)$$

$$\implies \mathbf{w} = \mathbf{w} + \mathbf{M}^{-1}(\mathbf{G}\mathbf{M}^{-1})^{-1}\left(\exp\left(\mathbf{G}\mathbf{M}^{-1}t\right) - \mathbf{I}\right)\mathbf{p}$$

$$\mathbf{w} = \mathbf{w} + \mathbf{G}^{-1}\left(\exp\left(\mathbf{G}\mathbf{M}^{-1}t\right) - \mathbf{I}\right)\mathbf{p}$$

$$\implies \Phi_{\epsilon, H_2(\mathbf{p})}\begin{bmatrix}\mathbf{w}\\\mathbf{p}\end{bmatrix} = \begin{bmatrix}\mathbf{w} + \mathbf{G}^{-1}\left(\exp\left(\mathbf{G}\mathbf{M}^{-1}\epsilon\right) - \mathbf{I}\right)\mathbf{p}\\\exp\left(\mathbf{G}\mathbf{M}^{-1}\epsilon\right)\mathbf{p}\end{bmatrix}$$

Eq. (4.1) is then generated by the map $\Phi_{\epsilon, H_{(\mathbf{w}, \mathbf{p})}} = \Phi_{\epsilon, H_1(\mathbf{w})} \circ \Phi_{\epsilon, H_2(\mathbf{p})} \circ \Phi_{\epsilon, H_1(\mathbf{w})}$. □

In the QIMHMC algorithm, we introduced another source of randomness in the form of a random mass matrix into MHMC. We thus need to show that the proposed algorithm converges to the correct steady-state distribution. This is provided in Theorem 4.1.2, which guarantees that the proposed algorithm produces the correct steady-state distribution.

Theorem 4.1.2. *Consider continuous-time non-canonical Hamiltonian dynamics with a deterministic time-varying positive-definite mass matrix* $\mathbf{M}(t)$ *in Eq. (4.1). The marginal* *density $\pi_{\mathbf{w}}(\mathbf{w}) \propto \exp(-U(\mathbf{w}))$ is a unique steady state distribution in the $\mathbf{w}$ space if momentum re-sampling steps $p_{\mathbf{p}}(\mathbf{p}) \propto \exp\left(\frac{\mathbf{p}^{\mathrm{T}} \mathbf{M}(t)^{-1} \mathbf{p}}{2}\right)$ are included.*

Proof. Following the approach of [128] for QIHMC, we consider the joint distribution of $(\mathbf{w}, \mathbf{p}, \mathbf{M})$ given by $\pi(\mathbf{w}, \mathbf{p}, \mathbf{M})$. Here we have dropped the explicit dependence of $\mathbf{M}$ on t because $\mathbf{M}(t)$ obeys the mass distribution $\mathbf{P_M}(\mathbf{M})$ for all t. Employing Bayes theorem we have that:

$$\pi(\mathbf{w}, \mathbf{p}, \mathbf{M}) = p(\mathbf{w}, \mathbf{p}|\mathbf{M}) \, \mathbf{P_M}(\mathbf{M})$$

$$\pi(\mathbf{w}, \mathbf{p}, \mathbf{M}) \propto \exp(-U(\mathbf{w})) \exp\left(\frac{\mathbf{p}^{\mathrm{T}} \mathbf{M}^{-1} \mathbf{p}}{2}\right)$$

$$\implies \pi(\mathbf{w}) = \int_{\mathbf{p}} \int_{\mathbf{M}} \pi(\mathbf{w}, \mathbf{p}, \mathbf{M}) \, d\mathbf{w} d\mathbf{M}$$

$$\pi(\mathbf{w}) \propto \exp(-U(\mathbf{w}))$$

(4.5)

which means that the marginal steady state distribution $\pi(\mathbf{w})$ is the correct posterior distribution.   □

An aspect that we are yet to address is which distribution $\mathbf{P_M}(\mathbf{M})$ should be used for the mass matrix. This is still an open area of research [128,162]. In this work, we consider the simple case where $\mathbf{M}$ is a diagonal matrix with the entries being sampled from a log-normal distribution where the mean is zero and the standard deviation, which we refer to as the volatility of volatility or vol-of-vol for short, is equal to a tunable parameter $\beta \in \mathbb{R}^{\geq 0}$. That is, for each $m_{ii} \in \mathbf{M}$ $\forall$ $i \in \{1, 2, ..., D\}$ is generated as $\ln m_{ii} \sim \mathcal{N}(0, \beta^2)$ and $m_{ij} = 0$ for $i \neq j$. We present the sensitivity analysis to the chosen value of β in Section 4.2.2.

4.2 Experiment description

In this section, we outline the settings used for the experiments, the performance metrics, and we present the sensitivity analysis for the vol-of-vol parameter β in QIMHMC.

4.2.1 Experiment settings

In all our experiments, we compare the performance of QIMHMC to HMC, MHMC and QIHMC using the multivariate ESS and the ESS normalised by execution time metrics presented in Section 2.2.1. We further assess the convergence behaviour of the MCMC methods using the $\hat{R}$ metric described in Section 2.2.2. The targets we consider in this chapter are the Banana shaped distribution, the multivariate Gaussian distributions with $D \in \{10, 50\}$ and BLR on the Pima, Australian and German credit datasets outlined in Table 2.2.

The vol-of-vol parameter β that we use depends on the particular target density. The sensitivity analysis for β is presented in Section 4.2.2. We set β to 0.1 for the Banana shaped distribution and Australian credit dataset, while β was set to 0.3 for the other targets. The trajectory length and step size parameters for the MCMC methods considered in this chapter were set to the values outlined in Table 2.5, with QIHMC and QIMHMC using the same step size as HMC and MHMC respectively. Ten independent chains were run for each method on each target distribution. Three thousand samples were generated for each target, with the first 1000 samples discarded as burn-in. This sample size and burn-in period were sufficient for all the algorithms to converge on all the targets. It is worth highlighting that we set the mass matrix **M** to the identity matrix for the HMC and MHMC methods. This setting for **M** is what is commonly used in practice [25,85,213,224].

4.2.2 Sensitivity to the vol-of-vol parameter

In this section, we present the sensitivity analysis for the chosen vol-of-vol parameter β. We considered values of $\beta \in \{0.0, 0.1, 0.2, 0.3, 0.4, 0.5, 0.6, 0.7, 0.9, 1.0\}$, with all the other settings being the same as those outlined in Section 4.2.1. It is worth highlighting that when $\beta = 0$, QIMHMC is equivalent to MHMC and QIHMC is equivalent to HMC. The results of the analysis are presented in Fig. 4.1. The results show that the ESS has a tendency of decreasing for both QIHMC and QIMHMC with increasing β on both the Australian and German credit datasets. In addition, the QIMHMC algorithm is able to maintain a high acceptance rate as the value of β is increased, while the acceptance rate of QIHMC decays to zero at a faster rate.

The results also indicate that smaller values of β are preferable, with the optimal value of the Australian credit dataset being 0.1 and around 0.5 for the German credit dataset. Furthermore, QIMHMC outperforms QIHMC for all values of β on both an ESS and normalised ESS basis, showing the robust results that can be obtained from QIMHMC.

4.3 Results and discussion

We present the performance of the HMC, MHMC, QIHMC, and QIMHMC methods using different performance metrics in Fig. 4.3 and Tables 4.1 to 4.3. In Fig. 4.3, the plots on the first row for each dataset show the ESS, while the plots on the second row show the ESS normalised by execution time. The results are for the ten runs of each algorithm. In Tables 4.1 to 4.3, each column corresponds to the results for a particular MCMC method. Values that are in **bold** indicate that the MCMC method outperforms the other MCMC algorithms on that particular metric. The execution time t in Fig. 4.3 and Tables 4.1 to 4.3 is in seconds. The results in Tables 4.1 to 4.3 are the mean results over the ten runs for each algorithm. We use the mean values over the ten runs in Tables 4.1 to 4.3 to form our conclusions about the performance of the algorithms.

The results in Tables 4.1 to 4.3 and Fig. 4.2 show that all the MCMC methods have converged as indicated by the $\hat{R}$ metric and the diagnostic trace-plots for the negative log-likelihood. It is also worth noting that the quantum-inspired algorithms consistently produce better convergence across the different targets based on the $\hat{R}$ metric, indicating that $\beta \neq 0$ improves the convergence behaviour of QIHMC and QIMHMC respectively.

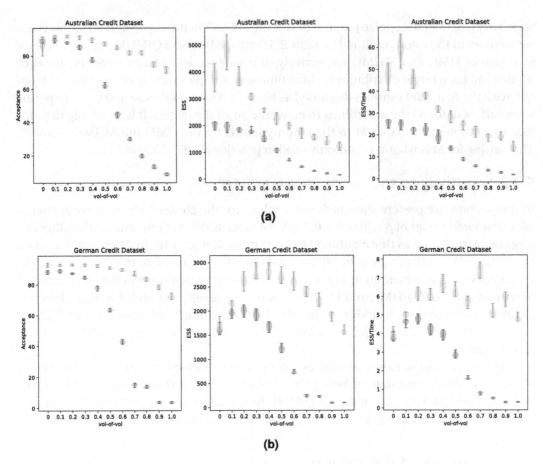

FIGURE 4.1 Acceptance rates, ESS and ESS/Time for ten runs of QIHMC (blue (dark gray in print version)) and QIMHMC (orange (light gray in print version)) on the a) Australian and b) German credit datasets with varying choices of the vol-of-vol β parameter. The results indicate that these metrics are a decreasing function of the vol-of-vol β parameter, with QIMHMC decreasing at a slower rate than QIHMC.

The results in Fig. 4.3 and Tables 4.1, 4.2, 4.3 show that the proposed QIMHMC method outperforms all the other methods across the ESS and normalised ESS performance metrics on all the targets. The outperformance also increases with increasing dimensionality of the problem, suggesting that QIMHMC is able to scale to larger models without a significant deterioration in sampling performance. It is also worth noting that MHMC sometimes outperforms QIHMC, for example on the Gaussian distribution with $D = 10$, suggesting that MHMC with an appropriately tuned magnetic field is able to outperform QIHMC.

As expected, MHMC outperforms HMC on the majority of the targets across all the metrics. This is in line with what has been previously observed [38,161,213]. The MHMC method underperforms HMC on the Banana and Australian target distributions, suggesting that the magnetic field chosen for these two targets might not be optimal. It is

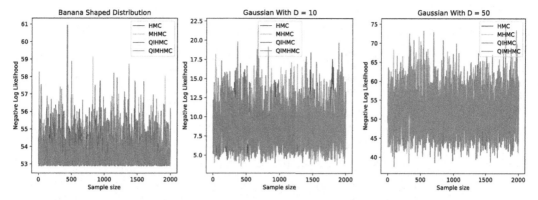

FIGURE 4.2 Diagnostic trace-plots of the negative log-likelihood across various targets averaged over ten runs of each method. These results show that all the MCMC methods have converged on all the targets.

Table 4.1 Banana shaped distribution results averaged over ten runs. The time t is in seconds. The values in **bold** indicate that the particular method outperforms the other methods on that specific metric.

Metric	HMC	MHMC	QIHMC	QIMHMC
		Banana shaped distribution		
ESS	964	878	1061	**1450**
t	19.24	**19.12**	19.34	20.63
ESS/t	50.1	46.1	54.8	**70.3**
$\hat{R}$ max	1.01	1.02	**1.00**	**1.00**

also worth noting that MHMC and HMC produce similar execution times, with HMC marginally outperforming MHMC on the majority of the targets on an execution time basis.

We also noted that QIHMC outperforms HMC across all the targets. This confirms the results observed by Liu and Zhang [128] using different target posteriors to those considered in this chapter. This shows the significant benefit that utilising a random mass can provide to the sampling properties of HMC based samplers. However, the real performance gains are only realised when the vol-of-vol parameter β has been appropriately tuned. Establishing an automated approach for tuning β is still an open research problem, which we aim to address in future work.

4.4 Conclusion

In this chapter, we introduced the QIMHMC method, which employs a random mass matrix for the auxiliary momentum variable in the non-canonical Hamiltonian dynamics of MHMC. This results in significant sampling improvements over MHMC. The new method

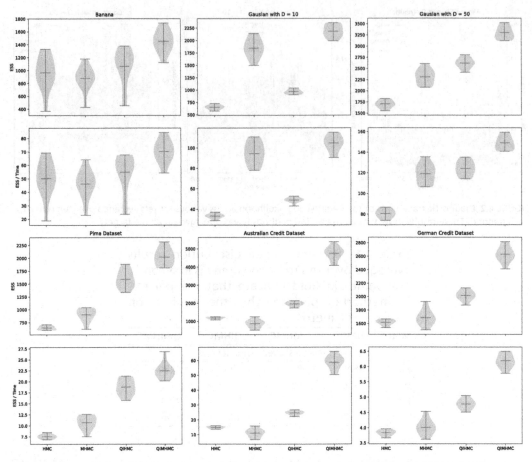

FIGURE 4.3 Results for the datasets over ten runs of each method. For each dataset, the plots on the first row show the multivariate effective sample size and the plots on the second row show the multivariate effective sample size normalised by execution time (in seconds). For all the plots, the larger the value the better the method. The dark horizontal line in each violin plot represents the mean value over ten runs of each algorithm.

is compared to HMC, MHMC and QIHMC. The methods are compared on the Banana shaped distribution, multivariate Gaussian distributions, and on real-world datasets modelled using BLR.

The empirical results show that the new method outperforms all the other methods on a time-normalised ESS basis across all the targets. Furthermore, QIHMC outperforms HMC as expected. This shows the significant benefit provided by using a random mass matrix for the momenta to the sampling properties of HMC based samplers in general.

A limitation of the method is the need to tune the vol-of-vol parameter. Although typically smaller values of the parameter improve the ESSs, a more robust approach to the selection of the parameter is still required. This work can be improved by establishing a heuristic or an automated approach to tune the vol-of-vol parameter. In addition, the tun-

Table 4.2 Multivariate Gaussian distribution results averaged over ten runs. The time t is in seconds. The values in **bold** indicate that the particular method outperforms the other methods on that specific metric.

Metric	HMC	MHMC	QIHMC	QIMHMC
		Gaussian with D = 10		
ESS	653	1844	965	**2184**
t	19.6	**19.5**	19.8	20.9
ESS/t	33.3	94.5	48.9	**104.7**
$\hat{R}$ max	1.03	1.02	**1.00**	**1.00**
		Gaussian with D = 50		
ESS	1 705	2313	2619	**3302**
t	21.1	**19.4**	21.2	23.3
ESS/t	80.7	119.11	124.3	**141.7**
$\hat{R}$ max	1.01	1.03	**1.00**	**1.00**

Table 4.3 Bayesian logistic regression results averaged over ten runs. The time t is in seconds. The values in **bold** indicate that the particular method outperforms the other methods on that specific metric.

Metric	HMC	MHMC	QIHMC	QIMHMC
		Pima dataset		
ESS	645	902	1591	**2019**
t	85.5	**84.2**	84.7	89.9
ESS/t	7.5	10.7	18.8	**22.5**
$\hat{R}$ max	**1.00**	1.02	**1.00**	**1.00**
		Australian credit dataset		
ESS	1184	867	1956	**4750**
t	79.2	**77.8**	79.0	81.0
ESS/t	15.0	11.1	24.8	**58.7**
$\hat{R}$ max	1.01	1.04	**1.00**	1.01
		German credit dataset		
ESS	1617	1686	1927	**2794**
t	453.9	**449.8**	456.41	459.3
ESS/t	3.56	3.75	4.22	**6.08**
$\hat{R}$ max	1.02	1.01	**1.00**	**1.00**

ing of the magnetic component could also be of interest as the outperformance of MHMC over HMC, and consequently, the outperformance of QIMHMC over QIHMC, depends on the chosen magnetic field. We also plan to incorporate a random mass matrix in S2HMC in future work.

In the following chapter, we extend MHMC and S2HMC by incorporating partial refreshment of the auxiliary momentum variable into MHMC and S2HMC respectively.

5

Generalised magnetic and shadow Hamiltonian Monte Carlo

5.1 Proposed partial momentum retention algorithms

The sampling process for HMC, MHMC and S2HMC follows a Gibbs sampling scheme where the auxiliary momentum variable is generated first, after which the position vector is generated based on the recently drawn momenta. The momenta are fully regenerated each time a new sample is drawn, with the old momenta being discarded. This is not always the optimal approach of treating the momenta across all possible target posterior distributions [42,98,107,192].

Horowitz [107] was amongst the first to observe this and employed a partial momentum update to HMC and found that it significantly improved the performance of HMC. That is, keeping some of the dynamics of the chain improved performance without harming the legitimacy of the Monte Carlo method [61,106,107]. The concept of partial momentum refreshment has been further developed in the context of sampling from integrator dependent shadow Hamiltonians [6,98,110,192]. Akhmatskaya et al. [6,192] apply partial momentum refreshment to shadow Hamiltonians on the Euclidean space, while Heide et al. [98] employ it when sampling from shadow Hamiltonians on the Riemannian manifold. The use of partial momentum refreshment is yet to be considered for MHMC and S2HMC in the literature. Given that MHMC is closely related to HMC, one would expect that employing partial momentum refreshment in MHMC would result in the same or better sampling performance as observed by Horowitz [107] on HMC. Similarly, utilising partial momentum refreshment in S2HMC should improve the sampling behaviour of S2HMC.

In this chapter, we combine the non-canonical dynamics of MHMC with partial momentum refreshment to create the PMHMC algorithm, which converges to the target distribution. We also combine the separable Hamiltonian in S2HMC with partial momentum refreshment to create the PS2HMC algorithm, which also converges to the correct stationary distribution. The performance of the proposed methods is compared against HMC, MHMC, S2HMC and PHMC respectively.

A key consideration when one implements partial momentum refreshment is what technique to use to update the momenta – that is, what should the momenta update equation be? Horowitz [107] mixes the momenta with a Gaussian random number with some user-specified mixing angle. In contrast, Akhmatskaya et al. [6,192] and Heide et al. [98] introduce a momentum refreshment parameter that controls the extent of the momentum refreshment between observations, with the new momentum being generated from

---

Algorithm 5.1 Magnetic Hamiltonian Monte Carlo with partial momentum refreshment algorithm.

    Input: $L, \epsilon, \rho, N, \mathbf{G}$ and $(\mathbf{w_0, p_0})$.
    Output: $(\mathbf{w}_i, \mathbf{p}_i)_{i=0}^{N}$
1: **for** $i \rightarrow 1$ to N **do**
2:     $(\mathbf{w}, \mathbf{p}) \leftarrow (\mathbf{w_{i-1}}, \mathbf{p_{i-1}})$.
3:     $u \sim \mathcal{N}(0, \mathbf{M})$
4:     $\bar{\mathbf{p}} \leftarrow \rho\mathbf{p} + \sqrt{1 - \rho^2}u$
5:     $(\hat{\mathbf{w}}, \hat{\mathbf{p}}) = \Phi_{\epsilon,H}^{L}(\mathbf{w}, \bar{\mathbf{p}}, \mathbf{G})$ in Eq. (1.23)
6:     $\zeta = \min\left[1, \exp(-\delta H)\right], u \sim \text{Unif}(0, 1)$
7:     **if** $\zeta > u$ **then**
8:         $(\mathbf{w}_i, \mathbf{p}_i, \mathbf{G}) \leftarrow (\hat{\mathbf{w}}, \hat{\mathbf{p}}, \mathbf{G})$
9:     **else**
10:        $(\mathbf{w}_i, \mathbf{p}_i, \mathbf{G}) \leftarrow (\mathbf{w}, -\mathbf{p}, -\mathbf{G})$
11:    **end if**
12: **end for**

---

a Gaussian distribution. This thesis utilises the approach outlined in [98,192,210]. In this approach, the updated momentum $\bar{\mathbf{p}}$ to generate the next state is then taken to be:

$$\bar{\mathbf{p}} = \rho\mathbf{p} + \sqrt{1 - \rho^2}u \tag{5.1}$$

with probability one, where ρ is the partial momentum refreshment parameter, u is Gaussian with mean zero and covariance $= \mathbf{M}$, and $\mathbf{p}$ is the momenta for the current state [192].

Note that $\bar{\mathbf{p}}$ has a Gaussian distribution and $\rho \in (0, 1)$. The two extremes that ρ can assume are: when $\rho = 1$, the momentum is never updated and thus possibly affecting the ergodicity [210] of the chain and when $\rho = 0$, the momentum is always updated, which is the behaviour of the original HMC based samplers. The resultant chain preserves some dynamics, with the exact amount depending on the value of ρ, between the generated samples [6,98,107,192]. The parameter ρ introduces an extra degree of freedom into the sampler and needs to be set [6,98]. In Section 5.2.2, we assess the sensitivity of the results on the chosen value of ρ. A key aspect to note is that the proposed algorithms will improve the performance without high additional computational cost and typically do not alter the acceptance rates of the original algorithms in practice [192].

The algorithmic description of the PMHMC and PS2HMC algorithms is presented in Algorithms 5.1 and 5.2 respectively. Theorem 5.1.1 guarantees that the proposed methods satisfy detailed balance and hence converge to the correct target density.

Theorem 5.1.1. *PMHMC and PS2HMC satisfy detailed balance.*

Proof. The guarantee that the proposed algorithms satisfy detailed balance provided by the use of the same argument in Horowitz [106] which is: after the MH step, the sign of the

---

Algorithm 5.2 Separable shadow Hamiltonian hybrid Monte Carlo with partial momentum refreshment algorithm.

Input: L, ϵ, ρ, N and $(\mathbf{w_0}, \mathbf{p_0})$.
Output: $(\mathbf{w_i}, \mathbf{p_i}, b_i)_{i=0}^{N}$
1: **for** $i \rightarrow 1$ to N **do**
2:      $(\mathbf{w}, \mathbf{p}) \leftarrow (\mathbf{w_{i-1}}, \mathbf{p_{i-1}})$.
3:      $u \sim \mathcal{N}(0, \mathbf{M})$
4:      $\bar{\mathbf{p}} \leftarrow \rho p + \sqrt{1 - \rho^2} u$
5:      Apply the pre-processing mapping in Eq. (1.34):
        $(\hat{\mathbf{w}}, \hat{\mathbf{p}}) = \mathcal{X}(\mathbf{w}, \bar{\mathbf{p}})$
6:      $(\hat{\mathbf{w}}, \hat{\mathbf{p}}) = \Phi_{\epsilon, \tilde{H}}^{L}(\hat{\mathbf{w}}, \hat{\mathbf{p}})$ in Eq. (1.20)
7:      Apply the post-processing mapping in Eq. (1.35):
        $(\hat{\mathbf{w}}, \hat{\mathbf{p}}) = \mathcal{X}^{-1}(\hat{\mathbf{w}}, \hat{\mathbf{p}})$
8:      $\zeta = \min\left[1, \exp(-\Delta\tilde{H})\right], u \sim \text{Unif}(0, 1)$
9:      **if** $\zeta > u$ **then**
10:         $(\mathbf{w}_i, \mathbf{p}_i) \leftarrow (\hat{\mathbf{w}}, \hat{\mathbf{p}})$
11:      **else**
12:         $(\mathbf{w}_i, \mathbf{p}_i) \leftarrow (\mathbf{w}, -\mathbf{p})$
13:      **end if**
14:      $b_i = \exp\left(\tilde{H}(\mathbf{w_i}, \mathbf{p_i}) - H(\mathbf{w_i}, \mathbf{p_i})\right)$
15: **end for**

---

momentum (and magnetic field for PMHMC) must be reversed in case of rejection. Given that $\bar{\mathbf{p}}$ in (5.1) is Gaussian, the proof that the proposed methods satisfy detailed balance follows that of MHMC and S2HMC respectively. □

Note that the algorithm for PHMC used in this thesis is the same as the PMHMC method outlined in Algorithm 5.1, except that we use Hamiltonian dynamics in step 6 instead of non-canonical Hamiltonian dynamics corresponding to MHMC.

5.2 Experiment description

In this section, we outline the settings used for the experiments, the performance metrics used, and we also present the sensitivity analysis for the partial momentum refreshment parameter α in PMHMC, PHMC and PS2HMC.

5.2.1 Experiment settings

In all our experiments, we compare the performance of PMHMC to HMC, MHMC, S2HMC and PHMC using the acceptance rate of the generated samples, ESS, ESS normalised by execution time and the $\hat{R}$ metric for convergence analysis of the MCMC chains. The target densities considered are multivariate Gaussian distributions with $D \in \{10, 50\}$, JDPs calibrated to financial market data and real-world datasets modelled using BLR. For all the target posteriors considered in this chapter, the momentum refreshment parameter ρ is set to 0.7. This setting worked well on all the targets. Further experiments of the sensitivity to ρ are presented in Section 5.2.2.

The trajectory length and step sizes parameters for the MCMC methods considered in this chapter were set to the values outlined in Table 2.5. The PMHMC method used the same step size as MHMC, while the S2HMC and PS2HMC methods used the same step size as HMC.

Ten independent chains were run for each method on each target distribution. Three thousand samples were generated for each target, with the first one-thousand samples discarded as burn-in. These settings were sufficient for all the algorithms to converge across all the targets.

5.2.2 Sensitivity to momentum refreshment parameter

To investigate the effects of varying the momentum refreshment parameter ρ, we ran ten independent chains of PHMC, PMHMC and PS2HMC on two targets for $\rho \in \{0.0, 0.1, 0.2, 0.3, 0.4, 0.5, 0.6, 0.7, 0.8, 0.9\}$. Note that we did not consider the case where $\rho = 1$ as for this case the momentum variable is not refreshed, and this could possibly affect the ergodicity of the proposed methods.

For this analysis, each chain used the same parameters as those in Section 5.2.1. The results are displayed in Fig. 5.1. The results show that PHMC, PMHMC and PS2HMC have stable acceptance rates across the different values of ρ on all the targets – indicating that ρ does not impact the acceptance rates of the proposed methods. This result is consistent with the observation of [192]. Furthermore, PS2HMC has the highest acceptance rate, and given that it uses the same step size as PHMC, it highlights the benefits that can be obtained from sampling from the shadow Hamiltonian instead of the true Hamiltonian.

The methods show a general trend of increasing ESS and normalised ESS with increasing ρ for both datasets, with a deterioration of performance occurring at $\rho = 0.9$ as the chain becomes "less ergodic". In addition, PS2HMC has higher ESSs than PHMC and PMHMC for these two targets, but has the lowest time-normalised ESS due to its large execution time. On the German credit dataset, the time-normalised ESS of all the methods jump to a higher level for $\rho > 0.5$, suggesting that the execution time improves for all the methods for $\rho > 0.5$. This phenomenon is not observed on the Australian credit dataset (which has $D = 14$) and is only present on the German credit dataset (which has $D = 25$). This seems to suggest that the impact of partial momentum refreshment becomes more pronounced on a time-normalised ESS as D increases. We intend to investigate this behaviour further in future work.

The automatic tuning of ρ is still an open research problem. We plan to address the automatic tuning of this parameter in future work. As a guideline, higher values of ρ seem to be associated with higher ESS.

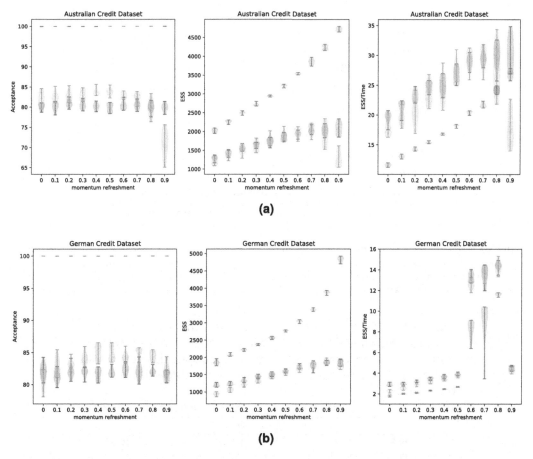

FIGURE 5.1 Acceptance rates, ESS and ESS/Time for ten runs of PHMC (blue (dark gray in print version)), PMHMC (orange (light gray in print version)), and PS2HMC (green (mid gray in print version)) on the a) Australian and b) German credit datasets with varying choices of the momentum refreshment parameter ρ. The results indicate that the ESS metrics are increasing functions of ρ, while the acceptance rate remains constant across all values of ρ.

5.3 Results and discussion

We first assess the convergence and mixing behaviour of the algorithms through plotting the convergence profile of the negative log-likelihood in Fig. 5.2. This plot is from the point at which the first sample is generated until the last sample is generated. The results indicate that the methods which employ partial momentum refreshment converge faster than the original algorithms. This shows that the mixing speed of Hamiltonian dynamics-based samplers can be improved by including partial momentum refreshment.

The performance of the algorithms across different metrics is shown in Fig. 5.3 and Tables 5.1 to 5.3. In Fig. 5.3, the plots on the first row for each dataset show the ESS, and the plots on the second row show the ESS normalised by execution time. The results are for ten runs of each algorithm. The execution time t in Fig. 5.3 and Tables 5.1 to 5.3 is in seconds.

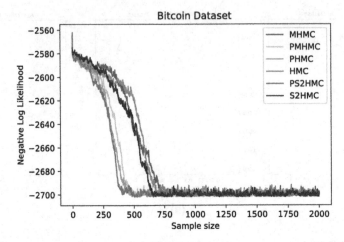

FIGURE 5.2 Diagnostic trace-plot of the negative log-likelihood showing the convergence behaviour of the algorithms on the Bitcoin dataset. The methods which employ partial momentum refreshment converge faster than the original algorithms. This plot was produced by using $\rho = 0.7$. Two thousand samples were generated with no burn-in period. The other settings are as outlined in Section 5.2.1. The results are for a single run of each algorithm.

Table 5.1 JDP results averaged over ten runs. The time t is in seconds. The values in **bold** indicate that the particular method outperforms the other methods on that specific metric. AR stands for the acceptance rate of the generated samples post the burn-in period.

Metric	HMC	MHMC	S2HMC	PHMC	PMHMC	PS2HMC
			USDZAR dataset			
AR	**99.99**	99.93	99.97	**99.99**	99.97	**99.99**
ESS	27	26	28	38	40	**41**
t	**179**	181	484	181	181	482
ESS/t	0.15	0.14	0.05	0.21	**0.22**	0.08
$\hat{R}$ max	1.03	1.02	1.03	1.01	1.02	**1.00**
			S&P 500 dataset			
AR	92.72	92.68	**99.3**	92.33	92.58	**99.3**
ESS	211	217	222	602	577	**715**
t	173	174	601	**172**	173	597
ESS/t	1.22	1.24	0.36	**3.49**	3.32	1.19
$\hat{R}$ max	1.03	1.02	1.04	**1.01**	1.02	**1.01**

The results in Tables 5.1 to 5.3 are the mean results over ten runs for each algorithm. We use the mean values over the ten runs in Tables 5.1, 5.2, 5.3 to form our conclusions about the performance of the algorithms.

The results in Fig. 5.3 and Tables 5.1 to 5.3 show that, as expected, MHMC outperforms HMC on all but one target being the Australian credit dataset. This is in line with the be-

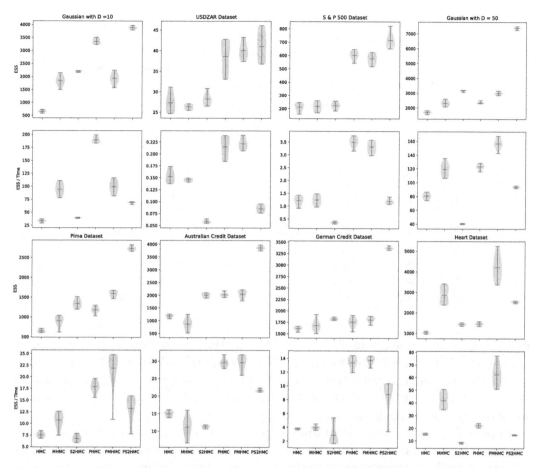

FIGURE 5.3 Results for the targets over ten runs of each method. For each dataset, the plots on the first row show the multivariate effective sample size and the plots on the second row show the multivariate effective sample size normalised by execution time (in seconds). The dark horizontal line in each violin plot represents the mean value over ten runs of each algorithm. For all the plots, the larger the value, the better the method.

haviour which we saw in Section 4.2 of Chapter 4. Furthermore, these results are in line with what has been previously observed in the literature [38,213].

We also notice that S2HMC produces higher acceptance rates than HMC across all the targets while using the same step size. This shows the benefits that can be derived from sampling from shadow Hamiltonians. We further find that the methods that partially refresh the momentum produce similar acceptance rates to the original algorithms. In addition, the results show that the PS2HMC and S2HMC algorithms consistently produce high acceptance rates across all the targets and outperform the other methods on this metric.

The results also indicate that PMHMC and PS2HMC outperform MHMC and S2HMC across all the targets considered on the ESS and ESS normalised by execution time met-

Table 5.2 Multivariate Gaussian distribution results averaged over ten runs. The time t is in seconds. The values in **bold** indicate that the particular method outperforms the other methods on that specific metric. AR stands for the acceptance rate of the generated samples post the burn-in period.

Metric	HMC	MHMC	S2HMC	PHMC	PMHMC	PS2HMC
			Gaussian with D = 10			
AR	86.21	80.96	**100.00**	86.22	82.86	**100.00**
ESS	653	1 844	2197	3345	1936	**3878**
t	19.61	**19.52**	55.67	17.63	**19.52**	56.25
ESS/t	33.33	94.45	39.48	**189.78**	99.17	68.95
$\hat{R}$ max	1.03	1.02	1.02	1.03	1.02	**1.01**
			Gaussian with D = 50			
AR	73.50	83.32	99.68	73.56	82.32	**99.92**
ESS	1705	2313	3164	2366	3008	**7 390**
t	21.12	19.42	78.28	19.22	**19.20**	78.73
ESS/t	80.71	119.11	40.43	123.14	**156.61**	93.86
$\hat{R}$ max	**1.01**	1.03	1.02	1.03	1.02	**1.01**

rics, respectively. Furthermore, PHMC outperforms HMC – which was also observed by Horowitz [107]. This result was also observed in the context of RMHMC in [98]. This shows the significant benefit partial momentum updates can provide to the sampling properties of HMC based samplers. However, the real performance gains are realised when the momentum refreshment parameter ρ has been appropriately tuned.

In general, we find that the algorithms with partial momentum refreshment have similar execution times compared to the original algorithms, except on the German credit dataset, where the execution time of the partial momentum refreshment algorithms drops. This is due to the phenomenon that we outlined in Section 5.2.2. This particular aspect of the method requires further investigation, which we plan to conduct in future work. It is worth highlighting that the S2HMC and PS2HMC algorithms have the most considerable execution times across all the targets. This is mainly due to the multiple times that the shadow Hamiltonian is evaluated. This affects the time-normalised ESS performance of these algorithms.

We find that PS2HMC outperforms all the methods on an ESS basis on all the targets, except on the Heart dataset where PMHMC outperforms all the methods. PMHMC outperforms all the methods on a time-normalised ESS basis on the BLR datasets, with mixed results on the Gaussian and JDP targets. We further find that S2HMC sometimes outperforms, on an ESS basis, all the other methods except for PS2HMC, for example, on the Gaussian targets and the German credit dataset. This indicates that S2HMC sometimes precludes, baring the slow execution time, the need for PMHMC in practice.

It is worth noting that all the methods produce low ESSs on the JDP datasets, indicating the difficulty of sampling from JDPs. The results of the $\hat{R}$ metric across all the targets show

Table 5.3   BLR results averaged over ten runs. The time t is in seconds. The values in **bold** indicate that the particular method outperforms the other methods on that specific metric. AR stands for the acceptance rate of the generated samples post the burn-in period.

Metric	HMC	MHMC	S2HMC	PHMC	PMHMC	PS2HMC
			Pima dataset			
AR	78.195	82.35	99.89	78.39	80.60	**99.94**
ESS	645	902	1339	1179	1595	**2731**
t	85.54	84.13	199	**65**	76	215
ESS/t	7.55	10.72	6.76	17.90	**21.88**	13.26
$\hat{R}$ max	**1.00**	1.02	**1.00**	**1.00**	1.01	**1.00**
			Heart dataset			
AR	81.69	79.10	99.96	81.93	83.67	**100.00**
ESS	1030	2864	1447	1460	**4215**	2528
t	**66**	68	170	**66**	67	170
ESS/t	15.48	41.96	8.48	22.09	**62.42**	14.83
$\hat{R}$ max	1.02	**1.01**	1.02	**1.01**	**1.01**	1.02
			Australian credit dataset			
AR	79.88	82.06	**100**	80.33	82.22	**100**
ESS	1184	867	2005	2030	2053	**3862**
t	79.18	77.82	178	**68**	69	178
ESS/t	14.96	11.14	11.21	29.61	**29.63**	21.62
$\hat{R}$ max	1.01	1.04	**1.00**	**1.00**	**1.00**	**1.00**
			German credit dataset			
AR	81.89	81.41	**100.0**	82.03	84.9	**100.0**
ESS	1617	1686	1828	1756	1808	**3375**
t	421.79	420.51	630.08	**130.01**	131.11	382.62
ESS/t	3.83	4.01	2.90	13.42	**13.77**	8.82
$\hat{R}$ max	1.02	**1.01**	1.02	**1.01**	**1.01**	**1.01**

that the methods have converged, with the algorithms displaying similar $\hat{R}$ metrics without an outright outperformer on all the targets.

5.4 Conclusion

In this chapter, we introduced partial momentum refreshment to MHMC and S2HMC. We showed that these modifications result in improved sampling performance over MHMC and S2HMC with minimal additional computational costs. We find that PS2HMC outperforms all the methods on an ESS basis on the majority of the targets, with PMHMC outperforming on the BLR datasets on a time-normalised ESS basis. These results indicate the overall efficacy of incorporating partial momentum refreshment in Hamiltonian dynamics-based samplers.

A limitation of the proposed methods is the need to tune the momentum refreshment parameter. Although typically larger parameter values improve the effective sample sizes, a more robust approach to selecting the parameter is still required. This work can be improved by establishing a heuristic or an automated approach to tune the momentum refreshment parameter. Furthermore, exploring techniques for accelerating the execution time of S2HMC and PS2HMC are worthwhile as these two algorithms produce the lowest execution times, which hampers their performance on a normalised ESS basis.

In the next chapter, we extend MHMC by deriving the fourth-order shadow Hamiltonian associated with the integration scheme used in MHMC. We then use this modified Hamiltonian to construct the novel SMHMC sampler.

Shadow Magnetic Hamiltonian Monte Carlo

6.1 Background

It has been previously confirmed that the performance of HMC suffers from the deterioration in acceptance rates due to numerical integration errors that arise as a result of large integration step sizes ϵ, or as the system size increases [98,110]. As MHMC is an extension of HMC, and becomes HMC when the magnetic component is absent, one would expect that it also suffers from the pathology of a rapid decrease in acceptance rates as the system size increases. The results in Fig. 6.1 suggest that MHMC may indeed suffer from a deterioration in acceptance rates.

The rapid decrease in acceptance rates results in significant auto-correlations between the generated samples, thus requiring large sample sizes. The deterioration of the acceptance rates can be reduced by using more accurate higher-order integrators, by using smaller step sizes, or by employing shadow Hamiltonians [192]. The first two approaches tend to be more computationally expensive than the latter approach [98,168,192]. In this chapter, we explore the approach of utilising shadow Hamiltonians to enhance the sampling performance of MHMC.

Samplers based on shadow Hamiltonians have been successfully employed to address the deterioration of sample acceptance as the system, and step sizes increase and also lead to more efficient sampling of the target posterior [6,110,212]. The shadow Hamiltonians are constructed by performing backward error analysis of the integrator and, as a result, are better conserved when compared to the true Hamiltonian [90]. Numerous approaches have been proposed for sampling from shadow Hamiltonians of various numerical integrators [6,98,110,212]. Sampling from the modified Hamiltonian associated with the numerical integrator employed in MHMC is yet to be explored in the literature. In this chapter, we address this gap in the literature by deriving the fourth-order modified Hamiltonian associated with the numerical integrator in MHMC. From this modified Hamiltonian, we create the new SMHMC method, which satisfied detailed balance. We compare the performance of the proposed method to MHMC and PMHMC across the Banana shaped distribution, multivariate Gaussian distribution, Protein dataset modelled using BNNs, and the Heart dataset modelled using BLR as highlighted in Table 2.2.

We proceed in this chapter by first deriving the shadow Hamiltonian corresponding to the leapfrog-like integration scheme in MHMC, after which we utilise this shadow Hamiltonian to construct the novel SMHMC algorithm.

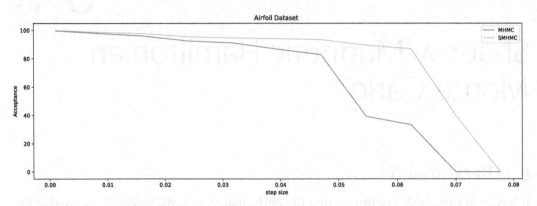

FIGURE 6.1 Impact of the step size on the acceptance rate of SMHMC and MHMC on the Airfoil dataset. The results show that SMHMC maintains higher acceptance rates than MHMC as the step size increases. Three thousand samples were generated for each run, with the first one thousand samples being the burn-in period. The results displayed in this plot were averaged over five runs of the algorithms.

6.2 Shadow Hamiltonian for MHMC

In this chapter, we focus on a fourth-order truncation of the shadow Hamiltonian under the leapfrog-like integrator in Eq. (1.23). Since the leapfrog-like integrator is second-order accurate ($\mathcal{O}^2$) [213], the fourth-order truncation is conserved with higher accuracy ($\mathcal{O}^4$) by the integrator than the true Hamiltonian. In Theorem 6.2.1, we derive the fourth-order shadow Hamiltonian under the leapfrog-like integrator.

Theorem 6.2.1. *Let $H : R^d \times R^d = R$ be a smooth Hamiltonian function. The fourth-order shadow Hamiltonian function $\hat{H} : R^d \times R^d = R$ corresponding to the leapfrog-like integrator used in MHMC is given by:*

$$\hat{H}(\mathbf{w}, \mathbf{p}) = H(\mathbf{w}, \mathbf{p}) + \frac{\epsilon^2}{12}[K_{\mathbf{p}}U_{\mathbf{ww}}K_{\mathbf{p}} + K_{\mathbf{p}}\mathbf{G}K_{\mathbf{pp}}U_{\mathbf{w}}] - \frac{\epsilon^2}{24}[U_{\mathbf{w}}K_{\mathbf{pp}}U_{\mathbf{w}}] + \mathcal{O}(\epsilon^4) \qquad (6.1)$$

Proof. As outlined in Tripuraneni et al. [213], the Hamiltonian vector field $\vec{H} = \nabla_{\mathbf{p}}H\nabla_{\mathbf{w}} + (-\nabla_{\mathbf{w}} + \mathbf{G}\nabla_{\mathbf{p}}H)\nabla_{\mathbf{p}} = \vec{A} + \vec{B}$ will generate the exact flow corresponding to exactly simulating the MHMC dynamics [213]. We obtain the shadow Hamiltonian via the separability of the true Hamiltonian [213]. The leapfrog-like integration scheme in Eq. (1.23) splits the Hamiltonian as: $H(\mathbf{w}, \mathbf{p}) = H_1(\mathbf{w}) + H_2(\mathbf{p}) + H_1(\mathbf{w})$ and exactly integrates each sub-Hamiltonian [213]. Using the Baker-Campbell-Hausdorff (BCH) [91] formula we obtain:

$$\Phi_{\epsilon,H}^{frog} = \Phi_{\epsilon,H_1(\mathbf{w})} \circ \Phi_{\epsilon,H_2(\mathbf{p})} \circ \Phi_{\epsilon,H_1(\mathbf{w})}$$

$$= \exp\left(\frac{\epsilon}{2}\vec{B}\right) \circ \exp(\epsilon\vec{A}) \circ \exp\left(\frac{\epsilon}{2}\vec{B}\right) \qquad (6.2)$$

$$= H(\mathbf{w}, \mathbf{p}) + \frac{\epsilon^2}{12}\{K, \{K, U\}\} - \frac{\epsilon^2}{24}\{U, \{U, K\}\} + \mathcal{O}(\epsilon^4)$$

where the non-canonical Poisson brackets [38,45] are defined as:

$$\{f, g\} = [\nabla_{\mathbf{w}}f, \nabla_{\mathbf{p}}f] \begin{bmatrix} \mathbf{0} & \mathbf{I} \\ -\mathbf{I} & \mathbf{G} \end{bmatrix} [\nabla_{\mathbf{w}}g, \nabla_{\mathbf{p}}g]^T$$
$$= -\nabla_{\mathbf{p}}f \nabla_{\mathbf{w}}g + \nabla_{\mathbf{w}}f \nabla_{\mathbf{p}}g + \nabla_{\mathbf{p}}f \mathbf{G} \nabla_{\mathbf{p}}g \tag{6.3}$$

and collapse to the canonical Poisson brackets when $\mathbf{G} = \mathbf{0}$ [38,45]. The corresponding derivatives from the non-canonical Poisson brackets are presented in Appendix A.3. The shadow Hamiltonian for the leapfrog-like integrator is then:

$$\hat{H}(\mathbf{w}, \mathbf{p}) = H(\mathbf{w}, \mathbf{p}) + \frac{\epsilon^2}{12}[K_{\mathbf{p}}U_{\mathbf{ww}}K_{\mathbf{p}} + \underbrace{K_{\mathbf{p}}\mathbf{G}K_{\mathbf{pp}}U_{\mathbf{w}}}_{A}] - \frac{\epsilon^2}{24}[U_{\mathbf{w}}K_{\mathbf{pp}}U_{\mathbf{w}}] + \mathcal{O}(\epsilon^4) \tag{6.4}$$

where A is the factor induced by the presence of the magnetic field $\mathbf{G}$. When $\mathbf{G} = \mathbf{0}$, the shadow in (6.4) becomes the shadow for Hamiltonian dynamics [110,212] in Eq. (1.31). It is worth noting that the shadow Hamiltonian in (6.4) is conserved to fourth-order [98, 192,212], and is thus more accurately conserved by leapfrog-like integrator than the true Hamiltonian [209]. □

6.3 Proposed Shadow Magnetic algorithm

We now present the SMHMC algorithm, which combines non-canonical Hamiltonian dynamics in MHMC with the high conservation property of shadow Hamiltonians. The benefits of employing non-canonical Hamiltonian dynamics in MHMC have already been established in [85,165,213], while the advantages of shadow Hamiltonians in general are presented in [6,98,145,161,212]. We combine these two concepts to create a new sampler that outperforms MHMC across various performance metrics.

An analysis of the shadow Hamiltonian corresponding to MHMC in Eq. (6.1) shows that the conditional density for the momenta $\pi_H(\mathbf{p}|\mathbf{w})$ is not Gaussian. This suggests that if we fully re-sample the momenta from a normal distribution, as we did in Chapter 5, we will attain a sampler that does not satisfy detailed balance [6,98]. This necessitates computationally intensive momentum generation [110] or partial momentum refreshment [6,192] with an MH step. In this chapter, we utilise the partial momentum refreshment procedure outlined in [6,98], in which a Gaussian noise vector $u \sim \mathcal{N}(0, \mathbf{M})$ is drawn. The momentum proposal is then produced via the mapping:

$$R(\mathbf{p}, u) = \left(\rho\mathbf{p} + \sqrt{1 - \rho^2}u, -\sqrt{1 - \rho^2}\mathbf{p} + \rho u\right) \tag{6.5}$$

The new parameter, which we refer to as the momentum refreshment parameter, $\rho = \rho(\mathbf{w}, \mathbf{p}, u)$ takes values between zero and one, and controls the extent of the momentum retention [98,165,192]. When ρ is equal to one, the momentum is never updated and when ρ is equal to zero, the momentum is always updated [165]. The momentum proposals are then accepted according to the modified non-separable shadow Hamiltonian given as $\bar{H}(\mathbf{w}, \mathbf{p}, u) = \hat{H}(\mathbf{w}, \mathbf{p}) + \frac{1}{2}u\mathbf{M}^{-1}u$. The updated momentum is then taken to be $\rho\mathbf{p} + \sqrt{1 - \rho^2}u$ with probability:

$$\omega := \max\left\{1, \exp(\bar{H}(\mathbf{w}, \mathbf{p}, u) - \bar{H}(\mathbf{w}, R(\mathbf{p}, u)))\right\}. \tag{6.6}$$

The incomplete refreshment of the momentum produces a chain which saves some of the behaviour between neighbourhood samples [6,98,107,165,192]. In Section 6.4.2, we assess the sensitivity of the sampling results on the user-specified value of ρ. An algorithmic description of the SMHMC sampler is provided in Algorithm 6.1. It is worth noting from Algorithm 6.1 that the SMHMC sampler uses two reversible MH steps, which implies that the resulting Markov chain is no longer reversible [6,98,192]. By breaking the detailed balance condition, it is no longer immediately clear that the target density is stationary, and so this must be demonstrated [98,168,192].

Theorem 6.3.1. *The SMHMC algorithm leaves the importance target distribution invariant.*

Proof. The proof of Theorem 6.3.1 is obtained in Appendix A of the paper by Radivojevic and Akhmatskay [192]. The proof involves showing that the addition of step 4 in Algorithm 6.1 leaves the target invariant. The result follows from [192] by making use of the fact that the explicit form of the shadow Hamiltonian, which has the additional magnetic component $A = K_{\mathbf{p}}\mathbf{G}K_{\mathbf{pp}}U_{\mathbf{w}}$ in Eq. (6.4) in our case, is not required for the proof [98,168,192]. $\qquad\square$

Algorithm 6.1 Shadow Magnetic Hamiltonian Monte Carlo algorithm.

  Input: $L, \epsilon, \rho, N, \mathbf{G}, (\mathbf{w_0}, \mathbf{p_0})$.
  Output: $(w_i, p_i, b_i)_{i=0}^N$
1: **for** $i \to 1$ to N **do**
2:     $(\mathbf{w}, \mathbf{p}) \leftarrow (\mathbf{w_{i-1}}, \mathbf{p_{i-1}})$.
3:     $u \sim \mathcal{N}(0, \mathbf{M})$
4:     $\bar{p} \leftarrow \rho p + \sqrt{1 - \rho^2}u$ with probability ω in Eq. (6.6).
5:     $(\hat{\mathbf{w}}, \hat{\mathbf{p}}) = \Phi_{\epsilon, H}^L(\mathbf{w}, \bar{\mathbf{p}}, \mathbf{G})$ in Eq. (1.23)
6:     $\zeta = \min[1, \exp(-\delta\hat{H})], u \sim \text{Unif}(0, 1)$
7:     **if** $\zeta > u$ **then**
8:         $(\mathbf{w}_i, \mathbf{p}_i, \mathbf{G}) \leftarrow (\hat{\mathbf{w}}, \hat{\mathbf{p}}, \mathbf{G})$
9:     **else**
10:         $(\mathbf{w}_i, \mathbf{p}_i, \mathbf{G}) \leftarrow (\mathbf{w}, -\mathbf{p}, -\mathbf{G})$
11:     **end if**
12:     $b_i = \exp(\hat{H}(\mathbf{w_i}, \mathbf{p_i}) - H(\mathbf{w_i}, \mathbf{p_i}))$
13: **end for**

6.4 Experiment description

In this section, we outline the settings used for the experiments, the performance metrics used, and we also present the sensitivity analysis for the partial momentum refreshment parameter ρ in SMHMC and PMHMC.

6.4.1 Experiment settings

In our analysis, we compare the performance of SMHMC against MHMC and PMHMC across the Banana shaped distribution, multivariate Gaussian distribution with $D = 10$, the Protein dataset modelled using a BNN and the Heart dataset modelled using BLR. We assess the performance using the acceptance rate, ESS, time-normalised ESS metrics and assess the convergence behaviour of the chains using the $\hat{R}$ metric. Note that for all our experiments in this chapter, we set $\mathbf{M} = \mathbf{I}$ which is the common approach in practice [25].

For all the target posteriors used in this chapter, the momentum refreshment parameter ρ is set to 0.7, which is consistent with the settings used in Chapter 5. This setting worked well on all the targets. Further experiments of the sensitivity to ρ are presented in Section 6.4.2. The trajectory length and step size parameters for the MCMC methods considered in this chapter were set to the values outlined in Table 2.5. Note that the SMHMC and PMHMC methods used the same step size as MHMC.

Ten independent chains were run for each method on each target distribution. Three thousand samples were generated for each target, with the first one-thousand samples discarded as burn-in. These settings were sufficient for all the algorithms to converge on all the targets.

6.4.2 Sensitivity to momentum refreshment parameter

We investigate the effects of varying the momentum refreshment parameter ρ on the sampling performance of the proposed shadow Hamiltonian method. A total of ten chains, starting from different positions, of the PMHMC and shadow MHMC algorithms were ran on the Australian credit dataset for $\rho \in \{0.0, 0.1, 0.2, 0.3, 0.4, 0.5, 0.6, 0.7, 0.8, 0.9\}$. Note that we exclude $\rho = 1.0$ from the analysis due to the same reasons outlined in Section 5.2.2. Fig. 6.2 shows the results for the Australian credit dataset. The results show that PMHMC and SMHMC have stable acceptance rates across the different values of ρ on all this target. SMHMC has higher acceptance rates and ESS than PMHMC for the same step size. However, due to the high execution time of SMHMC, PMHMC produced better time-normalised ESS compared to SMHMC. The methods show a general trend of increasing ESS and time-normalised ESS with increasing ρ, which is consistent with what was observed in Section 5.2.2 for other Hamiltonian methods that incorporate partial momentum refreshment.

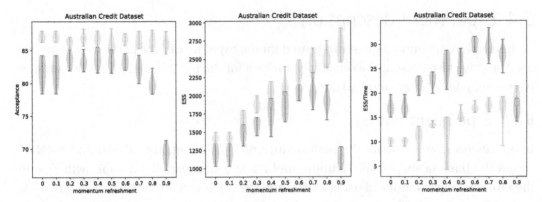

FIGURE 6.2 Acceptance rates, ESS and ESS/Time for ten chains of PMHMC (blue (dark gray in print version)) and SMHMC (orange (light gray in print version)) the Australian credit dataset with varying choices of ρ. The ESS metrics are an increasing function of ρ with the acceptance rate of SMHMC being larger than PMHMC for the same step size ϵ.

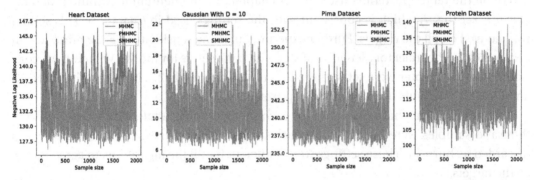

FIGURE 6.3 Diagnostic trace-plots of the negative log-likelihood across various targets averaged over ten runs of each method. These results show that all the MCMC methods have converged on all the targets.

6.5 Results and discussion

Fig. 6.3 shows the diagnostic trace-plots of the negative log-likelihood across various target posteriors. The results show that all three methods have converged on the four target densities analysed in this chapter.

The performance of the algorithms across different metrics is shown in Fig. 6.4 and Tables 6.1, 6.2, 6.3, 6.4. In Fig. 6.4, the plots on the first row for each dataset show the effective sample size, and the plots on the second row show the effective sample size normalised by execution time. The results are for the ten runs of each algorithm. The execution time t in Fig. 6.4 and Tables 6.1 to 6.4 is in seconds. The results in Tables 6.1 to 6.4 are the mean results over the ten runs for each algorithm. We use the mean values over the ten runs in Tables 6.1 to 6.4 to form our conclusions about the performance of the algorithms.

Tables 6.1 to 6.4 show that SMHMC produces the highest acceptance rate across all the targets, which is consistent with what we observed for other shadow Hamiltonian algo-

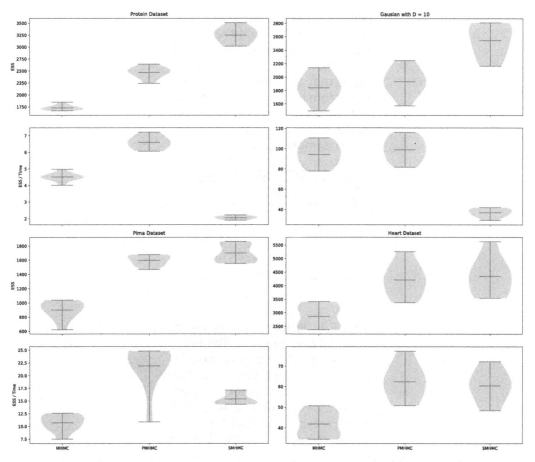

FIGURE 6.4 Results for the datasets over ten runs of each method. For each dataset, the plots on the first row show the multivariate effective sample size and the plots on the second row show the multivariate effective sample size normalised by execution time (in seconds). For all the plots, the larger the value, the better the method. The dark horizontal line in each violin plot represents the mean value over ten runs of each algorithm.

rithms in Chapter 5. Furthermore, the SMHMC algorithm produces the largest ESS on all the targets. In particular, it outperforms PMHMC, which shows that the method is doing something extra than just incorporating partial momentum refreshment into the MHMC. However, the source of the outperformance of SMHMC seems to be mostly driven by the incorporation of the partial momentum refreshment, highlighting the benefits of utilising partial momentum refreshment in Hamiltonian dynamics-based samplers in general.

The results show that the MHMC and PMHMC produce the lowest execution times across all the targets, with SMHMC having the largest execution time, sometimes as much as two times that of the MHMC method. The large execution time of SMHMC can be attributed to the multiple times that the shadow Hamiltonian is evaluated, as well as the extra MH step for the momenta generation. The slow execution time is the key drawback

Table 6.1 Multivariate Gaussian distribution with $D = 10$ results averaged over ten runs. The time t is in seconds. The values in **bold** indicate that the particular method outperforms the other methods on that specific metric. AR stands for the acceptance rate of the generated samples post the burn-in period.

Metric	MHMC	PMHMC	SMHMC
	Gaussian with $D = 10$		
AR	80.96	82.86	**84.64**
ESS	1844	1936	**2546**
t	**19.52**	**19.52**	69.01
ESS/t	94.45	**99.17**	36.90
$\hat{R}$ max	1.02	1.02	**1.01**

Table 6.2 Protein dataset results averaged over ten runs. The time t is in seconds. The values in **bold** indicate that the particular method outperforms the other methods on that specific metric. AR stands for the acceptance rate of the generated samples post the burn-in period.

Metric	MHMC	PMHMC	SMHMC
	Protein Dataset		
AR	80.28	79.4	**82.09**
ESS	1729	2467	**3244**
t	**373**	374	1579
ESS/t	4.51	**6.54**	2.05
$\hat{R}$ max	1.01	**1.00**	**1.00**

of SMHMC, and hinders the performance of the method on a time-normalised ESS basis. We find that PMHMC outperforms all the methods on a time-normalised ESS basis. SMHMC outperforms MHMC on the BLR datasets on a time-normalised ESS basis, with MHMC outperforming SMHMC on the other targets on the same basis. Furthermore, the $\hat{R}$ metric shows that all the methods have converged, with PMHMC and SMHMC producing marginally better convergence behaviour compared to MHMC.

Table 6.3 Heart dataset results averaged over ten runs. The time t is in seconds. The values in **bold** indicate that the particular method outperforms the other methods on that specific metric. AR stands for the acceptance rate of the generated samples post the burn-in period.

Metric	MHMC	PMHMC	SMHMC
		Heart Dataset	
AR	79.10	83.67	**84.66**
ESS	2864	4215	**4350**
t	68.24	**67.5**	71.90
ESS/t	41.96	**62.42**	60.50
$\hat{R}$ max	1.01	1.01	**1.00**

Table 6.4 Pima dataset results averaged over ten runs. The time t is in seconds. The values in **bold** indicate that the particular method outperforms the other methods on that specific metric. AR stands for the acceptance rate of the generated samples post the burn-in period.

Metric	MHMC	PMHMC	SMHMC
		Pima Dataset	
AR	82.35	80.60	**84.80**
ESS	902	1595	**1699**
t	84.13	**72.91**	110.66
ESS/t	10.72	**21.88**	15.35
$\hat{R}$ max	1.02	**1.01**	**1.01**

6.6 Conclusion

In this chapter, we introduced the novel SMHMC algorithm, which combines the non-canonical dynamics of MHMC with the benefits of sampling from a shadow Hamiltonian. This combination results in improved exploration of the posterior when compared to MHMC. The empirical results show that the new algorithm provides a significant improvement on the MHMC algorithm in terms of higher acceptance rates and larger effective sample sizes, even as the dimensionality of the problem increases.

A primary limitation of the proposed algorithm is the computational time associated with the method, mainly since it involves the computation of the Hessian matrix of the target distribution. This leads to poor performance on a time-normalised ESS basis. A straightforward approach to circumvent the computational burden is to use closed-form expressions for the first-order derivatives and the Hessian matrix. This approach, however, restricts the possible targets that can be considered. We aim to address this issue in the future by using a surrogate model to approximate the shadow Hamiltonian during the burn-in period of the method as an active learning task.

Another limitation of the method is the need to tune the momentum refreshment parameter. Although typically higher values of the parameter improve the effective sample sizes, a more robust approach to selecting the parameter is still required. In future work, we plan on improving the proposed method by establishing an automated approach to tune the momentum refreshment parameter.

In the next chapter, we address a crucial impediment in the general use of the S2HMC method, which is the tuning the parameters of S2HMC. Tuning of parameters of shadow Hamiltonian methods is yet to be explored in the literature. The next chapter aims to fill this gap and simultaneously make S2HMC more accessible to non-expert users.

Adaptive Shadow Hamiltonian Monte Carlo

7.1 Proposed adaptive shadow algorithm

The performance of HMC suffers from two significant practical issues. The first practical issue relates to the degeneration in acceptance rates due to numerical integration errors as the system size grows [98,110]. This deterioration in acceptance rates results in significant auto-correlations in the generated samples, necessitating the generation of large sample sizes. The second difficulty with HMC is the need to tune performance-sensitive parameters in the step size and trajectory length. A small trajectory length leads to the display of random walk behaviour [3,105], and one that is too large leads to wasted computation [3,105]. In contrast, small step sizes are computationally wasteful, leading to correlated samples and poor mixing. Large step sizes compound discretisation errors, which also lead to lousy mixing [3,105]. Finding the optimal values for these parameters is of paramount importance but is far from trivial [3,105].

An approach to address the rapid decrease in acceptance rates with increases in system size is to use modified or shadow Hamiltonian based samplers. These modified Hamiltonian methods leverage backward error analysis of the numerical integrator, which results in higher-order conservation of the shadow Hamiltonian relative to the true Hamiltonian [90]. Numerous methods have been put forward for sampling from a shadow Hamiltonian [6,98,110,145,212].

Sweet et al. [212] present S2HMC which leverages a processed leapfrog integrator that results in a separable shadow Hamiltonian. The separable shadow Hamiltonian reduces the need for computationally intensive momentum generation [110] or partial momentum refreshment [6,192] evaluations that are necessitated by non-separable shadow Hamiltonians. Heide et al. [98] derive a non-separable shadow Hamiltonian for the generalised leapfrog integrator in RMHMC, which results in improved performance relative to sampling from the true Hamiltonian. These methods still suffer from the practical impediment of setting the integration step size and trajectory length.

Hoffman and Gelman [105] present the NUTS methodolog which automatically sets the trajectory length of HMC by setting a termination criterion that avoids retracing of steps. Hoffman and Gelman [105] also address step size adaptation through primal-dual averaging in the burn-in phase. These two approaches for setting these parameters have been widely adopted in the literature [24,43,159,226].

There has been no attempt to adaptively set the step size and trajectory length parameters for shadow HMC methods. A particular constraint in trajectory length tuning is that most shadow Hamiltonian methods proposed in the literature rely on non-separable Hamiltonians. These non-separable Hamiltonian require special treatment of the auxiliary momentum variable as the momentum is no longer Gaussian. This precludes these methods from being directly used within the NUTS methodology [6,98,110,192]. We overcome this constraint by relying on a separable shadow Hamiltonian based sampler, which is the S2HMC algorithm. This allows for both tuning of step sizes through primal-dual averaging and the trajectory length via a binary tree recursion as in Hoffman and Gelman [105]. We refer to this new algorithm as adaptive S2HMC.

The sampling performance of the proposed adaptive S2HMC method is compared against NUTS, S2HMC with a fixed trajectory length and S2HMC with a uniform random trajectory length. We refer to the latter approach that uses a random trajectory length as Jittered S2HMC (JS2HMC). Note that the step size is tuned via primal-dual averaging during the burn-in period in all the methods. We show that our adaptive S2HMC method achieves better exploration of the posterior and higher effective sample sizes than S2HMC, JS2HMC and NUTS across various benchmarks while leaving the target density invariant. The analysis is performed on the Banana shaped distribution, a multivariate Gaussian distribution with $D = 10$, Neal's [174] funnel with $D = 25$ and BLR posterior targets using the Pima and Australian credit datasets as set out in Table 2.2.

The adaptive S2HMC method differs from NUTS in that a different integrator is used. Instead of using the leapfrog integrator associated with HMC, the processed leapfrog integrator, which is explicit and symplectic, corresponding to S2HMC is used. The processed leapfrog integrator used in the adaptive S2HMC sampler proceeds by first performing the pre-processing step and then passing the momenta, position, and the shadow density to the leapfrog integrator, after which a post-processing step is employed to recover the momenta and position. The post-processed position and momenta are then used in the stopping criterion to prevent a U-turn. Note that the stopping criteria in adaptive S2HMC are the same as in the original NUTS algorithm, except that now the target distribution is the shadow density, and the position and momentum are the post-processed position and momentum. That is, the criterion in Eq. (1.40) changes from using $\pi_{\mathbf{Z}}(\mathbf{z})$ to using the shadow equivalent $\hat{\pi}_{\mathbf{Z}^*}(\mathbf{z}^*)$ where $\mathbf{z}^*$ is the state representing the post-processed position and momenta. We then calculate the weights of the adaptive S2HMC method, as it is an importance sampler, by comparing the modified and true Hamiltonian at each generated state. Theorem 7.1.1 guarantees that the new method leaves the target distribution, which is the modified density, invariant.

Theorem 7.1.1. *Adaptive S2HMC satisfies detailed balance and thus leaves the target distribution invariant.*

Proof. To show that adaptive S2HMC satisfies detailed balance, we are required to show that the processed leapfrog algorithm is both symplectic and reversible as necessitated by the NUTS methodology. This is guaranteed by Theorem 1.8.2, with the proof presented in Section 1.8. □

Algorithm 7.1 Adaptive separable shadow hybrid Hamiltonian Monte Carlo algorithm.

Main loop same as NUTS in Algorithm 1.6. We are extending the BuildTree method in Algorithm 1.7 to support the processed leapfrog integration scheme.

function BuildTree($w, p, u, v, j, \epsilon, w^0, p^0$)
Output: $w^-, p^-, w^+, p^+, w', p', n', s', \alpha', n'_\alpha$

1: **if** $j = 0$ **then**
2:    Apply the pre-processing mapping $(\hat{w}, \hat{p}) = \mathcal{X}(w, p)$ in Eq. (1.34)
3:    $w^*, p^* = $ **Leapfrog**$(\hat{p}, \hat{w}, \epsilon v, \tilde{H})$
4:    Apply the post-processing mapping $(w', p') = \mathcal{X}^{-1}(w^*, p^*)$ in Eq. (1.35)
5:    $n' = \mathbf{I}[u < \exp(-\tilde{H}(w', p'))], s' = \mathbf{I}[u < \exp(\Delta_{max} - \tilde{H}(w', p'))]$
6:    $n_\alpha = 1, \alpha = \min\left(1, \exp(\tilde{H}(w^0, p^0) - \tilde{H}(w', p'))\right)$
7:    **return** $w', p', w', p', w', p', n', s', \alpha, n_\alpha$
8: **else**
9:    $w^-, p^-, w^+, p^+, w', p', n', s', \alpha', n'_\alpha = $ BuildTree$(w, p, u, v, j-1, \epsilon, w^0, p^0)$
10:    **if** $s' = 1$ **then**
11:       **if** $v = -1$ **then**
12:          $w^-, p^-, -, -, w'', p'', n'', s'', \alpha'', n''_\alpha = $ BuildTree$(w^-, p^-, u, v, j-1, \epsilon, w^0, p^0)$
13:       **else**
14:          $-, -, w^+, p^+, w'', p'', n'', s'', \alpha'', n''_\alpha = $ BuildTree$(w^+, p^+, u, v, j-1, \epsilon, w^0, p^0)$
15:       **end if**
16:       With prob. $\frac{n''}{n'+n''}$, set $w' = w'', p' = p''$
17:       $\alpha' = \alpha' + \alpha'', n' = n' + n'', n'_\alpha = n'_\alpha + n''_\alpha$
18:       $s' = s'' \mathbf{I}[(w^+ - w^-)p^- \geq 0] \mathbf{I}[(w^+ - w^-)p^+ \geq 0]$
19:    **end if**
20:    **return** $w^-, p^-, w^+, p^+, w', p', n', s', \alpha', n'_\alpha$
21: **end if**

We present the pseudo-code for the adaptive S2HMC sampler in Algorithm 7.1, with parts in blue (dark gray in print version) indicating the additions to NUTS with primal-dual averaging methodology of Hoffman and Gelman [105]. Suppose the blue (dark gray in print version) sections are omitted, and we now sample from the true Hamiltonian. In that case, the processed leapfrog reduces to the original leapfrog integration scheme, which then makes adaptive S2HMC to become NUTS. Note that when the dash "–" character is used as an output, it means that the corresponding argument is left unaltered.

For JS2HMC, we generate each sample using a random trajectory length drawn from a discrete uniform distribution. That is, $L \sim U(1, L_{max})$ with L_{max} specified by the user. The use of random trajectory lengths has been explored before in the context of HMC [102,224], but is yet to be considered for S2HMC. To show that JS2HMC preserves detailed balance, one would need to note that JS2HMC amounts to using a mixture of different S2HMC transition kernels which each preserve detailed balance, and hence JS2HMC preserves detailed

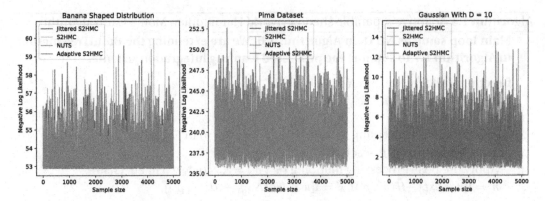

FIGURE 7.1 Diagnostic trace-plots of the negative log-likelihood across various targets averaged over ten runs of each method. These results show that all the MCMC methods have converged on all the targets.

balance. JS2HMC serves as a naive adaptive scheme for S2HMC, which should highlight if the more advanced adaptive schemes are adding any value.

7.2 Experiment description

We consider five test problems to demonstrate the performance of adaptive S2HMC over S2HMC, JS2HMC and NUTS. The targets are the Banana shaped distribution, a multivariate Gaussian distribution with $D = 10$, Neal's [174] funnel with $D = 25$ and BLR posterior targets using the Pima and Australian credit datasets as set out in Table 2.2.

Performance is measured via ESS and ESS per second, and we assess the convergence behaviour of the chains using the $\hat{R}$ metric. For all the algorithms, the step size was set by targeting an acceptance rate of 80% during the burn-in period. The trajectory length for the targets considered in this chapter was set to the values outlined in Table 2.5 for HMC. Ten independent chains were run for each method on each target distribution. Ten thousand samples were generated for each target, with the first 5 000 samples discarded as burn-in. These settings were sufficient for all the algorithms to converge on all the targets.

7.3 Results and discussion

Fig. 7.1 shows the diagnostic trace-plots of the negative log-likelihood across various target posteriors. The results show that all four methods have converged on the target densities considered.

The performance of the algorithms across different metrics is shown in Fig. 7.2 and Tables 7.1, 7.2, 7.3, 7.4. In Fig. 7.2, the plots on the first row for each dataset show the effective sample size, and the plots on the second row show the effective sample size normalised by execution time. The results are for the ten runs of each algorithm. The execution time t in Fig. 7.2 and Tables 7.1 to 7.4 is in seconds. The results in Tables 7.1 to 7.4 are the mean

Table 7.1 Banana shaped distribution results averaged over ten runs. The time t is in seconds. The values in **bold** indicate that the particular method outperforms the other methods on that specific metric. Average L represents the average trajectory length used to generate the post-burn-in samples.

Metric	NUTS	S2HMC	Jittered S2HMC	Adaptive S2HMC
Average L	7	15	7	12
ϵ	0.14	0.12	0.13	0.10
ESS	294	317	235	**582**
t	**17.26**	91.26	72.12	693.37
ESS/t	**16.83**	3.48	3.26	0.84
$\hat{R}$ max	**1.00**	**1.00**	**1.00**	**1.00**

Table 7.2 Multivariate Gaussian distribution with $D = 10$ results averaged over ten runs. The time t is in seconds. The values in **bold** indicate that the particular method outperforms the other methods on that specific metric. Average L represents the average trajectory length used to generate the post-burn-in samples.

Metric	NUTS	S2HMC	Jittered S2HMC	Adaptive S2HMC
Average L	6	15	7	7
ϵ	0.38	0.48	0.48	0.40
ESS	4735	1648	3408	**5342**
t	**14.84**	160.63	127.64	628.53
ESS/t	**318.99**	10.26	26.70	8.50
$\hat{R}$ max	**1.00**	**1.00**	**1.00**	**1.00**

Table 7.3 Neal's funnel density with $D = 25$ results averaged over ten runs. The time t is in seconds. The values in **bold** indicate that the particular method outperforms the other methods on that specific metric. Average L represents the average trajectory length used to generate the post-burn-in samples.

Metric	NUTS	S2HMC	Jittered S2HMC	Adaptive S2HMC
Average L	20	50	25	17
ϵ	0.30	0.30	0.33	0.017
ESS	7719	374	1116	**8441**
t	**120.80**	347.78	233.14	1 143.33
ESS/t	**65.25**	1.07	4.78	8.53
$\hat{R}$ max	**1.00**	**1.00**	**1.00**	**1.00**

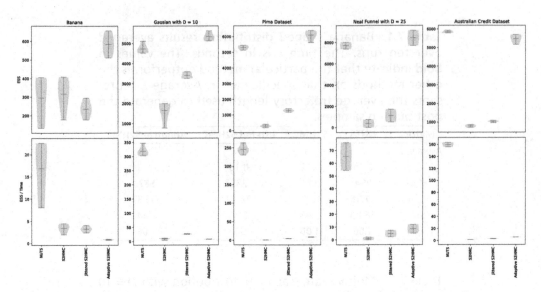

FIGURE 7.2 Results for the datasets over ten runs of each method. For each dataset, the plots on the first row show the multivariate effective sample size and the plots on the second row show the multivariate effective sample size normalised by execution time (in seconds). For all the plots, the larger the value, the better the method. The dark horizontal line in each violin plot represents the mean value over ten runs of each algorithm.

results over the ten runs for each algorithm. We use the mean values over the ten runs in Tables 7.1 to 7.4 to form our conclusions about the performance of the algorithms.

The results show that NUTS and adaptive S2HMC produce similar average trajectory lengths L across the targets, but with adaptive S2HMC producing the larger step size on the majority of the targets. Note that the average trajectory lengths L are calculated post the burn-in period. This combination of step size and trajectory length result in substantial execution times for adaptive S2HMC, which can be attributed to the multiple times the shadow density is evaluated as the adaptive algorithm moves forwards and backwards in time to ensure detailed balance. NUTS outperforms all the methods on an execution time basis, followed by JS2HMC. Note that JS2HMC uses, on average, half the trajectory length of S2HMC due to drawing the trajectory length from a uniform distribution, where the mean would be the upper bound divided by two. In our case, we set the upper bound to be equal to the trajectory length used in S2HMC. We also find that S2HMC and JS2HMC produce similar step sizes, with JS2HMC producing the largest step size of all the methods across all the target posteriors.

We find that adaptive S2HMC outperforms all the methods on an ESS basis across all the targets except for the Australian credit dataset, where it is outperformed by NUTS. More crucially, the adaptive S2HMC produces significantly higher ESSs when compared to S2HMC. What is interesting to note about the ESS performance of S2HMC is that when we target an acceptance rate of 80% as done in this chapter, it produces lower ESSs than when using the step size of HMC in Table 2.5 (as we saw in Chapter 5), which was a smaller step size. The drop in ESS is attributed to non-uniform weights that tend to be produced when

Table 7.4 BLR dataset results averaged over ten runs. The time t is in seconds. The values in **bold** indicate that the particular method outperforms the other methods on that specific metric. Average L represents the average trajectory length used to generate the post-burn-in samples.

Metric	NUTS	S2HMC	Jittered S2HMC	Adaptive S2HMC
		Pima Dataset		
Average L	7	50	25	7
ϵ	0.10	0.13	0.14	0.11
ESS	5302	288	1273	**6102**
t	**21.62**	485.28	306.41	724.87
ESS/t	**245.53**	0.59	4.16	8.42
$\hat{R}$ max	**1.00**	**1.00**	**1.00**	**1.00**
		Australian Credit Dataset		
Average L	10	50	25	8
ϵ	0.10	0.15	0.16	0.14
ESS	5853	794	1034	**5478**
t	**36.65**	484.87	335.68	943.27
ESS/t	**159.73**	1.63	3.11	5.80
$\hat{R}$ max	**1.00**	**1.00**	**1.00**	**1.00**

we target lower acceptance rates for the generated samples. This suggests that S2HMC prefers targeting higher acceptance rates; this is to ensure that the resultant weights of the importance sampler are uniform. JS2HMC outperforms S2HMC on an ESS basis across all the majority of the targets, suggesting that one can achieve more uniform weights in S2HMC by simply making the trajectory length random. This naive approach requires minimal modifications to already existing S2HMC implementations.

The adaptive S2HMC method outperforms S2HMC and JS2HMC on a normalised ESS basis on all the targets except on the Banana shaped distribution and multivariate Gaussian distribution. JS2HMC outperforms S2HMC across all the targets except on the Banana shaped distribution. Given the very insignificant change that is required to create JS2HMC from S2HMC, there seems to be little reason not to use it instead of S2HMC in practice. Overall, NUTS outperforms all the methods across all the targets on a time-normalised ESS basis, and all the methods produced good convergence on all the targets as measured by the $\hat{R}$ metric.

7.4 Conclusion

In this chapter, we introduced the novel adaptive S2HMC algorithm, which combines the benefits of sampling from a shadow Hamiltonian and adaptively sets the trajectory length and step size parameters for S2HMC, while leaving the target invariant. The new method was compared against S2HMC, JS2HMC and NUTS. The JS2HMC method utilises a random trajectory length, and we are the first to introduce such a concept for shadow Hamiltonians into the literature. The empirical results show that the new algorithms provide significant improvement on the S2HMC algorithm.

An important limitation of the adaptive S2HMC is the computational time associated with the method. This leads to poor performance on a normalised ESS basis. We aim to address this issue in the future by using a surrogate model as we intend to do for SMHMC outlined in Chapter 6. The naive JS2HMC method offers improvements to S2HMC without requiring much extra effort, and at half the execution time of S2HMC. It thus provides a practical adaptive scheme for non-expert users.

In the next chapter, we address a crucial impediment in the general use of the MHMC method, which is the tuning the step size and trajectory parameters of MHMC.

8

Adaptive noncanonical Hamiltonian
Monte Carlo

8.1 Background

MHMC improves the exploration of HMC by introducing a magnetic field in addition to the force field already in HMC. The magnetic field provides an extra degree of freedom over HMC and results in efficient exploration of the target posterior and consequently faster convergence and lower autocorrelations in the generated samples when compared to HMC [37,38,213]. When the magnetic component of MHMC is set to zero, MHMC has exactly the same dynamics as HMC [37,38,213]. We leverage this key characteristic of MHMC in developing our proposed method.

The main impediment of HMC and MHMC being broadly used in practice is that they are very sensitive to the trajectory length and step size parameters [3,105]. If these parameters are not set correctly, it can result in very inefficient sampling of the posterior distribution. A trajectory length that is too short leads to random walk behaviour akin to the Metropolis-Hasting method [105]. A trajectory length that is too long results in a trajectory that traces back [25,105]. On the other-hand, small step sizes are computationally inefficient leading to correlated samples and poor mixing, while large step sizes compound discretisation errors leading to low acceptance rates [3,25,105,144]. Tuning these two parameters requires the practitioner to conduct multiple time consuming pilot runs [3,25,105].

The NUTS method of Hoffman and Gelman [105] automates the tuning of the step size and trajectory length parameters for HMC. The step size parameter is tuned during the burn-in phase using the primal dual averaging methodology by targeting a user specified level of acceptance rate in the generated samples [3,105]. The trajectory length is set by iteratively doubling the trajectory length until specific criterion is met [3,105,143]. Empirical results show that NUTS performs at least as efficiently as and sometimes more efficiently than a well tuned standard HMC method, without requiring user intervention or costly tuning runs [105]. The tuning of the parameters of MHMC is yet to be explored in the literature. This work aims to fill this gap in the literature.

MHMC is closely related to HMC and only differs with it due to the magnetic term. In this work, we expand on the NUTS methodology of Hoffman and Gelman [105] by extending it to incorporate the magnetic field present in MHMC. This new algorithm will automatically tune the trajectory length as in NUTS, with the step size tuned using dual averaging during the burn-in phase while leaving the target distribution invariant. We refer to this new method as Adaptive MHMC.

Hamiltonian Monte Carlo Methods in Machine Learning. https://doi.org/10.1016/B978-0-44-319035-3.00020-3

Empirical results on the sampling of jump diffusion processes calibrated to real world financial market data, modelling of real world benchmark classification datasets using Bayesian logistic regression and simulation studies utilising multivariate Gaussian distributions show that Adaptive MHMC outperforms MHMC and NUTS on an effective sample size basis without the user having to manually set the trajectory length and step size. The proposed method is more computationally expensive compared to NUTS due to the extra matrix multiplications required to incorporate the magnetic field. This leads to the new method producing similar effective sample sizes normalised by execution time when compared to NUTS.

8.2 Proposed algorithm

The recently introduced MHMC algorithm enhances HMC by equipping it with a magnetic field [213]. This magnetic field encourages better exploration of the posterior [85,213]. This results in faster convergence and lower autocorrelations in the generated samples when compared to HMC [165,213].

MHMC uses the same Hamiltonian as in HMC in Eq. (1.14), but exploits non-canonical Hamiltonian dynamics where the canonical matrix now has a non-zero element on the diagonal. The MHMC dynamics are [161,168]:

$$\frac{d}{dt}\begin{bmatrix} w \\ p \end{bmatrix} = \begin{bmatrix} \mathbf{0} & \mathbf{I} \\ -\mathbf{I} & \mathbf{G} \end{bmatrix} \begin{bmatrix} \nabla_w H(w, p) \\ \nabla_p H(w, p) \end{bmatrix} \tag{8.1}$$

where $\mathbf{G}$ is the term that represents the magnetic field. The update equations for the non-canonical MHMC integration scheme are given as [213]:

$$\begin{aligned}
\mathbf{p}_{t+\frac{\epsilon}{2}} &= \mathbf{p}_t + \frac{\epsilon}{2}\frac{\partial H\left(\mathbf{w}_t, \mathbf{p}_t\right)}{\partial \mathbf{w}} \\
\mathbf{w}_{t+\epsilon} &= \mathbf{w}_t + \mathbf{G}^{-1}\left(\exp\left(\mathbf{G}\epsilon\right) - \mathbf{I}\right)\mathbf{p}_{t+\frac{\epsilon}{2}} \\
\mathbf{p}_{t+\frac{\epsilon}{2}} &= \exp\left(\mathbf{G}\epsilon\right)\mathbf{p}_{t+\frac{\epsilon}{2}} \\
\mathbf{p}_{t+\epsilon} &= \mathbf{p}_{t+\frac{\epsilon}{2}} + \frac{\epsilon}{2}\frac{\partial H\left(\mathbf{w}_{t+\epsilon}, \mathbf{p}_{t+\frac{\epsilon}{2}}\right)}{\partial \mathbf{w}}.
\end{aligned} \tag{8.2}$$

This means that MHMC only differs from HMC dynamics by $\mathbf{G}$ being non-zero [213]. When $\mathbf{G} = \mathbf{0}$, MHMC and HMC have the same dynamics. These MHMC dynamics cannot be integrated exactly and we resort to a numerical integration scheme with a Metropolis-Hastings acceptance step to ensure detailed balance [213]. The integrator for MHMC is not exactly the leapfrog integrator, but is very similar. This leapfrog-like integration scheme is shown as the *Integrator* function in Algorithm 8.1. As with HMC, the MHMC algorithm has trajectory length and step size parameters that need to be tuned. Tuning of these parameters often requires expert judgement, which makes the method difficult to use in practice for non-specialists.

We now introduce the adaptive Magnetic Hamiltonian Monte Carlo (Adaptive MHMC) algorithm which automatically tunes the parameters of MHMC. The proposed method addresses a key limitation of MHMC – which is how to tune the step size and trajectory length parameters of MHMC. Without a systematic algorithm for tuning an MHMC algorithm its utility becomes severely limited. The tuning of the parameters of MHMC is yet to be explored in the literature. The proposed algorithm addresses this gap in the literature and makes the MHMC accessible to non-experts.

This new algorithm is based on incorporating the magnetic field in MHMC into the NUTS methodology in Algorithm 1.6. In particular, the step size is tuned via primal dual averaging during the burn-in phase, while the trajectory length is set by a recursive doubling procedure until the particle traces back. The Adaptive MHMC method differs from NUTS in that a different integrator is used. Instead of using the leapfrog integrator associated with HMC, the leapfrog-like integrator (which is the explicit and symplectic) corresponding to MHMC is used. Thus the Adaptive MHMC algorithm combines the non-canonical dynamics of MHMC with the automation benefits of NUTS to create a new sampler.

The algorithmic difference of Adaptive MHMC with NUTS is highlighted in Algorithm 8.1. The stopping criteria in Adaptive MHMC is the same as in the original NUTS algorithm outlined in 1.40. It is crucial to note that when $\mathbf{G} = 0$, this new algorithm is equivalent to NUTS. This results in the proposed method inheriting the properties of NUTS such as detailed balance and time-reversibility.

Theorem 8.2.1. *Adaptive MHMC satisfies detailed balance and leaves the target distribution invariant.*

Proof. To show that Adaptive MHMC satisfies detailed balance one would need to show that a NUTS algorithm that uses the leapfrog-like numerical integrator is both symplectic and reversible, and hence satisfied detailed balance. This amounts to showing that the leapfrog-like integrator satisfies detailed balance as this is what is required to show that NUTS satisfies detailed balance [3,105].

We now argue that the leapfrog-like integrator used in Adaptive MHMC satisfies detailed balance. The map defined by integrating the non-canonical Hamiltonian system [213]

$$\frac{d}{dt}\begin{bmatrix} \mathbf{w} \\ \mathbf{p} \end{bmatrix} = \mathbf{A}\begin{bmatrix} \nabla_w H(\mathbf{w}, \mathbf{p}) \\ \nabla_p H(\mathbf{w}, \mathbf{p}) \end{bmatrix} \tag{8.3}$$

with initial conditions $(\mathbf{w}, \mathbf{p})$, where $\mathbf{A}$ is any square invertible, antisymmetric matrix induces a flow on the coordinates $(\mathbf{w}, \mathbf{p})$ that is still energy conserving with respect to $\mathbf{A}$ which also implies volume-preservation of the flow [213]. In addition, setting

$$\mathbf{A} = \begin{bmatrix} \mathbf{0} & \mathbf{I} \\ -\mathbf{I} & \mathbf{G} \end{bmatrix}$$

leads to MHMC dynamics and ensures that non-canonical dynamics have a (pseudo) time-reversibility symmetry as shown in [213]. These properties of being energy conserving, volume preserving and time-reversible guarantee that the leapfrog-like scheme satisfies detailed balance as required. Thus Adaptive MHMC satisfies detailed balance and hence leaves the target invariant.   □

It should be noted that the approach undertaken in this paper is not the only method that could have been used to tune the parameters of MHMC. Wang et al. [223,224] introduce a Bayesian optimisation framework for tuning the parameters of Hamiltonian and Riemann Manifold Hamiltonian Monte Carlo samplers. The authors show that their approach is ergodic and in some instances precludes the need for more complex samplers. Buchholz et al. [40] adapt Hamiltonian Monte Carlo kernels using sequential Monte Carlo. They show that their approach improves as the dimensionality of the problem increases. Hoffman et al. [102] propose an adaptive MCMC scheme for tuning the trajectory length parameter in HMC and show that this new technique typically yields higher effective samples sizes normalised by the number of gradient evaluation when compared to NUTS. We plan to consider these and other approaches for tuning the parameters of MHMC in future work.

The key advantage of the proposed Adative MHMC algorithm over MHMC is that it removes the need to manually tune the MHMC parameters. This makes MHMC more accessible as it removes the need for expert judgement in tuning the algorithm parameters. Note however that the magnetic component $\mathbf{G}$ would still need to be specified by the user.

It is important to note that the number of likelihood function evaluations for NUTS is not deterministic as the trajectory length used to generate each sample varies. As our proposed method is based on the NUTS methodology, the number of function evaluations is not deterministic and depends on the target posterior under consideration. The computational cost of the proposed method is inline with that of NUTS as MHMC has similar, albeit slightly higher, computational cost to HMC. Thus on targets where NUTS has high execution times, we would expect Adaptive MHMC to also have high execution times.

The magnetic field $\mathbf{G}$ in MHMC and Adaptive MHMC provides an extra degree of freedom for both these algorithms [213]. It is not immediately clear as to how one should set or tune this matrix, but this should ideally be conducted in an automated manner [161,165,213]. Tuning the magnetic component is still an open area of research. In this work, we follow the directions of the authors [161,165,166,213] and select only a few dimensions to be influenced by the magnetic field. In particular, $\mathbf{G}$ was set such that $\mathbf{G}_{1i} = \mathbf{G}_{5i} = g$, $\mathbf{G}_{i1} = \mathbf{G}_{i5} = -g$ and zero elsewhere for $g = 0.2$. Note that this particular form of $\mathbf{G}$ was chosen as $\mathbf{G}$ has to be antisymmetric [213]. In addition, we chose the first and firth dimensions as the target posteriors used in this paper include jump diffusion processes, which have only five parameters. Thus we did not consider higher dimensions as we wanted to use the same setting for $\mathbf{G}$ for all the target posterior distributions considered in this paper.

This is means that the choice of $\mathbf{G}$ is not necessarily the optimal choice for all the target distributions considered, but was sufficient for our purposes as this basic setting still leads to good performance of the algorithm. Tuning $\mathbf{G}$ for each target posterior should result in

---

Algorithm 8.1 Adaptive Magnetic Hamiltonian Monte Carlo.

    Main loop same as in NUTS

    function BuildTree($w, p, u, v, j, \epsilon, w^0, p^0$)

1: **if** $j = 0$ **then**

2:    $w', p' = $ **Integrator**$(p, w, \epsilon v, G)$ ← **only difference with NUTS**

3:    $n' = \mathbf{I}[u < \exp(-H(w', p'))], s' = \mathbf{I}[u < \exp(\Delta_{max} - H(w', p'))]$

4:    $n_\alpha = 1, \alpha = \min\left(1, \exp(H(w^0, p^0) - H(w', p'))\right)$

5:    **return** $w', p', w', p', w', p', n', s', \alpha, n_\alpha$

6: **else**

7:    $w^-, {}^-, w^+, {}^+, w', p', n', s', \alpha', n'_\alpha = \text{BuildTree}(w, p, u, v, j - 1, \epsilon, w^0, p^0)$

8:    **if** $s' = 1$ **then**

9:      **if** $v = -1$ **then**

10:        $w^-, p^-, -, -, w'', p'', n'', s'', \alpha'', n''_\alpha = \text{BuildTree}(w^-, p^-, u, v, j - 1, \epsilon, w^0, p^0)$

11:      **else**

12:        $-, -, w^+, p^+, w'', p'', n'', s'', \alpha'', n''_\alpha = \text{BuildTree}(w^+, p^+, u, v, j - 1, \epsilon, w^0, p^0)$

13:      **end if**

14:      With prob. $\frac{n'}{n'+n''}$, set $w' = w'', p' = p''$

15:      $\alpha' = \alpha' + \alpha'', n' = n' + n'', n'_\alpha = n'_\alpha + n''_\alpha$

16:      $s' = s''\mathbf{I}[(w^+ - w^-)p^- \geq 0]\mathbf{I}[(w^+ - w^-)p^+ \geq 0]$

17:    **end if**

18:    **return** $w^-, p^-, w^+, p^+, w', p', n', s', \alpha', n'_\alpha$

19: **end if**

    function Integrator(p, w, ϵ, G)

20: $p \leftarrow p + \frac{\epsilon}{2}\frac{\partial H}{\partial w}(w, p)$

21: $w \leftarrow w + G^{-1}(\exp(G\epsilon) - I)p$

22: $p \leftarrow \exp(G\epsilon)p$

23: $p \leftarrow p + \frac{\epsilon}{2}\frac{\partial H}{\partial w}(w, p)$

    return w, p

---

improved performance compared to the results presented in this manuscript. An alternative approach to the selection of **G** would have been to follow [38] and selecting **G** to be random antisymmetric matrix. We plan to explore this approach in future work.

8.3 Experiments

We consider three test problems to demonstrate the performance of Adaptive MHMC over MHMC and NUTS. We first study a jump diffusion process [149], whose transition density is an infinite mixture of Gaussian distributions with the mixing weights being probabilities from a Poisson distribution. We then perform a simulation study using multivariate Gaussian distributions with increasing dimensionality as in [165,192]. We proceed to consider performance on Bayesian Logistic Regression over various benchmark datasets outlined in [79].

Performance of the methods is measured via multivariate ESS and ESS per second. We also assess the convergence of the methods using the $\hat{R}$ metric of Gelman and Rubin [77, 202]. For all the algorithms, the step size was set by targeting an acceptance rate of 80% during the burn-in period. A total of 10 independent chains were run for each method on each target distribution. For MHMC, we considered the trajectory lengths to be in the set {10, 50, 100}. This allowed us to assess the sensitivity of the results to the trajectory length.

8.4 Results and discussion

The performance, in terms of $m\mathbb{ESS}$, of the algorithms for the simulation study and logistic regression datasets is shown in Fig. 8.1. The detailed results for the real world jump diffusion and logistic regression datasets across different metrics are shown in Tables 8.1 and 8.2. Note that the execution time t in Tables 8.1 and 8.2 is in seconds.

The first row in Fig. 8.1 shows the $m\mathbb{ESS}$ for the multivariate Gaussian distributions in the simulation study with increasing dimensionality D. The second row in Fig. 8.1 shows the $m\mathbb{ESS}$ for the logistic regression datasets. The results in Tables 8.1 and 8.2 are the mean results over the 10 runs for each algorithm. Note that we use the mean values over the 10 runs to form our conclusions about the performance of the algorithms.

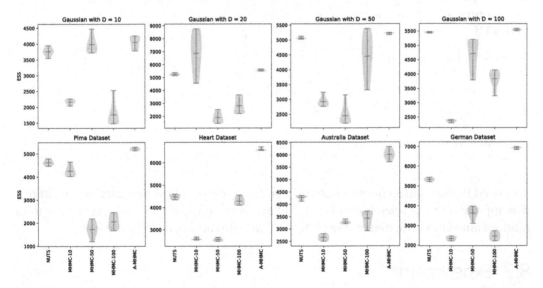

FIGURE 8.1 Results for the datasets over 10 runs of each method. For each dataset, the plots show the multivariate effective sample size. For all the plots, the larger the value the better the method. The dark horizontal line in each violin plot represents the mean value over 10 runs of each algorithm.

The first row of Fig. 8.1 shows that in all the values of D, Adative MHMC performs comparably or better than the MHMC method with fixed trajectory lengths. The results

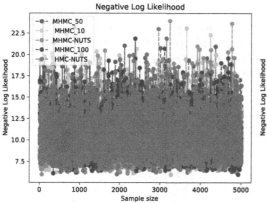

(a) Diagnostic negative log-likelihood trace plot for Gaussian $D = 10$.

(b) Diagnostic negative log-likelihood trace plot for Gaussian $D = 100$.

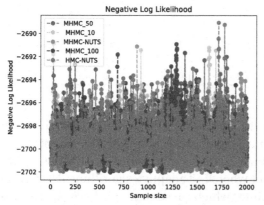

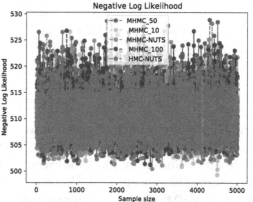

(c) Diagnostic negative log-likelihood trace plot for the Bitcoin dataset.

(d) Diagnostic negative log-likelihood trace plot for the German dataset.

FIGURE 8.2 Diagnostic negative log-likelihood trace plots for various targets. Similar results are observed for targets not included in the plot. Note that HMC-NUTS is the No-U-Turn Sampler while MHMC-NUTS is the Adaptive MHMC method.

also show that the optimal trajectory lengths to use for the MHMC for each D differs with no obvious pattern, illustrating how difficult it is to tune the trajectory length parameter. Adaptive MHMC tunes this trajectory length in an automated fashion, thus removing the manual process that would have been required by the practitioner to select the optimal trajectory length for each D. The results also show that for all the values of D, Adaptive MHMC outperforms NUTS.

The second row in Fig. 8.1 shows that across all the real world logistic regression datasets, Adaptive MHMC outperforms all the methods considered, with NUTS being sec-

Table 8.1 Jump diffusion results averaged over 10 runs. The time t is in seconds. NLL stands for negative log-likelihood. The values in **bold** indicate that the particular method outperforms the other methods on that specific metric. The relative speed up metric is with reference to the method with the lowest time normalised multivariate effective sample size. Note that A-MHMC represents Adaptive MHMC.

	NUTS	MHMC-10	MHMC-50	MHMC-100	A-MHMC
			Bitcoin dataset		
mESS	598	104	834	889	**1 068**
t (in secs)	1555	**178**	684	1397	2374
mESS/t	0.384	0.584	**1.219**	0.647	0.450
Test NLL	−2699	−2699	−2699	−2699	**−2767**
Relative Speed Up	1.00	1.52	**3.17**	1.68	1.17
$\hat{R}$	**1.00**	1.01	1.01	1.02	**1.00**
			USDZAR dataset		
mESS	40	137	43	172	**215**
t (in secs)	**45**	172	710	1 402	117
mESS/t	0.939	0.800	0.061	0.123	**1.835**
Test NLL	−4830	−4758	−4816	−4860	**−5121**
Relative Speed Up	15.39	13.11	1.00	2.02	**30.08**
$\hat{R}$	**0.99**	1.01	1.02	1.01	**1.00**

ond. This is also confirmed by the mean results, over 10 runs of the algorithms, shown in Tables 8.1 and 8.2. The Adaptive MHMC produces significantly more effective sample sizes, even after taking into account the execution time, than the other MHMC with different trajectory lengths – except on the Bitcoin dataset where the adaptive algorithms (NUTS and Adaptive MHMC) have very large execution times which causes poor normalised effective sample size performance. The Adaptive MHMC method can provide up to 40 times relative speed up when compared to MHMC. This shows the benefit of Adaptive MHMC's ability to automatically tune the trajectory length without user intervention. Adaptive MHMC and NUTS produce similar effective sample sizes normalised by execution time, and relative speed up, across all the datasets. With exception on the Bitcoin dataset, NUTS has the lowest execution time t on all the datasets, with Adaptive MHMC being a close second. The low execution time was to be expected as Adaptive MHMC does additional matrix operations, to take into account the magnetic term, when compared to NUTS.

Tables 8.1 and 8.2 show that the algorithms have similar predictive performance, with the MHMC algorithm with trajectory length equal to 100 marginally outperforming the other methods on all the logistic regression datasets. Adative MHMC outperforms on the jump diffusion datasets. It is also worth noting that Adaptive MHMC and NUTS have large executive times on the Bitcoin dataset and low execution times on the USDZAR dataset. The high execution time on the Bitcoin dataset is due to the high kurtosis of this dataset.

Table 8.2 Mean results over 10 runs of each algorithm. Each column represents the mean value for the specific method. For example, column three shows the mean results for MMHC-50. The execution time t is in seconds. The values in **bold** indicate that the particular method outperforms the other methods on that specific metric. The relative speed up metric is with reference to the method with the lowest time normalised multivariate effective sample size. AUC represents the area under the ROC curve. Note that A-MHMC represents Adaptive MHMC.

	NUTS	MHMC-10	MHMC-50	HMC-100	A-MHMC
			Pima dataset		
mESS	4601	4028	1686	2028	**5273**
t (in secs)	**18**	49	197	400	26
mESS/t	**245**	81	8	5	201
AUC	0.827	0.827	0.826	**0.828**	0.827
Relative Speed Up	**49.0**	16.2	1.6	1.0	40.2
$\hat{R}$	**0.99**	1.01	1.02	1.01	1.00
			Heart dataset		
mESS	4491	2539	2504	4011	**6621**
t (in secs)	**22**	48	194	388	31
mESS/t	199	51	12	10	**212**
AUC	0.896	0.896	0.895	**0.898**	0.896
Relative Speed Up	19.9	5.1	1.2	1.0	**21.2**
$\hat{R}$	1.01	**1.00**	1.01	**1.00**	**1.00**
			Australian credit dataset		
mESS	4311	2682	3359	3552	**5940**
t (in secs)	**30**	51	203	407	43
mESS/t	**143**	52	16	9	135
AUC	0.954	0.954	0.954	**0.955**	0.954
Relative Speed Up	**15.9**	5.8	1.8	1.0	15.0
$\hat{R}$	1.00	1.01	1.01	1.00	**0.99**
			German credit dataset		
mESS	5362	2307	3809	2428	**6945**
t (in secs)	**33**	58	228	471	40
mESS/t	161	39	16	5	**172**
AUC	0.764	0.764	0.763	**0.765**	0.763
Relative Speed Up	32.2	7.8	3.2	1.0	**34.4**
$\hat{R}$	**1.00**	1.02	1.01	1.01	**1.00**

Fig. 8.2 shows that all the MCMC methods have converged on all the target posteriors. This is further confirmed in Tables 8.1 and 8.2 where $\hat{R}$ is close to one for all the algorithms with Adaptive MHMC outperforming on the $\hat{R}$ metric on the majority of the datasets.

8.5 Conclusions

We present the adaptive Magnetic Hamiltonian Monte Carlo algorithm that automatically tunes the trajectory length and step size parameters of Magnetic Hamiltonian Monte Carlo without the user having to manually specify these parameters. We assess the performance of this new method against the No-U-Turn Sampler and Magnetic Hamiltonian Monte Carlo methods using 10, 50 and 100 trajectory lengths respectively. The methods are compared on the calibration of jump diffusion processes, Bayesian logistic regression and multivariate Gaussian targets.

The Adaptive MHMC algorithm significantly outperforms MHMC on both an effective sample size basis and normalised effective sample size basis on the majority of the datasets. The empirical results show that Adaptive MHMC outperforms NUTS on an effective sample size basis and produces similar normalised effective sample sizes when compared to NUTS.

This work can be improved by assessing the performance of the proposed method on deep neural networks and larger datasets such as MNIST. Comparing the performance of the method with Riemanian manifold based Markov Chain Monte Carlo methods would be an area of interest. Incorporating the adaptation of the magnetic field term in the proposed algorithm could also serve as an improvement on the method. We plan to also assess other methods for tuning parameters of MHMC, such as those based on utilising the variance of the change in the shadow Hamiltonian corresponding to the leapfrog-like integrator used in MHMC.

In the following chapter, we rely on the coupling theory of Hamiltonian samplers and incorporate antithetic sampling into the MHMC and S2HMC samplers. This approach leads to a reduction of the variance of their estimators or, equivalently, serves to increase their effective sample sizes.

9

Antithetic Hamiltonian Monte Carlo techniques

9.1 Proposed antithetic samplers

In their inspired work, Piponi et al. [189] combined antithetic sampling and control variate variance reduction techniques with Hamiltonian dynamics to create the A-HMC and control variate HMC methods respectively. The HMC based antithetic samplers have an advantage over antithetic Gibbs samplers presented in Frigessi et al. [71] in that they are applicable to problems where conditional distributions are intractable, and where Gibbs sampling may mix slowly [189]. The control variate HMC variance reduction technique is more generally applicable than the antithetic approach, which requires the target distribution to be symmetric about some vector. Control variate techniques rely on the practitioner being able to construct efficient and accurate approximate distributions, which is difficult for neural networks and is an impediment to general use [189]. Thus, this thesis focuses on the antithetic sampling approach, which is straightforward to implement for BNNs as well as for BLR. In particular, we expand on the work of Piponi et al. [189] by presenting two new antithetic sampling MCMC methods being the Antithetic Separable Shadow Hamiltonian Hybrid Monte Carlo (A-S2HMC) and Antithetic Magnetic Hamiltonian Monte Carlo (A-MHMC) algorithms.

The A-S2HMC algorithm is based on sampling from the shadow Hamiltonian using S2HMC [110,212]. Sampling using the S2HMC algorithm provides benefits over HMC – and the results in the preceding chapters of this thesis attest to this. One benefit is that the shadow Hamiltonian is better conserved by the numerical integrator, which allows one to use larger step sizes, and thus reducing auto-correlations, than in HMC without a significant drop in the acceptance rates [6,110,192,212]. In addition, S2HMC is an importance sampler and already offers variance reduction over HMC. The A-S2HMC algorithm thus combines the benefits of antithetic sampling with importance sampling, which should provide even more variance reduction than is provided by S2HMC over HMC. The disadvantage of S2HMC over HMC is that it consumes more computational resources than HMC, which reduces the outperformance on a time-normalised ESS basis.

The A-MHMC algorithm is based on adding antithetic sampling to the MHMC algorithm. The MHMC algorithms provide an improvement on HMC by adjusting the range of exploration via a magnetic field. This has the effect of enhancing the convergence speed and reducing the auto-correlations of the samples [85,213]. In the A-MHMC algorithm, we combine antithetic sampling with the benefits that MHMC already has over HMC intending to create a sampler that outperforms A-HMC. Unlike S2HMC, MHMC has comparable

Hamiltonian Monte Carlo Methods in Machine Learning. https://doi.org/10.1016/B978-0-44-319035-3.00021-5

Algorithm 9.1 Antithetic Magnetic Hamiltonian Monte Carlo algorithm.

Input: N, G, ϵ, L, w_{init}^x, w_{init}^y, $H(w, p)$
Output: $(w^x)_{m=0}^N$, $(w^y)_{m=0}^N$
1: $w_0^x \leftarrow w_{\text{init}}^x$
2: $w_0^y \leftarrow w_{\text{init}}^y$
3: **for** $m \rightarrow 1$ to N **do**
4:      $p_{m-1}^x \sim \mathcal{N}(0, \mathbf{M})$
5:      $p_{m-1}^y = -p_{m-1}^x$ ← **Momentum shared between the two chains**

6:      $p_m^x, w_m^x = \textbf{Integrator}(p_{m-1}^x, w_{m-1}^x, \epsilon, L, G, H)$
7:      $p_m^y, w_m^y = \textbf{Integrator}(p_{m-1}^y, w_{m-1}^y, \epsilon, L, G, H)$

8:      $\delta H^x = H(w_{m-1}^x, p_{m-1}^x) - H(w_m^x, p_m^x)$
9:      $\delta H^y = H(w_{m-1}^y, p_{m-1}^y) - H(w_m^y, p_m^y)$

10:     $\alpha_m^x = \min(1, \exp(\delta H^x))$
11:     $\alpha_m^y = \min(1, \exp(\delta H^y))$

12:     $u_m \sim \text{Unif}(0, 1)$ ← **Uniform random number shared between the two chains**
13:     **The Metropolis-Hastings step is the same as in Algorithm 1.3 for both chains.**
14: **end for**

---

execution time with HMC, which means that the computational burden should not outweigh the benefits of higher ESSs produced by MHMC and A-MHMC, respectively.

The pseudo-code for the new antithetic algorithms that we are proposing is presented in Algorithms 9.1 and 9.2. The difference between the antithetic algorithms and the original algorithms is that the momentum variable and the uniform random variable in the MH acceptance step are shared between the two chains. These differences are appropriately highlighted in the respective algorithms.

9.2 Experiment description

The performance of the algorithms is compared on real-world benchmark datasets. The real-world data used are the four classification datasets used in Girolami and Calderhead [79], which we model using BLR. We also apply BNNs to model real world regression benchmark datasets. The datasets, their number of features and their associated models are outlined in Table 2.2. For all the algorithms, we set the mass matrix $\mathbf{M} = \mathbf{I}$, which is the common approach in practice [25,175].

The performance metrics used in this chapter are the multivariate ESS, the execution time and the ESS normalised by the execution time. Note that the ESS for the variance

---

Algorithm 9.2 Antithetic Separable Shadow Hamiltonian Hybrid Monte Carlo algorithm.

Input: $N, \epsilon, L, w_{init}^x, w_{init}^y, H(w, p), \tilde{H}(w, p)$
Output: $(w^x)_{m=0}^N, (w^y)_{m=0}^N, (b^x)_{m=0}^N, (b^y)_{m=0}^N$

1:   $w_0^x \leftarrow w_{init}^x$
2:   $w_0^y \leftarrow w_{init}^y$
3: **for** $m \rightarrow 1$ to N **do**
4:     $p_{m-1}^x \sim \mathcal{N}(0, \mathbf{M})$
5:     $p_{m-1}^y = -p_{m-1}^x$ **Momentum shared between the two chains**

6:     Apply the pre-processing mapping to both chains
7:     $p_m^x, w_m^x = \textbf{Leapfrog}(p_{m-1}^x, w_{m-1}^x, \epsilon, L, \tilde{H})$
8:     $p_m^y, w_m^y = \textbf{Leapfrog}(p_{m-1}^y, w_{m-1}^y, \epsilon, L, \tilde{H})$

9:     Apply the post-processing mapping to both chains
10:    $\delta H^x = \tilde{H}(w_{m-1}^x, p_{m-1}^x) - \tilde{H}(w_m^x, p_m^x)$
11:    $\delta H^y = \tilde{H}(w_{m-1}^y, p_{m-1}^y) - \tilde{H}(w_m^y, p_m^y)$

12:    $\alpha_m^x = \min(1, \exp(\delta H^x))$
13:    $\alpha_m^y = \min(1, \exp(\delta H^y))$

14:    $u_m \sim \text{Unif}(0, 1) \leftarrow$ **Uniform random number shared between the two chains**
15:    **The Metropolis-Hastings step and the weight calculation is the same as in Algorithm 1.5 for both chains.**
16: **end for**

---

reduced chain is related to the ESS of the original chain as [189]:

$$ESS_{antithetic} = \frac{2 \times ESS_{original}}{1 + \eta} \tag{9.1}$$

where η is the correlation coefficient between the corresponding pairs of chains. In this thesis, the correlation is taken as the maximum correlation across all the parameter dimensions, which creates a lower bound for $ESS_{antithetic}$. Note that we estimate η using the Spearman rank correlation coefficient [230]. A careful analysis of Eq. (9.1) reveals that we can increase the ESS by ensuring that the correlation is as close as possible to -1, which is what the anti-coupling methodology aims to do. This also means that the $ESS_{antithetic}$ can be orders of magnitude greater than the total number of generated samples N.

For all the datasets, we generated three thousand samples with a burn-in period of one thousand samples. This was sufficient for all the algorithms to converge on all the datasets. The step sizes were chosen by targeting an acceptance rate of 95%, as suggested by Piponi et al. [189], through the primal-dual averaging methodology. Note that we only tune the step size of the primary chain X, and use this step size in the secondary chain Y. The tra-

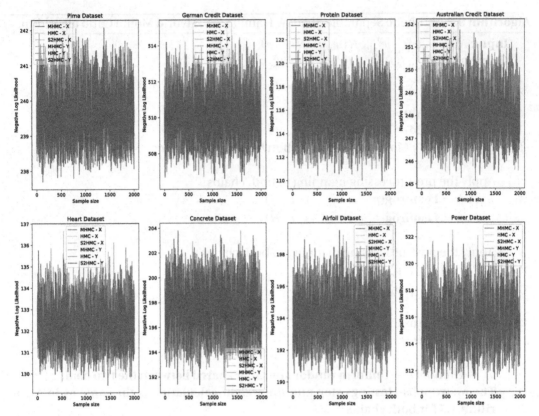

FIGURE 9.1 Diagnostic trace-plots of the negative log-likelihood across various targets averaged over ten runs of each method. These results show that all the MCMC methods have converged on all the targets. X is the primary chain and Y is the secondary chain for each method.

jectory length parameters for each target are the same as the ones in Table 2.5, with S2HMC using the same trajectory length as HMC, and the antithetic versions using the same trajectory length as the non-antithetic counterparts. In evaluating the S2HMC algorithm and its antithetic variant, we set a convergence tolerance of 10^{-6} or the completion of one-hundred fixed point iterations.

9.3 Results and discussion

Fig. 9.1 shows the diagnostic trace-plots of the negative log-likelihood averaged over ten runs for both the primary (X) and secondary/antithetic (Y) chains. The results show that all the MCMC methods have converged on all the targets, and on both the X and Y chains.

The performance of the algorithms across different metrics is shown in Fig. 9.2 and Tables 9.1 and 9.2. In Fig. 9.2, the plots on the first row of each dataset show the ESS, and the plots on the second row show the ESS normalised by execution time (which is in seconds).

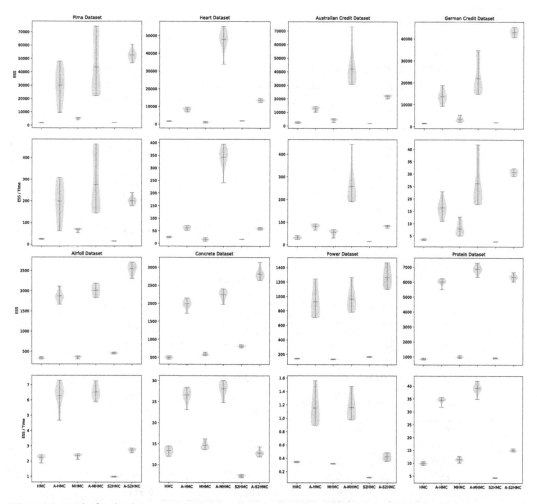

FIGURE 9.2 Results for the datasets over ten runs of each method across the BLR and BNN datasets. For each dataset, the plots on the first row show the multivariate effective sample size and the plots on the second row show the multivariate effective sample size normalised by execution time (in seconds). For all the plots, the larger the value, the better the method. The dark horizontal line in each violin plot represents the mean value over ten runs of each algorithm.

The results are for the ten runs of each algorithm. As with Fig. 9.2, the execution time t in Tables 9.1 and 9.2 is in seconds. The results in Tables 9.1 and 9.2 are the mean results over the ten runs for each algorithm. Note that we use the mean values over the ten runs in Tables 9.1 and 9.2 to form our conclusions about the performance of the algorithms.

We find that the shadow Hamiltonian methods produce the largest step size for the targeted 95% acceptance rate. This can be attributed to the leapfrog integration scheme better conserving the modified Hamiltonian compared to the true Hamiltonian. This has been a recurring observation in this thesis. Furthermore, we find that the MHMC methods

Table 9.1 Mean results over ten runs of each algorithm for the BLR datasets. Each column represents the mean value for the specific method. The execution time t is in seconds. The values in **bold** indicate that the particular method outperforms the other methods on that specific metric.

	HMC	A-HMC	MHMC	A-MHMC	S2HMC	A-S2HMC
			Pima Indian dataset			
ϵ	0.0577		0.0076		**0.1152**	
ESS	1831	30 152	5367	43 703	1970	**52 595**
t (in secs)	**76**	151	79	157	130	260
ESS/t	24.13	198.96	67.99	**275.38**	15.12	201.92
η	−0.8462		−0.6967		−0.9247	
			Heart dataset			
ϵ	0.08307		0.0058		**0.17799**	
ESS	1721	8418	1119	**47 917**	1912	13 545
t (in secs)	**67**	134	70	139	114	227
ESS/t	25.53	62.45	16.01	**342.41**	16.84	59.63
η	−0.5884		−0.9536		−0.7172	
			Australia credit dataset			
ϵ	0.0546		0.0068		**0.1213**	
ESS	2405	12 751	4515	**42 075**	1925	21 820
t (in secs)	**77**	154	81	162	130	260
ESS/t	31.178	82.64	55.45	**257.97**	14.76	83.63
η	−0.6209		−0.7624		−0.8232	
			German credit dataset			
ϵ	0.0295		0.0074		**0.0772**	
ESS	1465	13 630	3335	22 000	1899	**43 045**
t (in secs)	**416**	832	420	840	701	1 402
ESS/t	3.52	16.40	7.93	26.16	2.70	**30.69**
η	-0.7779		−0.6898		−0.9116	

produce the smallest step size. This is due to the presence of the magnetic field, which has the effect of reducing the step size required to reach the same level of sample acceptance rates when compared to HMC. This phenomenon is also clearly highlighted in Table 2.5 where MHMC is shown to produce lower step sizes consistently across all the target posterior distributions.

On the majority of the datasets, we find that MHMC and S2HMC have higher ESSs than HMC, with the outperformance being more pronounced on the BLR datasets. The A-MHMC and A-S2HMC methods produce superior ESSs on all 8 benchmark datasets when compared to A-HMC. A-MHMC produces higher ESSs than A-HMC and A-S2HMC on 7 of the 8 benchmark datasets, with A-MHMC underperforming A-S2HMC on the German credit dataset. These results show that the proposed methods produce significant outperformance on the BLR datasets, with the outperformance on the BNN datasets being less

Table 9.2 Mean results over ten runs of each algorithm for the BNN datasets. Each column represents the mean value for the specific method. The execution time t is in seconds. The values in **bold** indicate that the particular method outperforms the other methods on that specific metric.

	HMC	A-HMC	MHMC	A-MHMC	S2HMC	A-S2HMC
			Power dataset			
ϵ		0.0151		0.0115		**0.0307**
ESS	138	927	131	965	166	**1266**
t (in secs)	**402**	804	414	831	1499	2991
ESS/t	0.35	1.15	0.31	**1.16**	0.11	0.42
η		−0.6873		−0.7218		**−0.7332**
			Airfoil dataset			
ϵ		0.0290		0.0278		0.0627
ESS	336	1 874	363	2013	459	**2550**
t (in secs)	**149**	301	154	308	466	932
ESS/t	2.24	6.27	2.36	**6.53**	0.98	2.73
η		-0.6397		−0.6384		−0.6392
			Concrete dataset			
ϵ		0.0366		0.0367		**0.0935**
ESS	500	1 995	588	2250	813	**2822**
t (in secs)	**37**	74	40	80	110	219
ESS/t	13.34	26.63	14.70	**28.12**	7.41	12.85
η		**−0.4984**		−0.4766		−0.4226
			Protein dataset			
ϵ		0.0437		0.0438		**0.0790**
ESS	860	6 013	997	**6870**	914	6343
t (in secs)	**87**	174	88	175	211	422
ESS/t	9.88	34.54	11.39	**39.22**	4.32	14.99
η		**−0.7138**		−0.7096		−0.711

than on the BLR datasets. An explanation of this behaviour can be traced to two aspects: 1) the average correlations η produced by the methods – the proposed method produce very high correlations on the BLR datasets, with A-HMC producing comparable or better average correlations to MHMC and S2HMC on the BNN datasets, and 2) the magnetic field used for the MHMC methods may not be optimal for the BNN datasets, and this can be seen by the marginal outperformance of MHMC over HMC on an ESS basis on the BNN datasets.

As expected, HMC has the lowest execution time t on all of the datasets, with MHMC being a close second. The execution time for MHMC is similar to that of HMC on the BLR datasets and becomes slightly worse on the BNN datasets. This can be attributed to the larger dimensionality of the BNN models when compared to BLR models, which pronounces the computational costs of the extra matrix operations required for MHMC. The large compute time of the shadow Hamiltonian algorithms can be attributed to the fixed-point iterations in Eqs. (1.34) and (1.35). Note that the execution time for the antithetic variants is twice the execution time for the non-antithetic algorithms. This is because two chains are run for the antithetic versions. The execution time of all the algorithms increases with the dimensionality of the problem, which is expected. On a time-normalised ESS basis, A-MHMC outperforms A-HMC on all the datasets.

The results in this chapter show that although the proposed methods have, in general, a higher computational cost than HMC, they still provide improved normalised ESS rates. It is also worth noting that all the algorithms have similar predictive performance on all the benchmark datasets, with the predictive performance being similar between the antithetic and non-antithetic counterparts.

9.4 Conclusion

In this chapter, we introduced the antithetic S2HMC and antithetic MHMC variance reduction schemes based on approximate Markov chain coupling. We compare these two new algorithms to the A-HMC algorithm on classification tasks using BLR, and on regression tasks using BNN models. We find that the antithetic versions of all the algorithms have higher ESSs than their non-antithetic variants, which shows the usefulness of antithetic MCMC methods.

The work in this chapter can be improved by automatically tuning the magnetic term in MHMC and A-MHMC, which should improve the results on the BNN datasets. We plan to consider larger datasets and deeper neural networks in future work, albeit the computation cost will be higher. A comparison of the performance of the proposed algorithms to their control variate counterparts, and the exploration of the possibility of using Riemannian manifold-based Monte Carlo algorithms is also of interest.

In the following chapters, we apply the algorithms discussed in the previous chapters of this book to wind seed forecasting, covid-19 modelling, financial engineering and auditing of financial statements.

10

Bayesian neural network inference in wind speed nowcasting

10.1 Background

Climate change and the reduction of greenhouse gas emissions have become central items on the global sustainability agenda. This has culminated in the Paris climate accord of 2015 between over 192 state parties [215]. The agreements, amongst other things, commit these states to a just transition from fossil fuels to renewable energy sources such as wind and solar [143].

The main reservation around large-scale wind energy adoption is its intermittency as energy production is directly dependent on uncertain future atmospheric conditions [63]. Forecasting of short term wind energy production has thus become critical to operations management and planning for electricity suppliers [140]. Such forecasts can then be used for proactive reserve management and energy market trading to ensure that electricity load demands are optimally met [140,190].

Statistical and machine learning methods have become increasingly prominent in wind power forecasting. These are based on refining predictions from Numerical Weather Predictions (NWP) into localised predictions for the wind farms in question. Eseye et al. [65] propose a two-stage Adaptive Neuro-Fuzzy Inference System (ANFIS) with the first stage refining the NWP winds speeds. In contrast, the second stage uses the refined wind speed estimate for wind power prediction. Artificial neural networks (ANN) are used by Eseye et al. [64] for day ahead predictions trained based on both observed wind speed data and NWP windspeed data for wind speed predictions. A combination of Radial Basis Function (RBF) NNs and fuzzy inference is employed by Sideratos and Hatziargyriou [207] with significant improvement over baselines. Fugon et al. [72] finds that random forest models trained on NWP wind speed and direction forecasts outperform NNs, linear regression and other ensemble decision trees on prediction horizons of 1 to 60 hours. Daniel et al. [55] compares ANNs, boosted decision trees and generalised additive models for wind speed forecasting in South Africa. They find significant outperformance by ANNs with additional improvements given by forecast combination methods.

Mbuvha et al. [143] uses a Laplace approximation BNN to forecast wind power in a Norwegian wind farm. Mbuvha et al. [141] further shows that BNNs significantly outperform MLPs trained by maximum likelihood and are capable of identifying relevant inputs for prediction. In this work, we further explore the idea of BNNs in wind power prediction with parameter using more theoretically accurate MCMC methods.

Hamiltonian Monte Carlo Methods in Machine Learning. https://doi.org/10.1016/B978-0-44-319035-3.00022-7

MCMC methods are fundamental in performing inference on large scale BNN models. HMC [60] and its variants have been a popular choice of inference due to its ability to suppress random walk behaviour through the use of first-order gradient information [104]. While HMC has shown significant sampling efficiencies relative to its random walk counterparts, it still exhibits numerous pathologies that hinder its wide adoption for large scale practical applications. These include the need to tune highly sensitive parameters such as the discretisation step size ϵ and integration path length L as well as the requirement for the computation of posterior likelihood gradients. Another practical issue with HMC, particularly in relation to neural network applications is the exponentially decreasing acceptance rates and the related effective sample sizes as the number of sampling parameters D increases due to the compounding discretisation errors of the leapfrog integration.

Recent advances in HMC literature have primarily focused on setting adaptive step sizes, path lengths [104,224] and numerical or stochastic gradient approximations [21,48]. However, the issue of the degeneration of HMC with increases in model dimensionality or system size has received relatively little attention in machine learning literature.

Numerical integration errors which cause this degeneration in acceptance rates are analysed through modified equations that are exactly conserved by the discrete integrator [90,209]. These modified equations can be defined by suitably truncated asymptotic expansions in the powers of the discretisation step size parameter [110,209]. In Hamiltonian systems, such modified equations result in modified or shadow Hamiltonians which are conserved with higher-order accuracy relative to the true Hamiltonian.

Since the discrete integrator produces a more accurate flow of the shadow Hamiltonian, sampling from the shadow Hamiltonian thus facilitates efficient sampling with higher acceptance rates [32,110]. The bias in the canonical averages of parameters introduced by sampling from the shadow Hamiltonian is then addressed by an importance sampling scheme based on the true Hamiltonian as the target distribution.

Numerous approaches to shadow Hybrid Monte Carlo have been put forward such as Shadow Hybrid Monte Carlo (SHMC) [110], Targeted Shadow Hybrid Monte Carlo [6] and Mix & Match Hamiltonian Monte Carlo [192]. The computational performance of such approaches is limited by the need to either generate or partially refresh momenta to increase the probability of acceptance from a nonseparable shadow Hamiltonian [212].

In this chapter, S2HMC [212] which employs a processed leapfrog integrator to generate momenta through a separable shadow Hamiltonian, is introduced for sampling the posterior distribution efficiently. This work is the first such presentation of S2HMC in sampling parameters of BNNs.

10.1.1 Automatic relevance determination

The BNN formulation presented in Section 2.1.6 can be parameterised such that different groups of weights can come from unique prior distributions and thus have unique regularisation parameters α_c for each group. An ARD prior is one where weights associated with each network input have a distinct prior. Weights belonging to the same group (input) share the same regularisation parameter. The loss function in ARD is as follows [135]:

$$P(w|D, \alpha, \beta, H) = \frac{1}{Z(\alpha, \beta)} \exp\left(\beta E_D + \sum_c \alpha_c E_{W_c}\right) \qquad (10.1)$$

The regularisation hyperparameters for each group of weights can be estimated on-line during the inference stage. The resulting regularisation parameter α_c for each input can be inferred as denoting the relevance of each input. Irrelevant inputs will have high values of the regularisation parameter, meaning that their weights will be forced to decay to values close to zero. Conversely on the basis of the posterior variances $\frac{1}{\alpha_c}$, important inputs will have weights with high variances while less important inputs will have low variances. Since the mean for the weight priors is fixed at zero, it therefore follows that weights with high variances are allowed to take values far from zero (thus higher influence), while those with small variances are forced to take values close to zero (thus lower influence). Fig. 10.1 shows this rationale graphically where larger variances allow for more density far from zero, while low variances concentrate the density around zero.

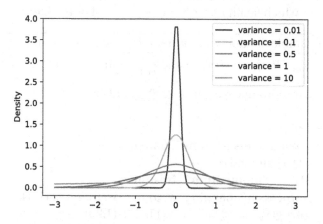

FIGURE 10.1 Prior distribution for weights under various variance settings.

10.1.1.1 Inference of ARD hyperparameters

Inference of ARD hyperparameters is a fundamentally complex inverse problem due to the multimodal and non-convex nature of the ARD loss function [135,172,206]. MacKay [135] obtains estimates of the ARD hyperparameters by maximising the evidence. This procedure only becomes possible because the simplifying assumptions of the Laplace approximation result in a tractable closed form calculation of the evidence.

Neal [175] employs an alternating framework between Gibbs sampling for ARD hyperparameters from Cauchy, Gamma and Dirichlet posteriors while using HMC for network weights. This approach, as it is based on MCMC converges to an asymptotically exact posterior. However numerous design choices are still required such as the choice of prior distribution.

In this chapter we employ a similar approach to Neal [175] by allowing the α_c parameters to follow a Gamma prior with a fixed shape parameter τ and a fixed rate parameter θ such that:

$$P(\alpha_c) = \frac{\theta^\tau}{\Gamma(\tau)}\alpha_c^{\tau-1}\exp(-\theta\tau) \qquad (10.2)$$

After taking into account the data likelihood on a given set of weights, the posterior for the parameter α_c corresponding to a particular group of parameters C becomes

$$P(\alpha_c|w_i \in C) \propto \alpha_c^{\tau+N_c-1}\exp\left(-\alpha_c(\theta + E_{W_c})\right) \qquad (10.3)$$

Where N_c is the number of weights in group C. Eq. (10.3) is still in the canonical form for a Gamma$(\tau + N_c, \theta + E_{W_c})$ distribution. This allows for Gibbs sampling of α_c parameters from the joint posterior given a fixed set of weights. Algorithm 10.1 shows a Gibbs step added to S2HMC at the beginning of each iteration. In practice alternating between Gibbs sampling for hyper-parameters and sampling for weights allows for several uninterrupted weight sampling iterations before the update of hyper-parameters. This creates stability in the potential energy, which facilitates the convergence of both chains.

Algorithm 10.1 Separable Shadow Hamiltonian Hybrid Monte Carlo algorithm with ARD.

Input: $N, \epsilon, L, w_{\text{init}}, H(w, p), \tilde{H}(w, p)$ and $\frac{N}{n_{\text{Gibbs}}}$ samples of parameters α_c.

Output: $(w)_{m=0}^N$, importance weights $= (b)_{m=0}^N$ and $(\alpha_c)_{m=0}^{\frac{N}{n_{\text{Gibbs}}}}$

1: $w_0 \leftarrow w_{\text{init}}$
2: **for** $m \rightarrow 1$ to N **do**
3:     Sample hyper-parameters α_c from Gamma$(\tau + N_c, \theta + E_{W_c})$ if mod$(m, n_{\text{Gibbs}}) = 0.$, otherwise use last sampled α_c
4:     $p_{m-1} \sim \mathcal{N}(0, \mathbf{M})$ $\leftarrow$ **momentum refreshment**
5:     Apply the pre-processing mapping $(\hat{\mathbf{w}}, \hat{\mathbf{p}}) = \mathcal{X}(\mathbf{w}, \mathbf{p})$ in Eq. (1.34)
6:     $p_m, w_m = $ **Leapfrog**$(p_{m-1}, w_{m-1}, \epsilon, L, \tilde{H})$ in Eq. (1.20)
7:     Apply the post-processing mapping $(\mathbf{w}, \mathbf{p}) = \mathcal{X}^{-1}(\hat{\mathbf{w}}, \hat{\mathbf{p}})$ in Eq. (1.35)
8:     $\delta H = \tilde{H}(w_{m-1}, p_{m-1}) - \tilde{H}(w_m, p_m)$
9:     $\alpha_m = \min(1, \exp(\delta H))$
10:    $u_m \sim \text{Unif}(0, 1)$
11:    $w_m = $ **Metropolis**$(\alpha, u_m, w_m, w_{m-1})$
12:    $b_m = \exp(-(H(w_m, p_m) - \tilde{H}(w_m, p_m)))$
13: **end for**

10.1.1.2 ARD committees

In order to rationalise the feature relevance measures emanating from each method, we propose a simple majority vote committee approach for feature selection. This approach minimises reliance on one inference approach and thus adds some robustness to the feature selection task. Table 10.1 gives an illustration of this committee framework with p

features and n samplers. In the ARD case each sampler gives a vote v_{ik} on the basis of some function of the posterior variance. In this work, a vote is attributed to a sampler if the posterior variance estimate $\frac{1}{\alpha_{ik}}$, corresponding to feature i is within the top five features on the basis of the ranked posterior variances from a particular sampler k. This can be defined as:

$$v_{ik} = f(\alpha_{ik}) = \begin{cases} 1, & \text{if } \frac{1}{\alpha_{ik}} \geq \frac{1}{\alpha_{i5}} \\ 0, & \text{otherwise} \end{cases} \tag{10.4}$$

where $\frac{1}{\alpha_{i5}}$ is the fifth highest ranked posterior variance value amongst the p, $\frac{1}{\alpha_{ik}}$ values for sampler k. Thus this voting mechanism looks for concordance between samplers with some allowance for differences in feature rankings. In general $f(\alpha_{ik})$ can be any well-defined function of a feature importance statistic of choice not limited to posterior variances (e.g. coefficients, gini impurity). The framework also allows for $f(\alpha_{ik})$ to include weighting of votes using metrics such as the predictive accuracy of the method that gives a specific feature importance statistic. This framework is consistent with Garcia-Chimeno et al. [76] who use of RF, Boosted Trees, LASSO and uni-variate variable selection to arrive at committee outputs. Pehlivanli et al. [185] also employs a similar approach using t-statistics, Fisher scores, the ReliefF algorithm and effective range based gene selection.

Table 10.1   An illustration of the ARD committee framework with p features and n samplers.

Feature	Sampler 1	Sampler 2	...	Sampler k	...	Sampler n	Total votes
Feature 1	v_{11}	v_{11}	...	v_{1k}	...	v_{1n}	$\sum_{k=1}^{n} v_{1k}$
Feature 2	v_{21}	v_{21}	...	v_{2k}	...	v_{2n}	$\sum_{k=1}^{n} v_{2k}$
...	...	...	...	...	...	...	...
...	...	...	...	...	...	...	...
Feature i	v_{i1}	v_{i2}	...	v_{ik}	...	v_{in}	$\sum_{k=1}^{n} v_{ik}$
...	...	...	...	...	...	...	...
...	...	...	...	...	...	...	...
Feature p	v_{p1}	v_{p2}	...	v_{kp}	...	v_{1n}	$\sum_{k=1}^{n} v_{pk}$

10.2 Experiment setup

MCMC methods for inference of BNN parameters are evaluated in wind speed forecasting tasks. On each dataset, HMC and MH are employed to draw 5000 samples for a BNN with a single hidden layer and 5 hidden neurons. This simple architecture was chosen based on an initial architecture search which showed reasonable performance across datasets. As the experiments are to evaluate the relative efficacy of the samplers – the architecture can be considered as a control variable.

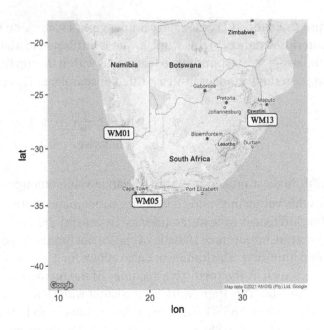

FIGURE 10.2 Map showing the locations of the locations of the weather stations included in the wind datasets.

10.2.1 WASA meteorological datasets

The wind speed datasets used in this work are based on meteorological observations collected from three weather stations participating in the Wind Atlas for South Africa (WASA) project [89]. The locations of the three weather stations considered in this work are indicated by the map in Fig. 10.2. The stations are selected to represent wind speed patterns along the coast of South Africa. The training and testing data split for this data is based on calendar dates. The training date range is 01/01/2016–31/12/2016, while the testing date range is 01/01/2017–30/06/2017 across all stations. Details of station-specific data characteristics are in Table 10.2. Observations at every station are recorded in 10-minute intervals. The date range across the stations is the same, minor differences in dataset sizes are purely because of short periods of equipment malfunction. The prediction task on these datasets is to forecast hour-ahead wind speed at the height of 62 meters given observations in the previous hour and some generalised features as described in Table 10.3. A height of 62 meters is selected as it is the typical hub height of wind turbines [55].

Table 10.2 Locations of weather stations considered for wind speed modelling.

Station Name	Features	N	Latitude	Longitude
WM01 Alexander Bay	19	78 642	−28.60	16.66
WM05 Napier	19	78 761	−34.61	19.69
WM13 Jozini	19	78 658	−27.43	32.17

Normalisation of attributes has been shown to improve the performance of neural network models [92]. Thus, each of the attributes of all the datasets above is pre-processed by projecting it onto the range [0, 1] using min-max normalisation.

Table 10.3 Descriptions of features utilised in the WASA data sets. All summary statistics (mean, max, etc.) are over ten minutes intervals.

Feature	Description
WS_62_mean	Mean wind speed in m/s at 62 meters
WS_62_min	Minimum wind speed in m/s at 62 meters
WS_62_max	Maximum wind speed in m/s at 62 meters
WS_62_stdv	Standard deviation of wind speed in m/s at 62 meters
WS_60_mean	Mean wind speed in m/s at 60 meters
WS_40_mean	Mean wind speed in m/s at 40 meters
WS_20_mean	Mean wind speed in m/s at 20 meters
WS_10_mean	Mean wind speed in m/s at 10 meters
WD_60_mean	Mean wind direction (angle) in m/s at 60 meters
WD_20_mean	Mean wind direction (angle) in m/s at 20 meters
Tair_mean	Mean air temperature in degrees Celsius at 20 meters
Tgrad_mean	Mean air temperature difference between 60 meters and 10 meters
Pbaro_mean	Barometric pressure in hpa
RH_mean	Relative Humidity (%)
Hour	Previous Hour
Month	Calender Month
ws_mean_lag_1	1 hour lagged mean wind speed at 62 meters
ws_mean_lag_2	2 hour lagged mean wind speed at 62 meters
ws_mean_lag_1_day	1 day lagged mean wind speed at 62 meters

10.2.2 Relationship to wind power

Wind speed is the main indicator of the wind power generation potential of a prospective site [46,72]. The generated output at a given location can be described by the equation:

$$P = C_p P_{\text{avail}} \tag{10.5}$$

Where C_p is a power coefficient which is a function of the turbine rotor and blade design. P_{avail} is the available wind power which is a function of localised wind conditions. The available wind power can be derived from Newtonian Mechanics as [46]:

$$P_{\text{avail}} = \frac{1}{2}\rho A v^3 \tag{10.6}$$

Where ρ is the localised air density, A is the sweep area of the turbine blades, and v is the wind speed at hub height. Since this work focuses on predicting wind speeds at prospective wind farm locations, it follows that the work contributes to the consequent area of wind power forecasting.

10.2.3 Performance evaluation

The metrics detailed in this section are utilised to evaluate predictive performance and sampling performance throughout this work.

Table 10.4   Experimental Settings for the BNNs and Sampling runs.

Setting	Value
BNN Number of Hidden Layers	1
BNN Number of Hidden Neurons	5
BNN Activation Function	ReLu
Sampling Trajectory Length (HMC)	100
Number of samples	5000
Number of samples between hyper-parameter samples (n_{Gibbs})	50

10.2.4 Preliminary step size tuning runs

The dual averaging method detailed in Section 1.9 is employed to inform the setting of step sizes for each dataset problem as step sizes are inherently dependent on the specific posterior likelihood landscape. These preliminary runs entail 5000 samples with a target acceptance rate of 75%. Table 10.5 shows the resultant step size after these tuning runs for each dataset.

Table 10.5   Step size selections for each dataset after initial dual averaging runs.

Dataset	Step Size
WM01 Alexander Bay	0.161
WM05 Naiper	0.146
WM13 Jozini	0.176

The regression datasets converged to relatively close step sizes. This is to be expected as they are of the same dimensionality and similar dataset sizes. These steps size are used for all BNNs across ARD and non-ARD models. The detailed parameter settings for the experiments are documented in Table 10.4.

10.3 Results and discussion

10.3.1 Sampling performance

Figs. 10.3, 10.4, 10.5 show the trace plots across datasets for MH, HMC and S2HMC. The rates and levels of convergence of HMC and S2HMC are almost identical as they both inherently use similar Hamiltonian dynamics in their proposals. If one looks at the negative log-likelihood as a goodness-of-fit measure, a consequence of this similarity is that these methods will have similar predictive performance in terms of Root Mean Square Error (MSE) (RMSE) for the two samplers.

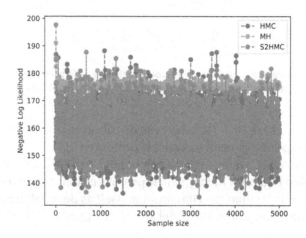

FIGURE 10.3 Negative log-likelihood trace plots for MH (orange (light gray in print version)), HMC (blue (dark gray in print version)), S2HMC (green (mid gray in print version)) for weather station WM01 Alexander Bay.

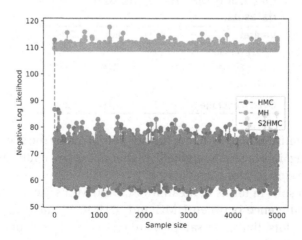

FIGURE 10.4 Negative log-likelihood trace plots for MH (orange (light gray in print version)), HMC (blue (dark gray in print version)), S2HMC (green (mid gray in print version)) for weather station WM05 Napier.

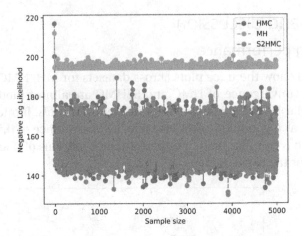

FIGURE 10.5 Negative log-likelihood trace plots for MH (orange (light gray in print version)), HMC (blue (dark gray in print version)), S2HMC (green (mid gray in print version)) for weather station WM13 Jozini.

The boxplots in Figs. 10.6, 10.7, 10.8 show the distribution of ESS across 10 independent chains with the corresponding mean statistics represented in Table 10.6. It can be seen that across the datasets, S2HMC yields higher ESSs relative to HMC. This experimental result supports the modified equation theory which postulates that the shadow Hamiltonian is conserved at a higher order than the Hamiltonian itself as detailed in Section 1.8 and suggested by zaguirre and Hampton [110], Skeel and Hardy [209] and Sweet et al. [212].

Table 10.6 Mean ESS statistics over ten independent chains each with 5000 samples using MH, HMC and S2HMC on all datasets.

Dataset	MH	HMC	S2HMC
WM01 Alexander Bay	0	4302	4352
WM05 Naiper	0	3714	3741
WM13 Jozini	0	4572	4616
Overall average	0	2848	2914

The higher ESS statistics of S2HMC are further reinforced by the acceptance rate results in Table 10.7. This again suggests marginally higher acceptance rates for S2HMC relative to HMC at the same step size for each dataset.

The regression results in terms of mean RMSEs and MAEs are indicated in Table 10.8. The performance difference between HMC and S2HMC is marginal, suggesting, as reflected in the trace plots, that their samples are relatively close geometrically. This phenomenon results in almost equal predictive performance.

In summing up the experimental results – an important finding is that both S2HMC and HMC can sample sufficiently representative parameters of the BNNs across datasets.

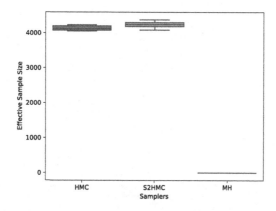

FIGURE 10.6 Boxplots showing the distribution of ESS over ten independent chains for the WM01 Alexandra Bay weather station.

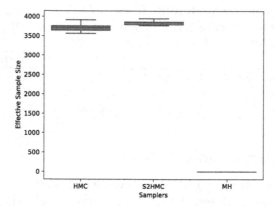

FIGURE 10.7 Boxplots showing the distribution of ESS over ten independent chains for the WM05 Naiper weather station.

Table 10.7 Mean acceptance rates (%) over ten chains of 5000 samples for each sampler on all datasets.

Dataset	MH	HMC	S2HMC
WM01 Alexander Bay	23.096	78.624	80.942
WM05 Naiper	26.05	79.516	81.980
WM13 Jozini	23.202	79.248	81.322
Overall average	36.242	76.803	79.087

When looking at sampling performance, the results suggest that the shadow Hamiltonian in S2HMC marginally improves the acceptance rates and consequently the ESS.

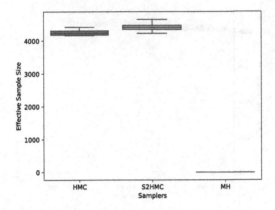

FIGURE 10.8 Boxplots showing the distribution of ESS over ten independent chains for the WM13 Jozini weather station.

Table 10.8 Mean testing RMSE (MAE) resulting from BNNs trained using ten independent chains of MH, HMC and S2HMC at each of the weather stations.

Dataset	MH	HMC	S2HMC
WM01 Alexander Bay	4.220 (3.061)	2.057 (1.657)	2.056 (1.893)
WM05 Napier	5.748 (4.852)	2.111 (1.984)	2.108 (1.687)
WM13 Jozini	2.934 (2.384)	1.856 (1.457)	1.858 (1.460)

10.3.2 Predictive performance with ARD

Table 10.9 shows the mean testing RMSE of the ARD BNNs on the windspeed datasets. As it follows from previous findings, MH-ARD is outperformed by HMC-ARD and S2HMC-ARD, respectively. It is important to note that with the introduction of the ARD prior on the wind speed datasets there was an improvement in RMSE compared to the results without ARD reported in Section 10.3. Thus ARD in the context of these regression datasets has the desired effect of introducing sparseness in their input space. This sparseness reduces the influence of noisy inputs. This finding is also similar to those of MacKay [135], Neal [175] and Mbuvha et al. [143] using both Laplace approximation and MCMC inference.

Table 10.9 Mean testing RMSE (MAE) resulting from BNNs trained using ten independent chains of MH, HMC and S2HMC at each of the weather stations.

Dataset	MH	HMC	S2HMC
WM01 Alexander Bay	8.939 (8.881)	1.642 (1.349)	1.651 (1.267)
WM05 Napier	8.466 (8.427)	1.496 (1.344)	1.527 (1.583)
WM13 Jozini	7.423 (4.336)	1.425 (1.112)	1.420 (2.128)

10.3.3 ARD committees and feature importance

The plots in Fig. B.1 and the ARD committees in Tables C.1–C.3 are utilised to decode the ARD relevance statistics. The ARD committee considers *votes* from each method based on the top 5 highest posterior variances. Features with more than 2 votes are then considered highly relevant. On an overall level, it can be seen from the posterior variance plots that HMC-ARD and S2HMC-ARD result in clearer sparsity when compared to regularisation by MH-ARD. Confidence in the relative feature importance can implicitly be assigned based on the predictive performance of each inference method.

In the WM01 Alexander Bay dataset, calendar month emerges as highly important, signalling a strong seasonal effect on wind speed patterns. Atmospheric pressure and relative humidity also have high posterior variance. This relationship between atmospheric pressure, relative humidity and wind speed is well documented in atmospheric physics literature [136]. One day lagged wind speeds for the same hour also are highly important, suggesting within-day cycles. Strong lagged dependencies were similarly found in a study of the Norwegian wind farm dataset by Mbuvha et al. [143]. Wind speeds at lower altitudes, i.e. 40 meters and 20 meters, are also found to be significant.

Posterior variances at WM05 Napier and WM13 Jozini sites show some overlap with the first site with a few site-specific variations. Air temperature and temperature gradients start to emerge as relevant features. This finding again reconciles well with atmospheric physics theory concerning causal links between atmospheric temperature, barometric pressure and wind speed [4]. Further evidence of intra-day and monthly cycles in wind speed patterns is also observed.

10.3.4 Re-training BNNs on relevant features

The robustness of the feature selections in the previous sections is investigated by retraining the BNNs on a reduced set of features corresponding to the ARD committee results.

Table 10.10 Mean Testing RMSE (MAE) resulting from BNNs re-trained using the relevant features identified in Tables C.1 to C.3 for each weather station.

Dataset	MH	HMC	S2HMC
WM01 Alexander Bay	4.245 (3.123)	2.515 (2.006)	2.517 (2.005)
WM05 Napier	3.85 (2.669)	2.750 (2.213)	1.527 (2.217)
WM13 Jozini	2.842 (2.470)	2.164 (1.698)	1.420 (1.697)

Retraining results on the WASA datasets are depicted in Table 10.10. While there is some deterioration in the HMC and the S2HMC based BNNs, MH based BNNs improve on all sites. A point worth noting is that the deterioration in the predictive performance of HMC/S2HMC based BNNs is not commensurate with the significant 59% reduction in the number of features. Again, the implication thereof is that the MH sampler gains additional efficiencies from the selection of high information quality features and the reduction in the dimensionality of the problem. Predictive performance robustness after dimensionality reduction through ARD is similarly found in the work of Mbuvha et al. [143] using the Gaussian approximation approach.

10.4 Conclusion

This chapter presented the first implementation in the literature of S2HMC in BNN inference. Initial experiments on simulated data show the robustness of S2HMC as both step sizes and problem dimensions increase. Experiments in wind speed forecasting show higher ESSs and acceptance rate statistics for S2HMC relative to HMC. The predictive performance of S2HMC and HMC based BNNs is found to be similar, suggesting that both samplers are effective in posterior exploration. When considering these findings, it is important to take into account the additional computations required in S2HMC (relative to HMC) for variable pre and post-processing as well as computation of the shadow Hamiltonians.

ARD through a hybrid of Gibbs sampling with MH, HMC and S2HMC is presented. It is observed that ARD improves predictive performance. An ARD committee framework is presented to add robustness to the feature selection procedure.

In terms of feature relevance: Calendar month, day lagged wind spends, and relative humidity emerged as influential features. These findings suggest highly cyclical patterns both within the day and the year. An inefficient sampler such as MH was shown to benefit from the ARD committees' dimensionality reduction. ARD provided a probabilistically principled structure for inference on the relative influences of various features on BNN predictions. Coupled with predictive uncertainty from BNNs, ARD facilitates troubleshooting and root-cause analysis of neural network predictions.

As avenues for future research and improvement, investigations into the computational efficiency of S2HMC to allow for speed up over HMC in BNNs can increase the attractiveness of the method. Such computational efficiencies could lead to greater adoption of MCMC methods in sampling larger scale deep neural networks.

Future work could include extensions to the proposed ARD committee feature selection approach to include other feature relevance metrics. A weighted committee voting scheme based on metrics such as predictive accuracy measures can also be explored. Additional prospective inputs from NWP models such as forecasts of wind speeds, temperature and pressure at future time points can also potentially improve the accuracy of the BNNs considered in this work. Inclusions of more complex BNN architectures, including increasing the network depth, remains an area of future investigation.

In the next chapter, we present a Bayesian framework for assessing the effectiveness of the Covid-19 lockdowns as implemented by the South African government in combating the spread of Covid-19.

A Bayesian analysis of the efficacy of Covid-19 lockdown measures

11.1 Background

The latest threat to global health has been the recent outbreak of the respiratory disease that was given the name Coronavirus Disease 2019 or COVID-19. COVID-19 is caused by the virus known as SARS-CoV-2 [18]. According to the World Health Organisation,[1] COVID-19 spreads primarily through droplets of saliva or discharge from the nose when an infected person coughs or sneezes. The high spread rates of COVID-19 in an unregulated environment prompted the South African government to introduce legislation that aimed to immediately and effectively protect its citizens from the potentially deadly coronavirus. Since the first case of COVID-19 in South Africa on the 5th of March 2020, the government has implemented a strategy of controlling the spread of this disease by introducing a *five-level* lockdown structure, further discussed in our section relating to methodology. This chapter investigates the adequacy of this regulation by inferring the basic reproduction number (R_0) of COVID-19 under each level of lockdown experienced.

R_0, also called the basic reproduction ratio or the basic reproductive rate, is an epidemiological metric used to describe the contagiousness or transmissibility of infectious agents [58]. It represents the expected number of secondary cases produced by a single infection in a completely susceptible population [115]. This definition also implies that vaccination roll-outs do not need to be explicitly accounted for in our analysis. However, it is essential to note that the value of R_0 is dependent on socio-behavioural factors, such as those affected by regulations stipulated by government legislation. Based on the above and for the interpretability of our results, we centre our investigation on this value. We will therefore infer the respective R_0's of COVID-19 for each lockdown alert level using Bayesian inference to ascertain the overall effectiveness and coherence of government legislation. The advantage of using the Bayesian framework is that it incorporates prior knowledge while allowing for uncertainty in estimating model parameters [144].

In order to establish the most appropriate disaster management regulations, the government must consider all factors specific to South Africa holistically. The considerations include the economic effects of imposing the various levels of lockdown. The implementation of lockdown alert levels which aims to reduce the contagion of COVID-19, leads to a forced reduction in production, changes in household demands for goods and services, a

---

[1] World Health Organisation Health Topics https://www.who.int/health-topics/coronavirus#tab=tab_1, accessed 21/04/2021.

decline in South African exports, and imposed uncertainty on business investment [13]. All these factors have a negative impact on the economy, with immediate loss of economic activity followed by medium-term and long-term economic effects [13]. Hence, the trade-off between preventing the spread of COVID-19 and the economic costs of these preventative measures is an essential factor in deciding the timing and level of lockdown be imposed.

According to de Villiers et al. [56], the COVID-19 virus and subsequent lockdown period have led to significantly reduced future taxable income as well as increased government borrowings. This combination places further constraints on the government's public finances, making it more challenging to address South Africa's basic social needs in the future. On a macroeconomic scale, a study conducted in the early days of COVID-19 in South Africa by Arndt et al. [13] suggests that a failure to contain the pandemic swiftly could lead to a contraction in Gross Domestic Product (GDP) for South Africa between 12% and 16%. On a microeconomic scale, the Gini coefficient in South Africa is considered the highest in the world [93]. This implies that a partial closure of the economy could lead to lower-income households not being able to afford their basic needs [13]. This results in a paradox whereby a lockdown is intended to reduce COVID-19 related deaths but may result in more people losing their lives from the subsequent effects of the reduction in economic activity.

In addition to the economic effects of lockdown, it is also essential to consider the social impacts of the lockdown on the South African population. Nguse and Wassenaar [179] explore the ramifications of COVID-19 on an already ineffective South African mental health system and conclude that public mental health has been negatively affected by the pandemic. Kim et al. [117] explore this further and conclude that the initial stages of the COVID-19 pandemic coincided with high rates of severe mental illness and low availability of mental healthcare in South Africa. One may therefore assume that these high rates of severe mental illness are borne from the government-imposed lockdowns. However, Kim et al. [117] clarify that increased symptoms of depression stem from a higher perceived risk of COVID-19 transmission rather than from the lockdown introduced to combat this spread. Therefore, this could imply that the various lockdown alert levels, which aim to reduce transmission rates, may improve public mental health. Thus, the social effects of the various lockdown implementations will need to be explored in more detail to determine an optimum disaster management strategy to be implemented by the South African government.

The main aim of this chapter is to analyse the effect of the South African government's disaster management act regulations on the disease patterns of the COVID-19 pandemic, with specific reference to the various levels of lockdown implemented. This aim will be achieved by comparing the contagiousness and transmissibility of the COVID-19 virus over the various levels of lockdown by answering the specific research question: To what extent are the disease patterns of COVID-19, namely the spreading rate and basic reproductive number R_0, affected by the various government-imposed lockdown alert levels? Answering this question will involve analysing which epidemiological models (or which combination of such models) are appropriate to infer R_0 and the spreading rate, finding appropriate initial values for the chosen model's parameters, and adjusting these initial parameter estimates using appropriate posterior techniques such as Bayesian inference. Finally, the different parameter values for the various levels of lockdown will be analysed and compared chronologically at each stage of government intervention.

James et al. [112] states that epidemiological models are essential tools to synthesise evidence for planning and forecasting, intending to provide analysis for decisions relating to policymaking for infectious diseases. This sentiment is echoed by Ives and Bozzuto [109], who states that estimates of R_0 are required for designing public health interventions for infectious diseases such as COVID-19. According to Dehning et al. [57], the framework proposed in their work can be used to measure the effectiveness and efficiency of government legislation that aims to reduce the spread of COVID-19. Therefore, given the social and financial cost of government interventions, it is critical to understand and analyse the effects of each level of lockdown imposed by the government to determine the optimal strategy for managing the COVID-19 pandemic in South Africa moving forward. The importance of this analysis extends further to inform policymakers of the most appropriate legislation to contain similar pandemics in the future. In addition to outlining the government's best course of action, the long-term consequences of the lack of appropriate government action can also be highlighted James et al. [112].

Contribution: This chapter presents a thorough and robust analysis of South Africa's lockdown policy framework that extends upon prior literature based on inferring change points in the spreading rate of COVID-19. This chapter builds on the work of Mbuvha and Marwala [144] by extending the analysis of the structure lockdown regulations presented by the government after the initial two-month period studied by Mbuvha and Marwala [144]. Furthermore, the work benefits of an additional 19 months for which COVID-19 data can be collected and updated, thus allowing for more accurate and reliable model specifications and results compared with previous literature [57,144]. This is due to the relatively low number of cases in the epidemic's initial stages, resulting in the possibility of statistical and systematic errors.

This chapter proceeds as follows: we begin by outlining further background and literature in Section 11.1.1. Section 11.2 details the data sources and methodology used to infer spreading rates and the R_0's of the different lockdown alert levels. Section 11.3 deals with the results obtained from our model, including posterior distributions for all the model parameters. Their estimated mean values, along with confidence intervals, are also discussed. Section 8.5 concludes our observations and proposes considerations to further research.

11.1.1 Review of compartment models for Covid-19

Brauer [35] extensively highlights the common compartmental models in epidemiology and their specific features in modelling different epidemics. One such model that seems of particular extensive use is the standard SIR model. Blackwood and Childs [29] and Mbuvha and Marwala [144] also demonstrate that this model has been widely dominant in COVID-19 modelling literature. With the information provided in this chapter and the unique characteristics of the COVID-19 pandemic, we have narrowed the search for a suitable model to an adjusted SIR model as suggested by Dehning et al. [57], who uses this model to infer spreading rates of COVID-19 in Germany. Dehning et al. [57] also suggest that their approach can be readily adapted to any other country or region. Further evidence to support this model selection in the South African COVID-19 landscape is drawn from the results of recent work by Mbuvha and Marwala [144] where the previously mentioned adjusted SIR model is found to be seemingly superior to the Susceptible-Exposed-Infected-Recovered (SEIR) model.

Mbuvha and Marwala [144] suggest that inference of the parameters of the SIR and SEIR compartmental models is best achieved through the utilisation of the Bayesian Framework. This is due to its incorporation of prior knowledge, and principled embedding of uncertainty in parameter estimation [144]. Mbuvha and Marwala [144] and Dehning et al. [57] explain the Bayesian formulation for inference of the main epidemiological parameters, namely the spreading rate (λ) and the recovery rate (μ), using MCMC, which we adopt in this chapter.

Raimúndez et al. [194] observe that posterior parameter estimates for epidemiological models may be unrealistic, regardless of the initially estimated priors. This observation specifically referred to the credibility intervals for the median incubation period, and basic reproductive number of the COVID-19 virus, which were both deemed too narrow. Raimúndez et al. [194] suggests instead of computing confidence intervals using MCMC samples; confidence intervals should instead be derived from profile likelihoods due to the additional realism and reliability provided. Despite this, MCMC sampling seems to be the most prevalent sampling process in epidemiological modelling for COVID-19, as seen in work by Mbuvha and Marwala [144], Dehning et al. [57], Safta et al. [204], Berihuete et al. [22] and Wang et al. [221]. O'Neill and Roberts [184] further justify the preference for the use of MCMC methods in epidemiological modelling, despite its shortfalls, by noting the greater degree of modelling flexibility.

Parameter updates for MCMC methods are often drawn probabilistically using an algorithm known as MH or its derivatives [144,145,161]. Alternative algorithms to MH include Slice Sampling, noted for its adaptive nature and robust theoretical properties [165,174], and the NUTS, which adds greater posterior exploration efficiency due to the use of first-order gradient information and the minimisation of user intervention or costly tuning runs [104]. For these reasons, we invoke NUTS for sampling the posterior distributions of our adjusted SIR model parameters.

From the point the first COVID-19 case was reported in South Africa, there was a 13-day period where no government interventions occurred (5th March 2020 to 17th March 2020). According to literature regarding COVID-19 in South Africa the R_0 for COVID-19 for this period was between 2 and 3.5, in the absence of any government policies or regulation [144]. This R_0 value is consistent with literature outlined by Ferguson et al. [68], Lourenco et al. [130] and [233] for R_0 estimates without any government policies or regulation. Dehning et al. [57] estimates a median recovery time of 8 days which corresponds to a mean recovery rate of 0.125. This estimation of the recovery rate accounts for the recovery of infected people as well as treatment measures. The adjusted SIR model proposed by Dehning et al. [57], explicitly accounts for the delay in reporting of COVID-19 cases using a variable 'D' denoting this delay in days. 'D' contains at least three distinct factors: the biological incubation period, which has a median of 5 to 6 days [57], an additional delay of 1 to 2 days for the experience of symptoms, and making the active decision to get tested [57], and the possible delay before test results return in approximately 1 to 2 days [57]. This results in an approximate 'D' of 8.6 days [57]

11.1.2 Lockdown alert levels

We will be dealing with data over the period from 5th March 2020 to 18 December 2021. The start date corresponds to the announcement of the first official COVID-19 case in South Africa. The levels of lockdown and their distinct periods are defined in Table 11.1 in chronological order.

Table 11.1   Date ranges corresponding to the different levels of restrictions imposed by the South African government.

Lockdown alert level	Time period	Number of Days
No restrictions	5 March 2020 – 18 March 2020	12
Initial restrictions	18 March 2020 – 25 March 2020	8
Alert level 5	26 March 2020 – 30 April 2020	36
Alert level 4	1 May 2020 – 31 May 2020	31
Alert level 3	1 June 2020 – 17 August 2020	78
Alert level 2	18 August 2020 – 20 September 2020	34
Alert level 1	21 September 2020 – 28 December 2020	99
Adjusted alert level 3	29 December 2020 – 28 February 2021	62
Adjusted alert level 1	1 March 2021 – 30 May 2021	91
Adjusted alert level 2	31 May 2021 – 15 June 2021	16
Adjusted alert level 3	16 June 2021 – 27 June 2021	12
Adjusted alert level 4	28 June 2021 – 25 July 2021	28
Adjusted alert level 3	26 July 2021 – 12 September 2021	49
Adjusted alert level 2	13 September 2021 – 30 September 2021	18
Adjusted alert level 1	1 October 2021 –	79

The specifications, regulations, and restrictions of each lockdown alert level as defined by the Disaster Management Act Regulations are summarised as follows[2]:

- No restrictions (Alert Level 0) correspond to the period preceding the introduction of any government intervention. No restrictions or regulations were specified or implemented on a national level.
- Initial restrictions (Alert Adjusted Level 0) are a revised lockdown alert level 0 whereby a travel ban on foreign nationals from high-risk countries is implemented. Additionally, the South African government initiated social distancing recommendations.

[2] https://www.gov.za/covid-19/about/about-alert-system.

- Alert Level 1 indicates a low COVID-19 spread with a high health system readiness. Regulations stipulate that most normal activity can resume, with precautions and health guidelines followed at all times.
- Adjusted Alert Level 1 is a revised lockdown alert level 1, where regulations are similar to those under Level 1 bar a few discretionary amendments and exceptions such as the sale of alcohol on specific days.
- Alert Level 2 indicates a moderate COVID-19 spread with a high health system readiness. Physical distancing and restrictions on leisurely/social activities, aiming to prevent a resurgence of the COVID-19 virus.
- Alert Level 3 indicates a moderate COVID-19 spread with a moderate health system readiness. Restrictions are placed on many activities, including social and workplace gatherings, to address the high risk of transmission.
- Adjusted Alert Level 3 is a revised lockdown alert level 3 where further restrictions were placed on all public and private gatherings. The government also introduced additional regulations stating that not wearing a mask in public would be deemed a criminal offense.
- Alert Level 4 indicates a moderate to a high COVID-19 spread with a low to moderate health system readiness. It is implemented through extreme precautions to limit community transmission and outbreaks while allowing some activity to resume.
- Alert Level 5 indicates a high COVID-19 spread with a low health system readiness. It is implemented when drastic measures are needed to contain the spread of the virus and save lives.

Overtime, due to economic considerations the South African government subsequently introduced *adjusted* versions of the lockdown alert levels described above. These adjusted alert levels have no clear chronological definitions such as the ones above as they often consider adhoc tactical combinations of restrictions typically associated with various lockdown alert levels.

11.2 Methods

We now detail the dataset and model settings that we utilise to perform inference on the spreading rates of COVID-19 under each lockdown alert level.

11.2.1 Infection data

We require population data pertaining to the disease patterns of COVID-19 in South Africa to infer the parameters of the proposed adjusted SIR model. This data is obtained from an open-source online dashboard provided by the center for Systems Science and Engineering at John Hopkins University [59]. Data for cumulative infected population, deaths, and recoveries are all available for each day of the analysis's time period, that is, 5th March 2020 to 18th December 2021.

11.2.2 The adjusted SIR model

The standard SIR model forms the basis of our methodology. This compartmental epidemiological model is used to model transitions between 3 stages of disease, namely *Susceptible*, *Infectious* and *Recovered* with associated spreading rates (λ) and recovery rates (μ) as shown below [35]. (See Fig. 11.1.)

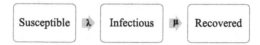

FIGURE 11.1 Diagram illustrating the three states and two transition rates of the SIR model.

The SIR model relies on solving the following system of ordinary differential equations [144]:

$$
\begin{aligned}
\frac{dS(t)}{dt} &= -\lambda S(t) I(t) \\
\frac{dI(t)}{dt} &= \lambda S(t) I(t) - \mu I(t) \\
\frac{dR(t)}{dt} &= \mu I(t)
\end{aligned}
\tag{11.1}
$$

This model is based on the following variable definitions [35]:

- $S(t)$ denotes the number of individuals who are susceptible to the disease, but who are not yet infected at time t.
- $I(t)$ denotes the number of infected individuals, assumed infectious and able to spread the disease by contact with susceptible individuals.
- $R(t)$ denotes the number of individuals who have been infected and then removed from the possibility of being infected again or of spreading infection, at time t.
- λ denotes the spreading rate, i.e., the rate of transition from $S(t)$ to $I(t)$.
- μ denotes the recovery rate, i.e., the rate of transition from $I(t)$ to $R(t)$.

The adjusted SIR model utilised by Mbuvha and Marwala [144] and Dehning et al. [57] is based on the standard SIR model, with the first adjustment proposed by Dehning et al. [57] to account for the delay in reporting of COVID-19 cases: D denotes the delay in becoming infected and being reported in the confirmed case statistics, such that the confirmed reported cases $CR(t)$ at some time t are in the form [57]:

$$
\mathbf{CR}(\mathbf{t}) = I^{new}(t - D)
\tag{11.2}
$$

I^{new} is the actual number of infected individuals for this adjusted model at a particular time point. This results in our simulations starting at time $t = 0$ with $I(0)$ infected cases, and the data of reported cases, $CR(t)$, starting from day $t > D$. Secondly, we approximate time-dependent spreading rates $\lambda(t)$ by episodes of constant spreading rates, as recommended by Mbuvha and Marwala [144] and Dehning et al. [57]. Each spreading rate corresponds to a level of lockdown – for example, λ_0 for before lockdown and λ_2 for lockdown alert level 5 that was instituted on 26 March 2020. This effectively means we have points in time where the spreading rate changes, each change point corresponding to the days in which a different lockdown alert level was implemented.

At this stage, it is important to note that R_0 can be expressed in terms of the spreading rate, λ, and the recovery rate, μ, as Mbuvha and Marwala [144], Brauer [35]:

$$\mathbf{R_0} = \frac{\lambda}{\mu} \tag{11.3}$$

11.2.3 Parameter inference using the No-U-Turn sampler

11.2.3.1 Prior distributions

Our goal is to analyse whether government intervention effectively reduced the spreading rate and R_0. Since this is the case, it is important that we do not impose prior assumptions relating to the decrease of these values. We, therefore, follow an approach shared by Dehning et al. [57] and Mbuvha and Marwala [144] by using weakly-informative Log-Normal distributions for the prior distributions of λ and μ such that the initial mean R_0 is 1.6 for all levels of lockdown. This places more weight on the data likelihood. The recovery rate prior distribution used corresponds to the approach outlined by Dehning et al. [57]and since utilised by Mbuvha and Marwala [144]. This distribution was LogNormal with parameters log(0.125) and 0.2.

Dehning et al. [57] suggests using Half-Cauchy priors for the weakly-informative initial distribution of the number of individuals initially infected, I(0). This ensures a flat prior from 0 to the parameter value, with heavy tails after that. Mbuvha and Marwala [144] suggest a parameter value of 20 for this prior distribution in a South African context. The prior distribution for the reporting delay 'D' will be based on LogNormal distributions with a mean of 8. [57] and with a variance of 0.2 [144].

Additionally, prior estimates of the change points in spreading rate are based on normal distributions with the mean values corresponding to the dates in which a different lockdown alert level was implemented, with variances of 1. This approach is consistent with that of Mbuvha and Marwala [144]. These estimates are excluded from Table 11.2 for brevity.

11.3 Results and discussion

The posterior distribution of the adjusted SIR model described in the previous section was sampled using NUTS. A total of 1 500 samples were drawn with 500 tuning samples during the burn-in phase.

Fig. 11.2 shows the model predictions and the actual new cases time series. It can be seen that the calibrated SIR is able to replicate four waves of infections in South Africa. This thus suggests, as expected, that a time-varying spread rate structure is indeed required to

Table 11.2   Table outlining the prior parameter distributions used in our approach (excluding change point estimates).

Parameter	Interpretation	Prior Distribution
λ_0	Spreading Rate No Restrictions	LogNormal(log(0.2),0.5)
λ_1	Spreading Rate Initial Restrictions	LogNormal(log(0.2),0.5)
λ_2	Spreading Rate Alert Level 5	LogNormal(log(0.2),0.5)
λ_3	Spreading Rate Alert Level 4	LogNormal(log(0.2),0.5)
λ_4	Spreading Rate Alert Level 2	LogNormal(log(0.2),0.5)
λ_5	Spreading Rate Alert Level 3	LogNormal(log(0.2),0.5)
λ_6	Spreading Rate Alert Level 1	LogNormal(log(0.2),0.5)
λ_7	Spreading Rate Adjusted Alert Level 3	LogNormal(log(0.2),0.5)
λ_8	Spreading Rate Adjusted Alert Level 1	LogNormal(log(0.2),0.5)
λ_9	Spreading Rate Adjusted Alert Level 2	LogNormal(log(0.2),0.5)
λ_{10}	Spreading Rate Adjusted Alert Level 3	LogNormal(log(0.2),0.5)
λ_{11}	Spreading Rate Adjusted Alert Level 4	LogNormal(log(0.2),0.5)
λ_{12}	Spreading Rate Adjusted Alert Level 3	LogNormal(log(0.2),0.5)
λ_{13}	Spreading Rate Adjusted Alert Level 2	LogNormal(log(0.2),0.5)
λ_{14}	Spreading Rate Adjusted Alert Level 1	LogNormal(log(0.2),0.5)
σ	Incubation to infectious rate	LogNormal(log(1/5),0.5)
μ	Recovery rate	LogNormal(log(1/8),0.2)
D	Reporting Delay	LogNormal(log(8),0.2)
I_0	Initial Infectious	Half-Cauchy(20)
E_0	Initial Exposed	Half-Cauchy(20)

capture the dynamics of the COVID-19 pandemic in South Africa. Fig. 11.3 showing the trace plots for each parameter suggests relative convergence of the sampler.

11.3.1 Spreading rate under various lockdown alert levels

Fig. 11.4 and Table 11.3 show the posterior distributions and mean estimates of spreading rates of our calibrated model. We now discuss the spreading rates in terms of R_0 for each lockdown alert level.

11.3.1.1 *No restrictions (alert level 0): 5 March 2020 – 18 March 2020*
The spreading rate of 0.349 for lockdown alert level 0 corresponds to an R_0 of 1.662 (CI[0.467,2.805]). As outlined before, the R_0 value represents the expected number of secondary cases produced by a single infection. This has the practical interpretation that under lockdown alert level 0, a single infected person would infect on average 1.662 persons.

11.3.1.2 *Initial restrictions (adjusted alert level 0): 18 March 2020 – 25 March 2020*
On the 18th of March 2020, the government introduced certain protocols which aimed to control the spread of COVID-19. This minor adjustment to lockdown alert level 0 cor-

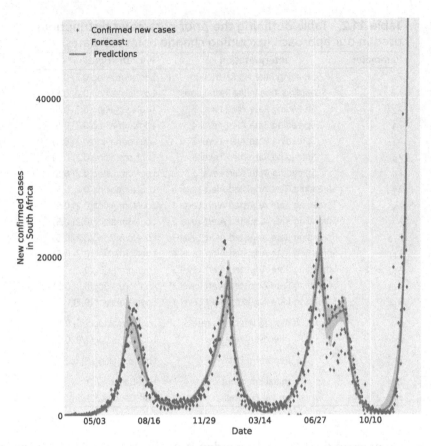

FIGURE 11.2 Fitted model and actual new cases data (until 18 December 2021) based on the adjusted SIR model with various change points.

responded to a decrease in the spreading rate from 0.349 to 0.198. Therefore, the R_0 value decreased by 43.261% from 1,622 ((CI[0.467,2.805]) to 0.943 (CI[0.424,1.571]). This is in line with findings by Mbuvha and Marwala [144] who postulate that the travel ban that was put in place under these measures reduced imported infections significantly.

11.3.1.3 Alert level 5: 26 March 2020 – 30 April 2020

On the 26th of March 2020, the first regulated lockdown was implemented, termed *lockdown alert level 5* by the government. This was seen as a drastic decision that aimed to reduce the spreading rate of the virus significantly through stringent regulations. Lockdown alert level 5 was put in place during a period where the spreading rate was found to be the highest at 0.369. This corresponded to an R_0 of 1.757 (CI[1.176, 2.008]), suggesting that this was indeed a period of high COVID-19 spread as suggested by Disaster Management Act regulations. Another explanatory factor, as indicated by [144] could be an increase in general public awareness around the COVID-19 virus, which could have in-

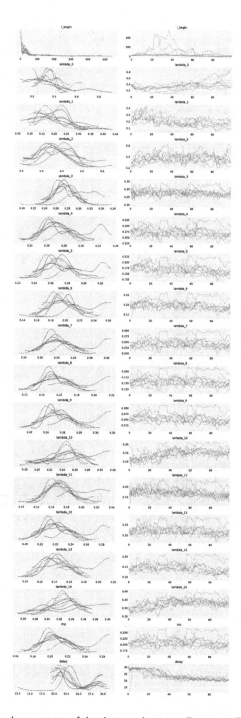

FIGURE 11.3 NUTS trace plots each parameter of the time varying spreading rate adjusted SIR model.

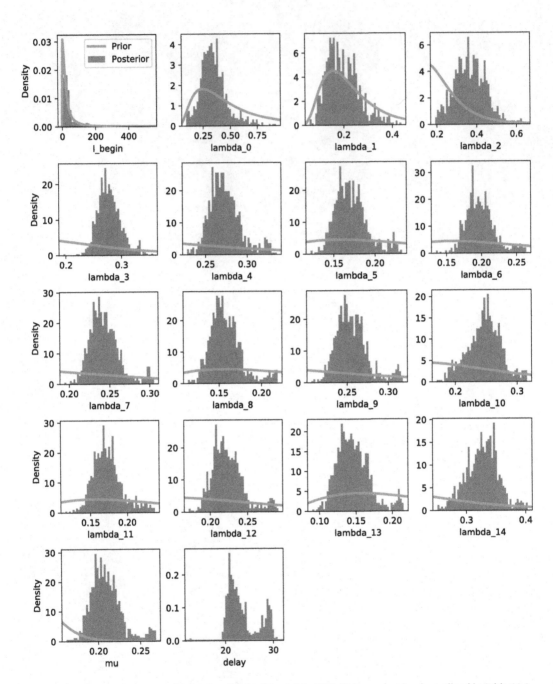

FIGURE 11.4 Posterior Parameter distributions for the SIR model with lockdown alert levels, outlined in Table 11.1, as change points.

Table 11.3 Mean posterior estimates of spreading at each level of lockdown including estimates and confidence intervals of R_0.

Parameter	Interpretation	Mean λ_i	Mean R_0	Confidence Interval R_0
λ_0	No Restrictions	0.349	1.662	[0.467 , 2.805]
λ_1	Initial Restrictions	0.198	0.943	[0.424, 1.571]
λ_2	Alert Level 5	0.369	1.757	[0.986, 2.390]
λ_3	Alert Level 4	0.278	1.324	[1.124 , 1.514]
λ_4	Alert Level 3	0.274	1.305	[1.167 , 1.533]
λ_5	Alert Level 2	0.171	0.814	[0.662 , 1.043]
λ_6	Alert Level 1	0.198	0.943	[0.795 , 1.195]
λ_7	Adjusted Alert Level 3	0.244	1.162	[1.000 , 1.357]
λ_8	Adjusted Alert Level 1	0.158	0.752	[0.600, 0.962]
λ_9	Adjusted Alert Level 2	0.256	1.219	[1.052, 1.429]
λ_{10}	Adjusted Alert Level 3	0.247	1.176	[0.886, 1.400]
λ_{11}	Adjusted Alert Level 4	0.174	0.829	[0.657, 1.043]
λ_{12}	Adjusted Alert Level 3	0.224	1.067	[0.881, 1.276]
λ_{13}	Adjusted Alert Level 2	0.146	0.695	[0.490, 0.910]
λ_{14}	Adjusted Alert Level 1	0.327	1.557	[1.262, 1.757]

fluenced more people to undergo the screening and testing processes. This also coincided with a state-led mass testing and screening programme.[3] Thus part of this rise in infections could be attributed to increased detection.

11.3.1.4 Alert level 4: 1 May 2020 – 31 May 2020

Lockdown alert level 4, implemented on 1st May 2020, when spreading rates had decreased from 0.369 to 0.278. This leads to a lower R_0 value of 1.324 CI([1.124,1.514]) than the previous period. This is positive because lockdown alert level 4 was introduced to partially relieve the stress placed on the South African economy while keeping the spreading rate of COVID-19 under control. The decline spreading rates over this time period again suggest that the government's decision to ease restrictions from Alert Level 5 was justified.

11.3.1.5 Alert level 3: 1 June 2020 – 17 August 2020

The decision to reduce restrictions and move to a lockdown alert level 3 on 1st June 2020 while there was a slight decrease spreading rate from 0.278 to 0.274, which corresponded to a new R_0 value of 1.305 CI([1.167,1.533]). Further easing the restrictions allows for more economic activity and mobility while keeping spreading rates relatively constant. This again suggests tactically correct action by the government in retrospect.

11.3.1.6 Alert level 2: 18 August 2020 – 20 September 2020

The implementation of lockdown alert level 2 on 18th August 2020 coincided with a large decrease in spreading rates from 0.274 to 0.171 leading to an R_0 of 0.814 ([0.662,1.043]).

---

[3] https://sacoronavirus.co.za/2020/04/20/update-on-covid-19-20th-april-2020/.

This is of significant importance as this value suggests that if the pandemic continues on this spread trajectory ($R_0 < 1$) – the virus will spread eventually dissipate (assuming no new variants and reinfections).

11.3.1.7 Alert level 1: 21 September 2020 – 28 December 2020

On 21st September 2020, the government decided to further ease restrictions by moving to lockdown alert level 1. This led to a increase in subsequent spreading rates from 0.171 to 0.198, resulting in an R_0 value of 0.943 CI([0.795,1.195]). This was an increase of 15.847%. It is important to note that lockdown alert level 1 is defined as 21st September 2020 to 28th December 2020.

The primary catalyst for this increase in R_0 is likely a combination of seasonal effects and social behaviour, leading to a so-called "second wave" of COVID-19 driven by the Beta variant. Additionally, the fact that this time period largely coincides with the start of summer and increased mobility could have contributed to the increase in the observed spreading rates and R_0's. This is because there is a high possibility of a positive relationship between temperature and COVID-19 growth [147].

11.3.1.8 Adjusted level 3: 29 December 2020 – 28 February 2021

The adjusted alert level 3 lockdown was introduced to combat the peak of the second wave that began under the previous lockdown and was implemented on 29th December 2020. This resulted in an increase in the spreading rate from 0.198 to 0.224. A relatively high R_0 of 1.162 CI([1.000,1.357]) is over the period. This thus suggests once more that a tactical increase in restrictions was justifiable.

Despite the efforts to combat the high spreading rate through more stringent regulations, it remained relatively high. This may have been due to a similar combination of factors in lockdown alert level 1. This includes a possible lack of social distancing adherence through the festive period and an increased average temperature during the summer months of January and February. The spreading rate for adjusted lockdown alert level 3 is significantly higher than the original level 3 spreading rate, with 0.244 and 0.612, respectively. This coincides with removing some of the original restrictions of alert level 3, such as the prohibition of inter-provincial travel, border closures, and strict alcohol bans.

11.3.1.9 Adjusted alert levels [1-4]: 1 March 2021 – 18 December 2021

As discussed earlier in the chapter, adjusted versions of alert levels 1 through 4 have been implemented between 1 March and 18 December 2021. These restriction levels encapsulate some of the elements in the original definitions of the alert levels with the discretionary removal of certain prohibitions. The results on a mean R_0 basis suggest that spreading rates are marginally lower than those of the corresponding original lockdown alert levels. An interesting consideration, however, is the break-in chronology between alert levels, with R_0 for adjusted alert level 1 being the highest of the adjusted lockdown regime. Given the government's previous actions, it has been expected that restrictions would have been increased to a higher alert level due to a relatively high R_0 of 1.55 in the period 1 October to 18

December 2021. This potentially suggests a shift in priorities, with economic impacts taking precedence. Furthermore, a vaccination campaign that began in February 2021 could have resulted in a reduction in the severity, in terms of the number of hospitalisations and deaths, of disease – leading to a justified removal of some restrictions. A final observation on adjusted alert levels is the spreading rates of the same adjusted alert level can vary significantly depending on the periods they are implemented due to confounding factors such as seasonality, new variant waves, population mobility cycles, and the aforementioned discretionary removal of restrictions.

11.3.1.10 Transitions between alert levels and efficacy of restrictions

The joint objective of minimising the economic opportunity cost of lockdown and reduction in the spread of COVID-19 is optimised when restrictions are imposed and lifted in a meaner that reflects the underlying dynamics of the pandemic. Thus transitions in spreading rates between adjacent time windows give insight as to whether the decision to move between lockdown alert levels is tactically justifiable. Based on the sequence of R_0 values between March and September 2020, the staged easing of restrictions was in line with the inferred spreading rates. This relationship, however, breaks down when looking at adjusted alert levels between March and December 2021.

11.3.1.11 Recovery rate

The inferred recovery rate parameter, μ, is fixed as a constant over the time horizon of the study. As a result, our model estimates a mean value for μ of 0.210 CI([7.257,21.286]). According to literature referenced in section 11.1.1 a recovery rate of approximately 0.125 was expected. Mbuvha and Marwala [144], further support this fact by inferring a recovery rate of 0.151. However, both of these values are estimated based on initial COVID-19 data gathered at the earliest stages of the pandemic. This difference in the recovery rates could be due to medical facilities operating at a much higher capacity during specific points of the study, as detailed by Silal et al. [208]. Since the focus of this work is on spreading rates alternative values, the constant recovery rate will have little impact on the conclusions.

11.4 Conclusion

Overall, the SIR model parameters inferred via the application of the NUTS sampler give rise to our analysis which aims to effectively quantify the South African government's implementation of lockdown over a 654-day period since the first COVID-19 case in South Africa.

The inference results suggest that government's actions in imposing and lifting lockdown restrictions were broadly in line with the underlying spreading rate levels as envisaged in the initial Disaster Management Act regulations. This relationship breaks down with the introduction of adjusted lockdown alert levels with the discretionary lifting of restrictions. The adjusted alert level period is also confounded by an ongoing vaccination campaign.

Other considerations that could be explored in further work are directly assessing the seasonal effects on social behaviour, particularly the disease characteristics of COVID-19. These extensions will effectively isolate the impact of the various government implemented lockdown alert levels by accounting for a more significant number of explanatory variables. Further extensions could include *explicit modelling of incubation time distributions, spatial heterogeneity, isolation effects, sub-sampling effects, and undetected cases beyond the reporting delay or the age and contact patterns of the population.* Further, constraining our recovery rate to be constant over a sizable time horizon may be impractical. This parameter may be more effectively be expressed as time-varying between the different lockdown alert levels, as detailed by Yang et al. [227].

In the next chapter, we use the Bayesian framework to infer South African equity option prices under the Merton jump diffusion model.

12

Probabilistic inference of equity option prices under jump-diffusion processes

12.1 Background

In their seminal work, Black and Scholes [28] introduced their Black-Scholes option pricing framework, which has gone on to revolutionise finance. Their framework is based on constructing a self-financing portfolio of the underlying and cash that replicates the payoff of a European option. The approach makes various assumptions such as that markets are friction-less, constant risk-free interest rate, and that the underlying process is driven by geometric Brownian motion dynamics, among others. The last assumption implies that the returns are normally distributed, which empirical results have shown that this assumption is violated as asset returns have fatter tails than those implied by the normal distribution [51,122,155]. Furthermore, the empirical analysis also reveals the stylised facts of volatility clustering (where squared returns are highly correlated) and implied options volatility smile (where the volatility various for each strike for the same maturity option) [122]. Various models have been proposed to address these three stylised facts. These models include models driven by fractal Brownian motion [146], stochastic volatility [2], and jump-diffusion models [122,149], among others.

Unlike models driven by Brownian motion, models driven by fractal Brownian motion can produce self-similarity due to dependent increments [137]. The disadvantage of these models is that, in some instances, they may result in the presence of arbitrage opportunities [200]. Stochastic volatility models were originally designed to capture the volatility clustering effect [122]. These models include discrete-time models such as the ARCH and GARCH [10] models and continuous-time versions such as the Heston model [100]. The Heston model extends geometric Brownian motion by allowing the diffusive volatility to be a stochastic process and is thus able to capture the dynamics of the volatility skew. Jump-diffusion models, first introduced by Merton [149] into the financial literature, enhance geometric Brownian motion by adding a jump component driven by a Poisson process to the drift and diffusion terms already present in geometric Brownian motion. The addition of the jump component allows the models to capture the fat tails of the returns and the volatility skew [122]. Closed-form expressions exist for European options under jump-diffusion models, with the price being the weighted Black-Scholes option prices, with the weights being probabilities from the Poisson distribution.

Hamiltonian Monte Carlo Methods in Machine Learning. https://doi.org/10.1016/B978-0-44-319035-3.00024-0

139

This chapter calibrates the one-dimensional Merton [149] jump-diffusion model to three-month European call and put options on the South African FTSE All-Share Index traded on the Johannesburg Stock Exchange. We intend to produce a distribution of the calibrated model parameters and also naturally incorporate confidence intervals for any predictions produced by the model. To this end, we calibrate the Merton [149] model by employing the Bayesian inference framework.

In this chapter, we aim to infer the posterior distribution of the parameters $P(\mathbf{w}|M)$ for the jump-diffusion model so we can perform predictions using the model and establish how well the model fits the volatility skew. The posterior distribution $P(\mathbf{w}|M)$ is typically not available in close form, and thus, numerical techniques are often required to determine the posterior [134]. The common approaches for training models, that is, determining the posterior distribution, within the Bayesian framework are variational inference techniques [101,103] and MCMC algorithms. MCMC algorithms are preferable to variational techniques as they are guaranteed to converge to the correct target distribution if the sample size is sufficiently large [203,205], and are thus the focus of this chapter.

We present the first-in-literature application of the MALA [79], HMC [60], and the NUTS [105] methods in the calibration of the Merton jump-diffusion models for inference of South African European option prices. The MALA improves on the seminal MH [95] algorithm by employing Langevin dynamics to explore the target posterior more efficiently via the utilisation of first-order gradient information of the unnormalised target posterior distribution. HMC utilises Hamiltonian dynamics to guide its exploration, with the MALA being a particular case of HMC. HMC is a popular MCMC method that has been extensively used in various applications such as finance, energy, and health [144,145,163]. NUTS is a state-of-art method that provides an adaptive scheme for tuning the step-size and trajectory length parameters of HMC [105].

The empirical results show that the MALA and NUTS algorithms can reproduce the put option prices regardless of their level of moneyness, with HMC not fitting the skew. Except for very deep in the money options, all the MCMC methods can fit the call option price data. The Bayesian approach also produces posterior distributions of the parameters, which allows the practitioner to establish confidence intervals on the calibrated parameters. These parameters would be used to simulate the asset paths that could be used to price exotic options such as Barrier options and options embedded in life insurance contracts.

12.1.1 Merton jump diffusion option pricing model

In this chapter, we study the jump-diffusion model of Merton [149], which is a one-dimensional Markov process $\{X_t, t \geq 0\}$ with the following dynamics under the risk neutral measure $\mathbf{Q}$ [149,155]:

$$d \ln X_t = r dt + \sigma dZ_t + (J-1) dK_t \tag{12.1}$$

where r is the risk free interest rate, σ is the diffusive volatility, Z_t and K_t are the Brownian motion process and Poisson process with intensity λ respectively, and

$$J \sim \mu_{jump} \exp\left(-\frac{\sigma_{jump}^2}{2} + \sigma_{jump}\mathcal{N}(0, \sigma_{jump}^2)\right)$$

is the size of the jump size as a multiple of the stock price X_t, μ_{jump} is the average jump size and σ_{jump} is the volatility of the jump size. Thus, the parameters that we are interested in calibrating are $\{\sigma, \mu_{jump}, \sigma_{jump}^2, \lambda\}$. Note that all the parameters have positive support. The first two terms of Eq. (12.1) are the same as in the Black-Scholes [28] model, with the last term being the jump component introduced by Merton [149].

Closed-from solutions for European options under the jump-diffusion model exist and are written as functions of Black-Scholes option prices. If the Black-Scholes option price is given as $P_{BS}(S, K, T, \sigma, r)$, then the corresponding jump diffusion option price P_{JD} is given as:

$$P_{JD}(S, K, T, \sigma_k, r, \lambda, \mu_{jump}, \sigma_{jump}) =$$

$$\sum_{i=0}^{\infty} \frac{\exp(-\mu_{jump}\lambda T)(\mu_{jump}\lambda T)^i}{i!} P_{BS}(S, K, T, \sigma_i, r_i) \qquad (12.2)$$

where $\sigma_i = \sqrt{\sigma^2 + \frac{\sigma_{jump}^2}{T}}$ and $r_i = r - \lambda(m-1) + k\frac{\log(\mu_{jump})}{T}$. Note that i represents the number of jumps that occur during the life of the option. Eq. (12.2) shows that the jump diffusion option price P_{JD} is a weighted average of Black-Scholes P_{BS} option prices with the weights derived from the Poisson process driving the jump component.

In this chapter, we aim to calibrate Eq. (12.2) to market observed put and call option prices by minimising the difference between the observed and the predicted option prices – which is a sum of squared errors. This is undertaken by assuming that the sum of squared errors follows a Gaussian distribution with mean zero and unit standard deviation. Furthermore, we place a log-normal prior, with mean zero and standard deviation equal to one, on all the parameters. This target posterior is trained using the MCMC methods described in the following section.

12.2 Numerical experiments

In this section, we present the data used in all the experiments. We also describe the experiments performed as well as the performance metrics utilised.

12.2.1 Data description

The data used is for all three-month European options on the All Share Index expiring on 22 July 2019. The data consists of the strikes, 3MJIBAR rate, and time to expiry for both puts and calls. Two hundred call options and 200 put option prices were divided into train and test using a 90-10 split.

12.2.2 Experiment description

We generate five chains of ten thousand samples with a burn-in period of five thousand samples using the MALA, HMC, and NUTS MCMC methods. The step size of all the methods was tuned during the burn-in period using the primal-dual averaging methodology as described in Section 1.9 targeting a sample acceptance rate of 80%. A trajectory length of ten was used for HMC. Any required tuning of algorithm parameters was performed during the burn-in period. For the HMC and NUTS algorithms we set the pre-conditioning matrix $\mathbf{M} = \mathbf{I}$, which is the common approach in practice [161,164,172].

We then assess the performance of the MCMC algorithms by the effective sample sizes of the generated samples, the effective sample sizes of the generated samples normalised by execution time, and predictive performance on unseen option price data. Note that the execution time is the time taken to generate the samples after the burn-in period and that higher values of the effective sample size are preferable. To assess the predictive performance, we compare the predicted option prices based on the calibrated jump-diffusion model parameters and market observed strike, interest rate, and time to expiry of the option.

The effective sample calculation used in this chapter is the multivariate effective sample size metric outlined in Vats et al. [159,218]. We further analyse the convergence behaviour using the potential scale reduction factor, which is also called the $\hat{R}$ metric, of Gelman and Rubin [77]. Values of around one for the $\hat{R}$ metric indicates that the chain has converged.

12.3 Results and discussions

The results in Table 12.1 show the sampling performance of the MCMC methods, Fig. 12.1 and Table 12.2 show the calibrated jump-diffusion model parameters, Fig. 12.2 shows the distribution of the error on the predictions while Fig. 12.3 shows the predicted option prices for both calls and puts of varying strikes.

Table 12.1 shows that NUTS outperforms the other two methods in terms of sampling performance as NUTS produces the largest effective sample size as well as the lowest test negative log-likelihood. MALA has the lowest execution time, which leads to it outperforming all the methods on time normalised effective sample size basis. It is interesting to note that NUTS produces an execution time of orders of magnitude more than the other methods. The large execution time can be attributed to the highly multi-modal nature of the target posterior distribution, with similar results having been observed in Mongwe et al. [160,164]. In Mongwe et al. [160,164,169], jump-diffusion processes were calibrated to historical market data across various financial markets using various MCMC methods.

Fig. 12.1 and the corresponding summary in Table 12.2 show that the calibrated for HMC and NUTS broadly agree on the call option data, with the parameters for MALA being different. This also results in NUTS and HMC having similar predictive performance on the call option data as shown in Fig. 12.2 and the test negative log-likelihood in Table 12.1, with MALA being the worst performer based on these metrics. Fig. 12.1 also shows that

Table 12.1 Sampling performance of the MCMC methods.
A cell that is **bold** indicates
that the method outperforms
on that particular metric. The
results are averaged over five
runs of each algorithm. NLL is
the negative log-likelihood.

Metric	MALA	HMC	NUTS
Call option data			
ESS	131	140	**408**
t	**144**	536	4100
ESS/t	**0.910**	0.262	0.099
$\hat{R}$ max	1.01	**1.00**	**1.00**
Test NLL	922	847	**812**
Put option data			
ESS	59	55	**311**
t	**152**	558	8296
ESS/t	**0.388**	0.099	0.037
$\hat{R}$ max	**1.00**	1.02	**1.00**
Test NLL	332	5 094	**227**

Table 12.2 Merton jump-diffusion parameter estimates averaged over the five runs of each algorithm. This table summarises the results in Fig. 12.1. The values in the parenthesis
are the standard deviations rounded to two decimal places.

Method	σ	μ_{jump}	σ_{jump}	λ
Call option data				
MALA	0.061 (0.00)	1.099 (0.01)	0.040 (0.01)	0.409 (0.08)
HMC	0.000 (0.00)	1.054 (0.00)	0.012 (0.00)	2.587 (0.16)
NUTS	0.009 (0.00)	1.054 (0.00)	0.014 (0.00)	2.518 (0.19)
Put option data				
MALA	0.104 (0.00)	1.149 (0.01)	0.387 (0.01)	0.401 (0.02)
HMC	0.000 (0.00)	0.893 (0.00)	0.005 (0.00)	3.608 (0.04)
NUTS	0.122 (0.00)	2.932 (0.27)	5.243 (3.78)	0.026 (0.00)

although MALA and NUTS have different calibrated parameters, they have similar predictive performance as shown in Figs. 12.2 and 12.3. This can be attributed to the parameters
of the jump component in Eq. (12.2) not being separable (with λ being a latent variable),
meaning that different combinations of the parameters can lead to the same predictive
performance.

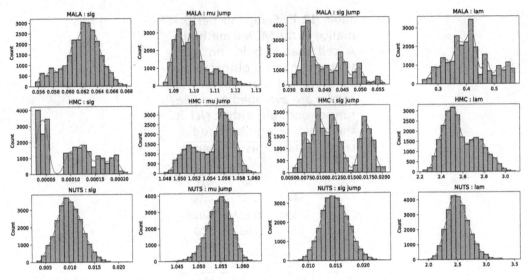

(a) Calibrated parameters using the call option data.

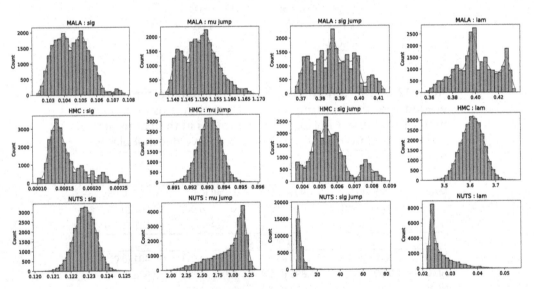

(b) Calibrated parameters using the put option data.

FIGURE 12.1 Calibrated jump-diffusion parameters from the MALA, HMC and NUTS algorithms.

Fig. 12.3 shows that, in general, the MCMC methods can capture the overall shape of the skew, with HMC performing poorly on the put option data. We find that MALA and NUTS can reproduce the put option prices for all moneyness levels. The methods can also replicate the call option prices on the call option data, except for very deep in the money

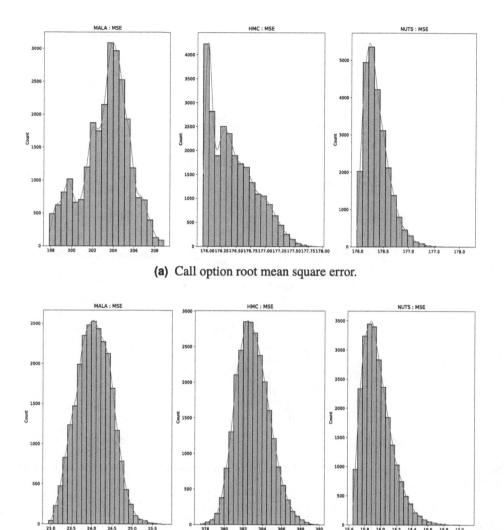

(a) Call option root mean square error.

(b) Put option root mean square error.

FIGURE 12.2 Root mean square error distribution for the call and put option data using the MALA, HMC and NUTS methods.

call options. The worst performer for the call option data is the MALA method. The overall predictive performance of the MCMC methods on the call option data is much worse than on the put option data, with all methods predicting that the skew is a lot steeper than what has been observed in the market. The results could be improved by using more call option price data in the training of the jump-diffusion model, particularly in the deep in the money region.

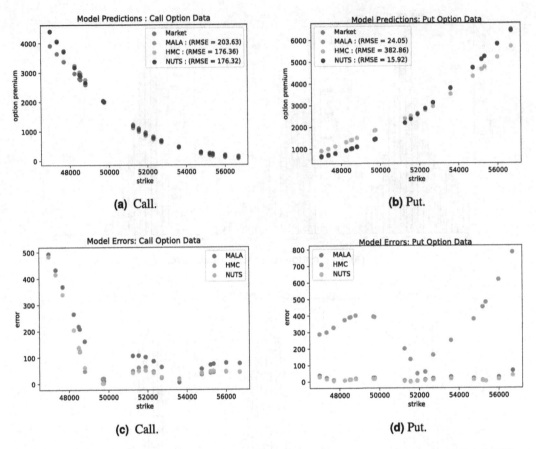

FIGURE 12.3 Averaged option price predictions for the call and put option data using the MALA, HMC and NUTS algorithms.

12.4 Conclusion

We present a probabilistic approach to infer South African equity option prices and volatility skew by calibrating jump-diffusion models to call and put data on the All-Share Index. The inference of the models is performed using Metropolis Adjusted Langevin Algorithm, Hamiltonian Monte Carlo, No-U-Turn Sampler methods.

The results show that NUTS produces the best sampling behaviour on both the call and put option data. The analysis also shows that NUTS produces the best out-of-sample predictions for both put and call options of various moneyness, with slight miss-pricing on very deep in the money call options. These results could prove to be helpful to practitioners interested in calibrating jump-diffusion processes with the aim of pricing non-traditional exotic options such as those present in life insurance contracts.

The work in this chapter can be enhanced by considering the entire volatility surface instead of limiting the data to only three-month options. Furthermore, a comparison with results from calibrating other models such as the Heston model and Kou's [122] double exponential jump-diffusion model could be of interest. We plan to explore these themes in future work.

In the following chapter, we present the first application of MCMC methods to the modelling of financial statement audit outcomes, with a focus on South African local government entities.

13

Bayesian inference of local government audit outcomes

13.1 Background

The Auditor General of South Africa (AG-SA) revealed that South African local government entities lost over $2 billion in irregular expenditure in the 2018–2019 financial year [16, 158]. This irregular expenditure has consequently harmed service delivery and returns on the rapidly increasing government debt [16]. The manipulation of financial statements is not only limited to the public sector, with the Steinhoff collapse being a prime example of management fraud in the private sector [52,53]. Steinhoff is a South African retailer that lost over R200 billion in market capitalisation on the JSE over a short space of time after allegations of accounting fraud [53,158].

The recent scandal of Wirecard, and previously Enron, also indicate that financial statement fraud is not only a problem for South Africa, but the world at large [97,181]. Wirecard is a German payment processing company, which filed for insolvency in 2020, that manipulated its financial statements by misstating its profit [181]. Enron was an American natural gas company that lost over $60 billion in market capitalisation in the early 2000s after the allegations of fraud emerged [97].

The use of automated techniques for the analysis and detection of financial statement fraud has been on the increase in the past decade, as highlighted in Appendix D [67,80,87,118,127,154,157,158,187]. In our literature survey of 52 papers, which we summarise in Appendix D, we outline how artificial intelligence and other automated methods can be used to construct decision support tools for various stakeholders. For example, auditors may use the decision support tool to flag entities who are at risk of having committed financial statement fraud and reduce the turnaround time of the audit, amongst other benefits [157,158]. A prime example within the South African context is the AG-SA having to audit all local and provincial government entities at the end of each financial year [16,157].

As shown in Table D.3, logistic regression has been successfully used in the literature for the detection of financial statement fraud [9,67,108,116,121,153,182,186,188]. Moepya et al. [153] use logistic regression in the detection of fraud in companies listed on the Johannesburg Stock Exchange (JSE), while Boumediene et al. [33] performed a similar study for entities listed in Tunisia. Logistic regression has advantages over more complicated models such as artificial neural networks in that the results are more easily interpretable by the stakeholders, which is an important consideration when building a decision support tool [118,153,157].

Hamiltonian Monte Carlo Methods in Machine Learning. https://doi.org/10.1016/B978-0-44-319035-3.00025-2

In logistic regression, as with any other machine learning model, one has to decide on the input features to use. Correctly selecting the variables to use as inputs for the models is essential because it can influence the performance of the models [141]. Utilising feature selection techniques can improve the model's predictive performance and reduce the model complexity as fewer features would be required [44,158]. Examples of feature selection methods used in the financial statement fraud detection literature include correlation, t-test, analysis of variance, decision trees, and principal component analysis [33,47,49,69,153,158,211]. In this chapter, we limit ourselves to only using financial ratios to predict financial statement audit outcomes. Thus feature selection in this context amounts to selecting which financial ratios are the most important or relevant for inferring financial statement audit opinions.

In this chapter, we present the first use of BLR with automatic relevance determination (BLR-ARD) for the inference of audit outcomes. The Bayesian approach allows us to measure the uncertainty in our predictions, which gives a sense of how much confidence we have in a particular prediction. The use of ARD allows us to automatically determine which of the input features are the most relevant, with uncertainty measures around these as well [133,141]. This formulation of the problem results in the model outcomes being more interpretable, allowing stakeholders to understand the model results better.

This chapter's motivation is to understand the financial performance of South African municipalities in terms of audit outcomes, particularly the features or financial ratios that drive these audit outcomes. We approach this problem from a Bayesian perspective as it provides a probabilistically principled framework for predicting and understanding the audit performance of local government entities. This framework also enables us to provide uncertainty levels in the predictions produced by the models and further allows us to automatically identify and rank the most important financial ratios for audit outcome modelling using prior distributions – which is an essential contribution of this chapter.

We train the BLR-ARD model parameters with MCMC methods. This chapter also presents the first use of the random walk MH, HMC, MALA, MHMC, S2HMC algorithms in the training of BLR-ARD models for inference of financial statement audit opinions.

13.2 Experiment description

13.2.1 Data description

The data used is obtained from South African municipalities' audited financial statement data for the period 2010 to 2018. The years 2010 to 2012 had missing data and were excluded from our analysis. The data was sourced from the South African National Treasury website[1] [171]. The dataset had a total of 1 560 records from 2012 to 2018. This dataset contains, for each municipality in South Africa, the income statement, balance sheet, and cash flow statement for each year. The dataset also contains reports that outline audit opinions, conditional grants, and capital expenditure. In this thesis, we create financial ratios based

[1] https://municipaldata.treasury.gov.za/.

on each municipality's income statement, balance sheet statement, cash flow statement, and capital acquisition report. The conversion of the financial statements into financial ratios is discussed in Section 13.2.2.

The municipalities in South Africa are governed by the Municipal Finance Management Act, and are audited by the AG-SA [16]. The distribution of audit opinions for the dataset shows that the unqualified data instances are just under 55%, with the rest being qualified or worse cases. This distribution also means that there is no large class-imbalance problem for this dataset. Note that outstanding audit opinions, which were only 3 in the data set, are assigned to the disclaimer audit opinion class [15].

13.2.2 Financial ratio calculation

The financial ratios used in this thesis are based on the municipal circular number 71 issued by the National Treasury of the Republic of South Africa [170]. The financial ratios considered can be grouped into two broad categories, namely financial performance and financial position. The financial performance ratios can be further broken down into efficiency, distribution losses, revenue management, expenditure management, and grant dependency. The financial position ratios can be subdivided into asset management/utilisation, debtors management, liquidity management, and liability management. The specific ratios considered in this thesis are [170]:

1. *Debt to Community Wealth/Equity* – Ratio of debt to the community equity. The ratio is used to evaluate a municipality's financial leverage.
2. *Capital Expenditure to Total Expenditure* – Ratio of capital expenditure to total expenditure.
3. *Impairment of PPE, IP and IA* – Impairment of Property, Plant and Equipment (PPE) and Investment Property (IP) and Intangible Assets (IA).
4. *Repairs and Maintenance as a percentage of PPE +IP* – The ratio measures the level of repairs and maintenance relative to assets.
5. *Debt to Total Operating Revenue* – The ratio indicates the level of total borrowings in relation to total operating revenue.
6. *Current Ratio* – The ratio is used to assess the municipality's ability to pay back short-term commitments with short-term assets.
7. *Capital Cost to Total Operating Expenditure* – The ratio indicates the cost of servicing debt relative to overall expenditure.
8. *Net Operating Surplus Margin* – The ratio assesses the extent to which the entity generates operating surpluses.
9. *Remuneration to Total Operating Expenditure* – The ratio measures the extent of remuneration of the entity's staff to total operating expenditure.
10. *Contracted Services to Total Operating Expenditure* – This ratio measures how much of total expenditure is spent on contracted services.

11. *Own Source Revenue to Total Operating Revenue* – The ratio measures the extent to which the municipality's total capital expenditure is funded through internally generated funds and borrowings.
12. *Net Surplus / Deficit Water* – This ratio measures the extent to which the municipality generates surplus or deficit in rendering water service
13. *Net Surplus / Deficit Electricity* – This ratio measures the extent to which the municipality generates surplus or deficit in rendering electricity service.

The first six ratios above are measures of financial position, while the rest are measures of financial performance. Table 13.1 provides descriptive statistics of the financial ratios in the dataset. None of the financial ratios had missing values. Furthermore, the financial ratios were not strongly correlated, with the maximum absolute pairwise linear correlations being less than 0.5.

Table 13.1   Five number summary of the thirteen financial ratios in the South African local government financial statement audit opinion dataset. Note that mil represents a million. Q1 and Q3 are the lower and upper quartiles.

Ratio	Min	Q1	Median	Q3	Max
1	−2046.45	11.97	19.43	35.49	6640.18
2	−3.81	11.22	17.85	25.36	77.66
3	−15.34	3.67	4.94	6.58	159.27
4	−1.86	0.00	0.83	1.91	170.67
5	−0.09	0.28	0.43	0.63	2.64
6	−0.88	0.56	1.16	2.19	23.06
7	−0.31	0.207	0.98	2.33	13.97
8	−147.32	−7.08	4.71	15.34	81.07
9	−67.61	26.31	32.51	41.17	159.98
10	−11.31	0.00	0.97	4.91	51.83
11	7.87	98.14	99.85	100.00	103.54
12	−114100 mil	0	0	83	1436 mil
13	−555400 mil	0	0	21	14970 mil

13.2.3 Bayesian logistic regression with ARD

We model the local government audit outcomes using BLR due to the simplicity of this model and the fact that it is one of the commonly used methods in the FSF literature as shown in Table D.4. The negative log-likelihood $l(D_x|\mathbf{w})$ function, where $\mathbf{w}$ are the model parameters, associated with logistic regression is given by:

$$l(D_x|\mathbf{w}) = \sum_i^{N_{obs}} y_i \log(\mathbf{w}^T x_i) + (1 - y_i)\log(1 - \mathbf{w}^T x_i) \tag{13.1}$$

where D_x is the data and N_{obs} is the number of observations. Thus, the target unnormalised posterior log distribution is given as:

$$\ln p(\mathbf{w}|D_x) = l(D_x|\mathbf{w}) + \ln p(\mathbf{w}|\boldsymbol{\alpha}) + \ln q(\boldsymbol{\alpha}) \tag{13.2}$$

where $\ln p(\mathbf{w}|\boldsymbol{\alpha})$ is the log of the prior distribution placed on the parameters given the hyperparameters, and $\ln q(\boldsymbol{\alpha})$ is the marginal distribution of the hyperparameters. We model the parameters $\mathbf{w}$ as having a Gaussian prior with each parameter having zero mean and its own standard deviation α_i. The $\alpha_i's$ are assumed to follow a log-normal distribution with mean zero and variance 1. The α_i indicates how vital the parameter associated with the input feature is. The larger the value of α_i, the more critical the input feature is in predicting the audit outcomes and election results, respectively.

The aim is to infer the parameters $\mathbf{w}$ and hyperparameters α using MCMC methods. In the literature, this problem is typically formulated as a Gibbs sampling scheme, where the hyperparameters are sampled first and then the parameters and so on [141,172]. The approach taken in this chapter is to jointly infer the parameters $\mathbf{w}$ and hyperparameters α. This approach has the advantage of resulting in a more stable exploration of the posterior, at least for the current dataset. However, it results in the effective parameter space being doubled – which can significantly reduce the sampling time compared to the Gibbs sampling approach.

For each of the random walk MH, MALA, HMC, MHMC and S2HMC algorithms used in this chapter, we generate ten Markov chains of 10 000 samples. The first 5000 samples were used as the burn-in period, and any required tuning of algorithm parameters was performed during the burn-in period. For the HMC, MHMC and S2HMC algorithms we set the pre-conditioning mass matrix $\mathbf{M} = \mathbf{I}$, which is the common approach in practice [25,172].

We target a 25% acceptance rate for random walk MH [198], 60% for MALA [198] and 80% acceptance rates for the remaining MCMC algorithms. A trajectory length of 50 was used for HMC, MHMC and S2HMC. We then assess the performance of the algorithms by generating the trace-plots of the unnormalised target posterior distribution, the ESSs of the generated samples, the ESSs of the generated samples normalised by execution time, and predictive performance on unseen data. Note that the execution time is the time taken to generate the samples after the burn-in period.

The ESS calculation used is described in Section 2.2.1. The predictive performance on unseen data is performed using the ROC as well as AUC. The ranking of the importance of the financial ratios is performed by calculating the mean or average α, which are the standard deviations in Eq. (13.2), for each model parameter over the ten chains. The higher the α value, the more important the input financial ratio is for modelling the audit outcomes.

13.3 Results and discussion

In evaluating the S2HMC algorithm, we set a convergence tolerance of 10^{-6} or the completion of 100 fixed point iterations. Fig. 13.1 shows the inference results, while Figs. 13.2 and

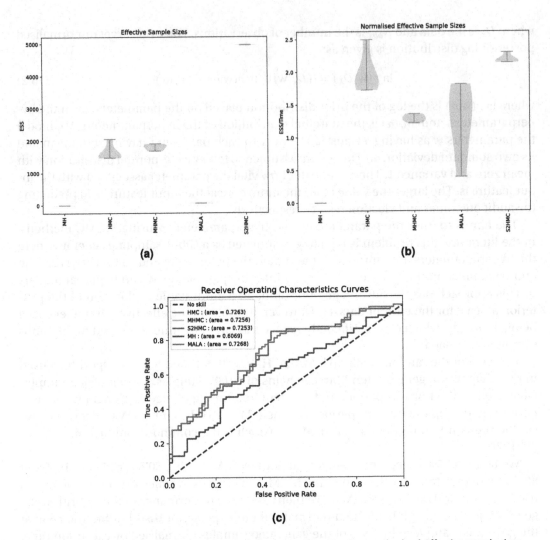

FIGURE 13.1 Inference results for the BLR-ARD model across various sampling methods. a) Effective sample sizes, b) Effective sample sizes normalised by execution time and c) Predictive performance based on the AUC.

13.3 shows the input feature importance or relevance for the considered MCMC methods. The results in Figs. 13.2 and 13.3 are summarised, as rankings for each financial ratio, in Table 13.2.

Fig. 13.1 (a) shows that the S2HMC produces the largest effective sampling sizes, indicating that the algorithm produces less correlated samples when compared to the other methods. HMC and MHMC have the second-highest ESSs, with random walk MH and MALA having very low ESSs, indicating that these two methods produce significantly correlated samples.

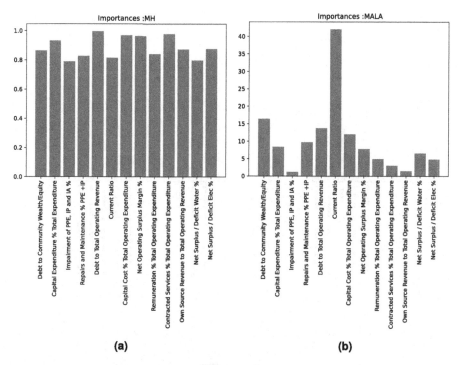

FIGURE 13.2 Average posterior standard deviations from the random walk MH and MALA algorithms. The higher the value, the more important the financial ratio is to modelling audit opinions.

Fig. 13.1 (b) shows that on a normalised (by execution time) ESS basis, the HMC and S2HMC have similar time normalised ESSs and outperform the other methods. Although MH is also relatively fast, since the ESS it produces is very low, it still underperforms on a normalised ESS basis. Fig. 13.1 (c) shows that the MH algorithm has the lowest predictive performance. S2HMC and MHMC have the joint highest predictive performance, which corresponds with the high ESSs generated by these methods. Note that a convergence analysis of the chains was performed using the $\hat{R}$ metric. We found that all the methods had converged on the target.

Figs. 13.2 and 13.3 shows the relative importance or relevance of each of the financial ratios produced by each of the MCMC methods. The results show that the MH algorithm struggles to distinguish between important and not-so-important financial ratios. This is because of the poor exploration of the target. On the other hand, the other MCMC methods can extract the importance or most relevant features for the audit opinion modelling task. Table 13.2 shows the ranking of the importance of the financial ratios produced by each of the methods. The most commonly featured financial ratios in the top five rankings are:

- Ratio 5 – *Debt to Total Operating Revenue*: This ratio is selected by all the five methods
- Ratio 7 – *Capital Cost to Total Operating Expenditure*: This ratio is selected by all the five methods

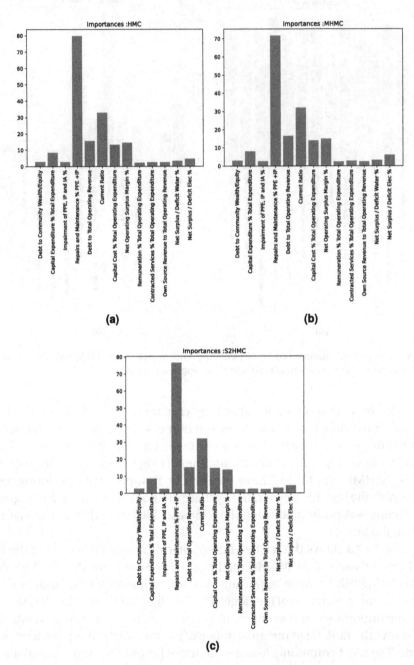

FIGURE 13.3 Average posterior standard deviations from the HMC, MHMC and S2HMC algorithms. The higher the value, the more important the financial ratio is to modelling audit opinions.

Table 13.2 Ranking of the financial ratios by each method. For example, MHMC ranks ratio four as the most important, while MH ranks ratio seven as the third most important. The financial ratios are described in more detail in Section 13.2.2.

Ranking	MH	MALA	HMC	MHMC	S2HMC
1	5	6	4	4	4
2	10	1	6	6	6
3	7	5	5	5	5
4	8	7	8	8	7
5	2	4	7	7	8
6	13	2	2	2	2
7	11	8	13	13	13
8	1	12	12	12	12
9	9	9	1	1	1
10	4	13	3	10	3
11	6	10	11	3	10
12	12	11	10	11	11
13	3	3	9	9	9

- Ratio 4 – *Repairs and Maintenance as a percentage of PPE +IP*: This ratio is selected by MALA, HMC, MHMC and S2HMC
- Ratio 6 – *Current Ratio*: This ratio is selected by MALA, HMC, MHMC and S2HMC
- Ratio 8 – *Net Operating Surplus Margin*: This ratio is selected by the MH, MHMC and S2HMC algorithms.

Our analysis in this chapter shows that the most relevant financial ratios are the repairs and maintenance as a percentage of PPE and IP, current ratio, net operating surplus margin, and the debt to total operating revenue, with the last relevant ratio being the capital cost to total operating expenditure ratio.

These results make intuitive sense as, for example, high repairs and maintenance ratio means that the municipality is undertaking more repairs to assets than the assets' total value. This is likely an indication of a lack of adherence to proper corporate governance as repairs to assets should typically be less than the value of those assets – else those assets should be written-off. Furthermore, a high capital cost to total expenditure ratio means that debt repayments are the most significant component of total expenditure, indicating that the entity has a large debt. This might prompt the entity to act in a manner that flouts corporate governance procedures to hide its dire financial situation.

Furthermore, a high current ratio means that the entity has more current assets than current liabilities, meaning that it is in an excellent financial position and less likely to be fraudulent. On the other hand, a high debt to total operating revenue ratio means that the entity has too much debt compared to the revenue that it is generating, which makes it more likely to act fraudulently. In addition, entities with high net operating surplus margins are profitable and less likely to be fraudulent. In contrast, entities with meager and negative net operating surplus margins are more likely to act fraudulently. These results are in line with what has been observed for listed entities in previous studies [84,180].

These results can prove to be particularly useful for auditors as focusing on these ratios can speed up the detection of inadequate corporate governance behaviour in municipal entities and improve the overall quality of the audits.

13.4 Conclusion

This chapter presented the first-in-literature fully Bayesian approach to inferring financial statement audit opinions. This Bayesian approach is applied to South African local government entity audit outcomes using financial ratios as inputs. The inference is performed using random walk MH, MALA, HMC, MHMC and S2HMC. The sampling was applied to BLR-ARD. Automatic relevance determination allows one to determine which features are the most important in an automated manner and thus implicitly perform feature selection.

In our approach, the parameters and the hyperparameters, which measure the relevance of the financial ratios, are jointly sampled. The results show that the S2HMC produces the best sampling results, with the largest ESSs. However, the predictive performance of MALA, HMC, MHMC and S2HMC is found to be the same. The random walk MH algorithm produces the worst sampling behaviour due to its random walk nature and has both the lowest effective sample rates and predictive performance.

The results further show that the five most essential features in the modelling of audit outcomes for municipalities are the 1) repairs and maintenance as a percentage of total assets ratio, 2) current ratio, 3) debt to total operating revenue, 4) net operating surplus margin, and 5) capital cost to total operating expenditure ratio. These results could prove helpful for auditors as focusing on these ratios can speed up the detection of possible fraudulent behaviour of municipal entities. The work in this chapter can be improved upon by comparing the performance of the BLR with ARD model with other models such as the BNN with ARD model. Furthermore, we plan to perform this analysis for listed entities and compare the results to the local government entities considered in this chapter. The consideration of a more extensive set of financial ratios could also improve the results.

14

Conclusions

14.1 Summary of contributions

In this book, we explore and propose novel extensions and enhancements to the MHMC and S2HMC algorithms. These methods are descendants of HMC, which is a popular and go-to method for performing Bayesian inference of complex machine learning models. We compare the extensions to MHMC and S2HMC that we introduce to the original algorithms across numerous performance metrics and various benchmark problems. We also present a first-in-literature application of MCMC methods to the prediction of South African municipal financial statement audit outcomes.

We begun the book by revisiting the MH algorithm, which forms the core of more advanced methods, with the aim of improving its sampling behaviour without adding a significant computational cost. We introduced the SVMH and LSMH methods. These algorithms extend random walk MH by treating the scale matrix as being stochastic and allowing it to depend on the local geometry of the target respectively. These approaches provide improved sampling behaviour when compared to MH, with SVMH provided a better time-normalised ESS performance over NUTS as the dimensionality of the problem increases.

HMC is the preferred MCMC algorithm due to its ability to intelligently explore the posterior through the use of first-order gradient information of the target via Hamiltonian dynamics. It turns out that when a magnetic field is added to HMC to produce non-canonical Hamiltonian dynamics, the target can be explored even more efficiently. This enhancement of HMC with a magnetic field leads to the MHMC algorithm. The MHMC method is a key focus of this book, and we enhance it in the following ways:

- We employ a random mass matrix for the auxiliary momentum variable to mimic the behaviour of quantum particles to create the QIMHMC algorithm. We prove that this new algorithm converges to the correct stationary distribution. Furthermore, experiments across various target distributions show that QIMHMC outperforms HMC, MHMC and QIHMC on a time-normalised effective sample size basis. A limitation of the proposed algorithm is the requirement for the user to manually specify the distribution of the mass matrix and tune the parameters of the distribution. As with MHMC, the magnetic component of QIMHMC still needs to be tuned. These are open areas of research.

- We utilise partial momentum refreshment, instead of a total refreshment, of the momentum variable to create PMHMC which enhances the performance of MHMC. The results show that this approach leads to significant improvements in performance over

HMC, MHMC and PHMC on a time-normalised effective sample size basis. A drawback of this method is the need to tune the partial momentum refreshment parameter, which determines the extent of the momentum retention. Our analysis shows that higher parameter values are favourable, but these values tend to vary between different target distributions. Tuning this parameter is still an open area of research.

- We obtain the fourth-order modified Hamiltonian associated with the numerical integrator employed in MHMC to create the new SMHMC method, which employs partial momentum refreshment for the generation of the momentum. The results show that the new method outperforms MHMC and PMHMC on an effective sample size basis across numerous targets. This method has two main drawbacks. The first relates to having to tune the partial momentum refreshment parameter as with PMHMC. The second relates to the method's high execution time due to the computation of the non-separable Hamiltonian. The high execution time leads to a decrease in performance on a time-normalised basis. Reducing the execution time is a crucial area of improvement of the proposed algorithm.

Previous studies have shown that HMC's sampling performance decreases as the step size or the system size increases. Methods based on sampling from the shadow Hamiltonian instead of the true Hamiltonian have been shown to address this pathology. This is due to the shadow Hamiltonian being better conserved by the numerical integrator than the true Hamiltonian. One such method is the S2HMC algorithm, which utilises a processed leapfrog integrator to avoid the computationally expensive generation of the momentum. In this book, we extend S2HMC in the following ways:

- We employ partial momentum refreshment to enhance the performance of S2HMC. This was achieved by partially retaining the momentum used to generate the previous sample in the current momenta generation before passing these momenta to the processed leapfrog integrator. The results showed that this approach results in outperformance over S2HMC and PMHMC on an ESS basis. As with SMHMC, the drawback of this method is the requirement to tune the partial momentum refreshment parameter as well as the associated long execution times typical of shadow Hamiltonian methods.
- We propose a method for tuning the parameters of S2HMC which is based on substituting the leapfrog integrator in NUTS with the processed integrator. This is a first-in-literature on methods for tuning parameters of algorithms based on shadow Hamiltonians. This removes the need for the user to manually specify and tune the trajectory length and step sizes parameters. Tuning these parameters would otherwise require time-consuming pilot runs. The results show that the method produces better ESSs than NUTS, outperforms S2HMC on a time-normalised ESS basis but underperforms NUTS on a normalised ESS basis due to the long execution time of the proposed algorithm.

MCMC estimators have a higher variance when compared to classical Monte Carlo estimators due to auto-correlations present between the generated samples. In this book, we use antithetic sampling to tackle the high variance problem in HMC based methods. Antithetic sampling involves running two chains concurrently, with one of the chains having a negated momentum variable compared to the other chain. In this book, we present the antithetic versions of MHMC and S2HMC. The results show that the antithetic versions of the algorithms produce higher time-normalised effective sample sizes when compared to antithetic HMC and the non-antithetic versions of the algorithms. These results show the usefulness of incorporating antithetic sampling into samplers that employ Hamiltonian dynamics. As this approach is straightforward and requires minimal assumptions about the target, there seems very little reason not to deploy it in practice.

This book presents various applications of the Bayesian framework using MCMC methods to energy, epidemiology, financial engineering and auditing. In particular, we provide a first-in-literature application of Bayesian inference to:

- BNN inference in wind speed forecasting. Accurate wind speed and consequently wind power forecasts form a critical enabling tool for large scale wind energy adoption. BNNs trained using HMC methods are used to forecast one hour ahead wind speeds on the Wind Atlas for South Africa datasets. A generalisable ARD committee framework is introduced to synthesise the various sampler ARD outputs into robust feature selections.
- Analysing South Africa's efforts in combating the spread of the SARS-CoV-2 using lockdown levels. We utilise the NUTS algorithm in sampling posterior distributions of parameters induced by a SIR model configured change points corresponding to the different levels of lockdown put in place by the South African Government in terms of the Disaster Management Act. We utilise these results to analyse the effectiveness of the distinct lockdown alert levels entailed by South Africa's regulations to the Disaster Management Act.
- Infer South African equity option prices. We calibrate the one-dimensional Merton jump-diffusion model to European put and call option data on the All-Share price index using MCMC methods. Our approach produces a distribution of the jump-diffusion model parameters, which can be used to build economic scenario generators and price exotic options such as those embedded in life insurance contracts.
- Modelling audit outcomes of South African local government entities. Furthermore, we perform ARD using MCMC methods to identify which financial ratios are essential for modelling audit outcomes of municipalities. Stakeholders could use these results in understanding what drives the audit outcomes of South African municipalities.

14.2 Ongoing and future work

The analysis performed in this book relied on the minimal tuning of the magnetic field in MHMC. We plan to address this drawback by assessing various methods for automatically tuning the magnetic field in future work. The manual tuning of the magnetic component performed in this book suggests that if the magnetic field is optimally tuned, it could significantly improve the performance of the MHMC algorithm. We are also currently investigating possible heuristics and automated approaches to automatically tune the partial momentum refreshment parameter in the PMHMC and PS2HMC methods. The QIMHMC algorithm can also be refined by developing automated approaches to select an optimal distribution from a user-specified class of distributions.

The slow execution times associated with evaluating shadow Hamiltonians in S2HMC and SMHMC can be addressed through the use of surrogate model approaches. A surrogate approach that could be considered is the use of Sparse grid [231] interpolation to pre-compute the gradients of the Hamiltonian before the sampling process begins. This would improve the time-normalised performance of the methods, but possibly at the cost of accuracy. Furthermore, the shadow Hamiltonian itself could be learned during the burn-in period using Gaussian Processes. As evaluating the shadow Hamiltonian is the most expensive part of the algorithms, this should reduce the execution time post-burn-in period and consequently improve the time-normalised effective sample size performance. Furthermore, when we developed SMHMC, we only focused on a shadow Hamiltonian that is only conserved up to fourth-order. The results could be improved by considering higher-order shadow Hamiltonians, albeit at a higher computation cost.

One of the key issues in machine learning is model selection. Within the Bayesian framework, model selection and comparison are conducted via the Bayesian evidence metric. We are currently extending the MHMC methods presented in this book so that they are also able to produce the evidence metric. The approach that we are currently considering is creating a continuously tempered version of MHMC in a similar fashion to continuously tempered HMC outlined in [83]. Given than MHMC outperforms HMC across various targets, one would expect continuously tempered MHMC to outperform continuously tempered HMC.

The application areas of the methods presented in this book could be extended to larger datasets such as MNIST and deeper neural networks as opposed to the small neural networks considered in this book. This will consequently result in longer execution times. This could be improved by considering stochastic gradient versions of the algorithms proposed in this work. Currently, the literature does not cover stochastic gradient approaches for shadow Hamiltonian based samplers. Addressing this gap in the literature could prove to be a significant contribution to knowledge.

Lastly, in this book, we only considered variance reduction techniques based on using antithetic sampling. In the future, we plan to create a control variate version of MHMC. As control variate techniques are more generally applicable compared to antithetic sampling (which assumes symmetry of the target distribution), we expect control variate MHMC and the combination of control variate and antithetic sampling MHMC to outperform the antithetic MHMC method presented in this book. Furthermore, comparing the antithetic methods introduced in this book with the antithetic versions of RMHMC and QIHMC could be of interest.

A

Separable shadow Hamiltonian

A.1 Derivation of separable shadow Hamiltonian

Using the BCH [91] formula, it can be shown that the fourth-order shadow Hamiltonian is given as:

$$\tilde{H}^{[4]}(\mathbf{w}, \mathbf{p}) = H(\mathbf{w}, \mathbf{p}) + \frac{\epsilon^2}{12} K_{\mathbf{p}}^T U_{\mathbf{ww}} K_{\mathbf{p}} - \frac{\epsilon^2}{24} U_{\mathbf{w}}^T K_{\mathbf{pp}} U_{\mathbf{w}} + \mathcal{O}(\epsilon^4) \tag{A.1}$$

One can interpret the first error term in Eq. (A.1) as a perturbation to the kinetic energy K and the next as a perturbation to the potential energy U. The perturbation to the kinetic energy K alters the fixed mass matrix $\mathbf{M}$ into a different and likely position-dependent matrix. In most situations, this makes the distribution of the momentum variable non-Gaussian.

We now seek a canonical transformation that can transform the Hamiltonian in Eq. (A.1) to a separable Hamiltonian. Sweet et al. [225] use the following canonical transformation [129]:

$$\begin{aligned}
\mathbf{W} &= \mathbf{w} + \epsilon^2 \lambda K_{\mathbf{pp}} U_{\mathbf{w}} + \mathcal{O}(\epsilon^2) \\
\mathbf{P} &= \mathbf{p} - \epsilon^2 \lambda U_{\mathbf{ww}} K_{\mathbf{p}} + \mathcal{O}(\epsilon^2)
\end{aligned} \tag{A.2}$$

After substitution of (A.2) into (A.1) the shadow Hamiltonian becomes:

$$\begin{aligned}
\tilde{H}^{[4]}(\mathcal{X}(\mathbf{w}, \mathbf{p})) &= H(\mathbf{W}, \mathbf{P}) + \frac{\epsilon^2}{12} K_{\mathbf{P}} U_{\mathbf{ww}} K_{\mathbf{P}} - \frac{\epsilon^2}{24} U_{\mathbf{w}} K_{\mathbf{PP}} U_{\mathbf{w}} + \mathcal{O}(\epsilon^4) \\
&= \underbrace{U(\mathbf{W})}_{A} + \underbrace{K(\mathbf{P})}_{B} + \underbrace{\frac{\epsilon^2}{12} K_{\mathbf{P}} U_{\mathbf{ww}} K_{\mathbf{P}}}_{C} - \underbrace{\frac{\epsilon^2}{24} U_{\mathbf{w}} K_{\mathbf{PP}} U_{\mathbf{w}}}_{D} + \mathcal{O}(\epsilon^4)
\end{aligned} \tag{A.3}$$

where taking the first order Taylor expansion of U(W) at $\mathbf{w}$ and substituting $\mathbf{W}$ gives:

$$\begin{aligned}
A &= U(\mathbf{w}) + U_{\mathbf{w}} (\mathbf{W} - \mathbf{w}) + \frac{1}{2} (\mathbf{W} - \mathbf{w}) U_{\mathbf{ww}} (\mathbf{W} - \mathbf{w})^T + \mathcal{O}(\epsilon^4) \\
&= U(\mathbf{w}) + U_{\mathbf{w}} \left(\epsilon^2 \lambda K_{\mathbf{pp}} U_{\mathbf{w}} \right) + \left(\epsilon^2 \lambda K_{\mathbf{pp}} U_{\mathbf{w}} \right) U_{\mathbf{ww}} \left(\epsilon^2 \lambda K_{\mathbf{pp}} U_{\mathbf{w}} \right)^T + \mathcal{O}(\epsilon^4) \\
&= U(\mathbf{w}) + U_{\mathbf{w}} \epsilon^2 \lambda K_{\mathbf{pp}} U_{\mathbf{w}} + \mathcal{O}(\epsilon^4)
\end{aligned} \tag{A.4}$$

and substituting $\mathbf{P}$ into B gives:

$$\begin{aligned}
B &= \frac{1}{2} \left(\mathbf{p} - \epsilon^2 \lambda U_{\mathbf{ww}} K_{\mathbf{p}} + \mathcal{O}(\epsilon^2) \right) K_{\mathbf{pp}} \left(\mathbf{p} - \epsilon^2 \lambda U_{\mathbf{ww}} K_{\mathbf{p}} + \mathcal{O}(\epsilon^2) \right) \\
&= K(\mathbf{p}) - \epsilon^2 \lambda K_{\mathbf{p}} U_{\mathbf{ww}} K_{\mathbf{p}} + \mathcal{O}(\epsilon^4)
\end{aligned} \tag{A.5}$$

By using the second order Taylor approximation of $U(\mathbf{W})$ at $\mathbf{w}$ and substituting $\mathbf{W}$, we have that:

$$U(\mathbf{W}) = U(\mathbf{w}) + U_{\mathbf{w}}(\mathbf{W} - \mathbf{w}) + \frac{1}{2}(\mathbf{W} - \mathbf{w})U_{\mathbf{ww}}(\mathbf{W} - \mathbf{w})^T + \mathcal{O}(\epsilon^4)$$

$$U_{\mathbf{W}} = U_{\mathbf{w}} + U_{\mathbf{ww}}(\mathbf{W} - \mathbf{w}) + \mathcal{O}(\epsilon^4) \tag{A.6}$$

$$U_{\mathbf{WW}} = U_{\mathbf{ww}} + \mathcal{O}(\epsilon^4)$$

We then have that:

$$C = \frac{\epsilon^2}{12}K_{\mathbf{p}}U_{\mathbf{ww}}K_{\mathbf{p}}$$

$$= \frac{\epsilon^2}{12}K_{\mathbf{p}}\left(U_{\mathbf{ww}} + \mathcal{O}(\epsilon^4)\right)K_{\mathbf{p}} \tag{A.7}$$

$$= \frac{\epsilon^2}{12}K_{\mathbf{p}}U_{\mathbf{ww}}K_{\mathbf{p}} + \mathcal{O}(\epsilon^4)$$

Similarly, from the first order Taylor approximation of $U(\mathbf{W})$ at $\mathbf{w}$, it follows that $U_{\mathbf{W}} = U_{\mathbf{w}} + \mathcal{O}(\epsilon^2)$ and noting that $K_{\mathbf{PP}} = K_{\mathbf{pp}}$ as K is quadratic, we have that:

$$D = \frac{\epsilon^2}{24}U_{\mathbf{W}}K_{\mathbf{PP}}U_{\mathbf{W}}$$

$$= \frac{\epsilon^2}{24}\left(U_{\mathbf{w}} + \mathcal{O}(\epsilon^2)\right)K_{\mathbf{pp}}\left(U_{\mathbf{w}} + \mathcal{O}(\epsilon^2)\right) \tag{A.8}$$

$$= \frac{\epsilon^2}{24}U_{\mathbf{w}}K_{\mathbf{pp}}U_{\mathbf{w}} + \mathcal{O}(\epsilon^4)$$

It then follows that:

$$\tilde{H}^{[4]}(\mathcal{X}(\mathbf{w}, \mathbf{p})) = A + B + C + D$$

$$= H(\mathbf{w}, \mathbf{p}) + \epsilon^2\left(\frac{1}{12} - \lambda\right)K_{\mathbf{p}}U_{\mathbf{ww}}K_{\mathbf{p}} + \epsilon^2\left(\lambda - \frac{1}{24}\right)U_{\mathbf{w}}K_{\mathbf{pp}}U_{\mathbf{w}} + \mathcal{O}(\epsilon^4) \tag{A.9}$$

To remove the second term which contains mixed derivatives of $\mathbf{w}$ and $\mathbf{p}$ and noting that $K_{\mathbf{pp}}$ is a constant, we set $\lambda = \frac{1}{12}$ and have that:

$$\tilde{H}^{[4]}(\mathcal{X}(\mathbf{w}, \mathbf{p})) = H(\mathbf{w}, \mathbf{p}) + \frac{\epsilon^2}{24}U_{\mathbf{w}}K_{\mathbf{pp}}U_{\mathbf{w}} + \mathcal{O}(\epsilon^4) \tag{A.10}$$

which is the required separable shadow Hamiltonian which is used in S2HMC.

A.2 S2HMC satisfies detailed balance

Theorem A.2.1. *S2HMC satisfies detailed balance.*

Proof. This proof is taken from Sweet et al. [212] Section III A. To show that S2HMC satisfies detailed balance, we need to show that the processed leapfrog integration scheme is both sympletic and reversible. That is, we need to show that the processing map $(\hat{\mathbf{w}}, \hat{\mathbf{p}}) = \mathcal{X}(\mathbf{w}, \mathbf{p})$ commutes with reversal of momenta and preserves phase space volume so that the resulting processed leapfrog integrator used in S2HMC is both sympletic and reversible and thus ensures detailed balance.

We can get a symplectic map using a generating function of the third kind [129]:

$$S(\mathbf{w}, \hat{\mathbf{p}}) = \mathbf{w}\hat{\mathbf{p}} + \frac{\epsilon}{24}\left[U_{\mathbf{w}}(\mathbf{w} + \epsilon\mathbf{M}^{-1}\hat{\mathbf{p}}) - U_{\mathbf{w}}(\mathbf{w} - \epsilon\mathbf{M}^{-1}\hat{\mathbf{p}})\right] \tag{A.11}$$

The map $(\hat{\mathbf{w}}, \hat{\mathbf{p}}) = \mathcal{X}(\mathbf{w}, \mathbf{p})$ is then given by:

$$\hat{\mathbf{w}} = \frac{\partial S}{\partial \hat{\mathbf{p}}}; \quad \mathbf{p} = \frac{\partial S}{\partial \mathbf{w}}. \tag{A.12}$$

The map $(\hat{\mathbf{w}}, \hat{\mathbf{p}}) = \mathcal{X}(\mathbf{w}, \mathbf{p})$ from Eq. (A.11) is given precisely by Eqs. (1.34). This map is the pre-processing step of S2HMC. In other words, it is the canonical change in variables that preserves the symplectic property of the processed leapfrog algorithm. The inverse mapping $(\mathbf{w}, \mathbf{p}) = \mathcal{X}^{-1}(\hat{\mathbf{w}}, \hat{\mathbf{p}})$ is given by Eq. (1.35). The inverse mapping is the post-processing step of S2HMC. The reversibility of the processed leapfrog algorithm can be shown by $\mathcal{X}(\mathbf{w}, -\mathbf{p}) = \text{diag}(I, -I)\mathcal{X}(\mathbf{w}, \mathbf{p})$. Thus, since the processed leapfrog algorithm is both symplectic and reversible, S2HMC preserves detailed balance. □

A.3 Derivatives from non-canonical Poisson brackets

In this appendix, we present the derivatives derived from the non-canonical Poisson brackets:

$$\begin{aligned}
\{K, U\} &= -\nabla_{\mathbf{p}}K\nabla_{\mathbf{w}}U + \nabla_{\mathbf{w}}K\nabla_{\mathbf{p}}U + \nabla_{\mathbf{p}}K\mathbf{G}\nabla_{\mathbf{p}}U - K_{\mathbf{p}}U_{\mathbf{w}} \\
\{K, \{K, U\}\} &= -K_{\mathbf{p}}U_{\mathbf{ww}}K_{\mathbf{p}} - K_{\mathbf{p}}\mathbf{G}K_{\mathbf{pp}}U_{\mathbf{w}} \\
\{U, K\} &= U_{\mathbf{w}}K_{\mathbf{p}} \\
\{U, \{U, K\}\} &= U_{\mathbf{w}}K_{\mathbf{pp}}U_{\mathbf{w}}
\end{aligned} \tag{A.13}$$

where $\nabla_a f = \frac{\partial f}{\partial a}$ for some function f which is a function of some variable a. Note that the derivatives from the non-canonical Poisson brackets differ from the canonical derivatives through the presence of the magnetic field $\mathbf{G}$. When $\mathbf{G} = \mathbf{0}$, the non-canonical Poisson bracket derivatives collapse to the canonical derivatives.

ARD posterior variances

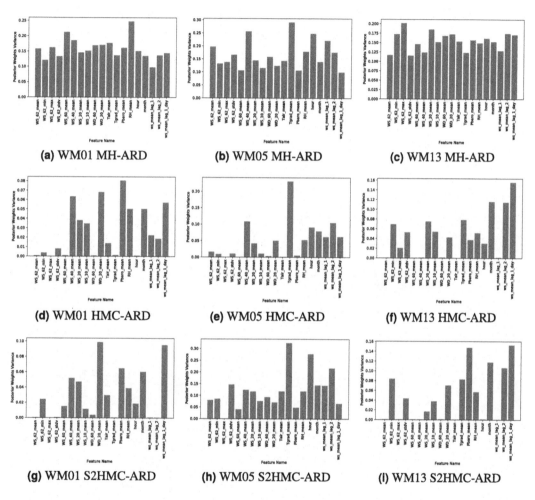

FIGURE B.1 Mean posterior variances from the MH, HMC and S2HMC ARD model which indicate the relevance of each attribute for each of the datasets.

C

ARD committee feature selection

Table C.1 Committee table of ARD feature selections based on the top 5 features from each inference method on the WM01 Alexander Bay dataset.

Feature	MH	HMC	S2HMC	Total votes
WS_62_mean	1			1
WS_62_min				
WS_62_max				
WS_62_stdv				
WS_60_mean	1			1
WS_40_mean	1		1	2
WS_20_mean		1	1	2
WS_10_mean				
WD_60_mean				
WD_20_mean				
Tair_mean				
Tgrad_mean				
Pbaro_mean		1	1	2
RH_mean	1	1		2
hour				
month		1	1	2
ws_mean_lag_1				
ws_mean_lag_2				
ws_mean_lag_1_day		1	1	2

Table C.2   Committee table of ARD feature selections based on the top 5 features from each inference method on the WM05 Napier dataset.

Feature	MH	HMC	S2HMC	Total votes
WS_62_mean	1			1
WS_62_min	1			1
WS_62_max				
WS_62_stdv				
WS_60_mean				
WS_40_mean				
WS_20_mean	1	1	1	3
WS_10_mean				
WD_60_mean				
WD_20_mean				
Tair_mean	1	1	1	3
Tgrad_mean			1	1
Pbaro_mean				
RH_mean	1	1	1	3
hour				
month	1	1	1	3
ws_mean_lag_1	1	1		2
ws_mean_lag_2				
ws_mean_lag_1_day				1

Table C.3   Committee table of ARD feature selections based on the top 5 features from each inference method on the WM13 Jozini dataset.

Feature	MH	HMC	S2HMC	Total votes
WS_62_mean				
WS_62_min	1	1	1	3
WS_62_max	1			
WS_62_stdv				
WS_60_mean				
WS_40_mean				
WS_20_mean	1	1	1	3
WS_10_mean				
WD_60_mean	1			1
WD_20_mean	1			1
Tair_mean				
Tgrad_mean		1	1	2
Pbaro_mean			1	1
RH_mean				
hour				
month		1	1	2
ws_mean_lag_1				
ws_mean_lag_2	1	1	1	3
ws_mean_lag_1_day	1	1	1	3

D

Summary of audit outcome literature survey

In this appendix, we present a summary of the findings from the FSF detection and audit outcomes literature survey that we provide in our article in [158]. This summary uses the themes of the most common: 1) definitions of fraud, 2) features used for detecting fraud, 3) region of the case study, dataset size and imbalance, 4) algorithms used for detection, 5) approach to feature selection / feature engineering, 6) treatment of missing data, and 7) performance measure used in the literature.

Tables D.1 to D.3 provide a summary of some of the aspects of FSF detection as reflected in the 52 papers surveyed in [158], with a visual representation of changes over time. Table D.1 shows three different definitions of FSF and the total number of studies from the survey that have used each definition. In the table, each digit '1' under a time period indicates a study using the given definition of fraud. Similarly, Tables D.2 and D.3 show the data feature type and the most commonly used detection methods, respectively. In Table D.3, the digit '2' is used to indicate two studies using the given method. Note that most studies used multiple methods, so the totals do not correspond to the number of studies for each period. Table D.4 summarises the overall findings from the survey, where the percentages in the brackets show the proportion of studies in the survey that used the particular approach.

Table D.1 FSF definitions used through time. Each digit 1 in the table represents a study that used a given definition of FSF in the time period, where A: Investigation by authorities, Q: Qualified audit opinion, C: Combination of both definitions.

Definition	Total	1995–1999	2000–2004	2005–2009	2010–2014	2015–2018
A	33 (63%)	111	1	111111	111111111111	11111111111
Q	12 (23%)			1111	11111	111
C	7 (13%)	1	1	111	11	
Totals	52	4	2	13	19	14

Table D.2   FSF data features used through time. Each digit 1 in the table represents a study that used a given type of data feature in the time period, where F: financial ratios, F&NF: financial and non-financial ratios, T: text, and F&T: financial variables and text.

Data feature	Total	1995–1999	2000–2004	2005–2009	2010–2014	2015–2018
F	27 (52%)	111	11	1111111111	11111111	1111
F&NF	16 (31%)	1		111	11111111	1111
T	7 (13%)				111	1111
F&T	2 (4%)					11
Totals	52	4	2	13	19	14

Table D.3   The FSF detection methods through time. Each digit 2 in the table represents two studies that used the given detection method in the time period, where LR: logistic regression, ANN: artificial neural network, SVM: support vector machine, DT: decision tree, DA: discriminant analysis, and OTH: other.

Method	Total	1995–1999	2000–2004	2005–2009	2010–2014	2015–2018
LR	24 (18%)	2	2	222	22222	22
ANN	26 (21%)	2		222	22222	2222
SVM	16 (13%)			2	222	2222
DT	14 (12%)			22	222	22
DA	6 (6%)	2		22		
OTH	36 (29%)			22222	2222222222	222
Totals	122	6	2	32	52	30

Table D.4   Summary of findings from the FSF detection literature survey.

Implementation issue	Most common approach in the literature
Fraud definition	Investigations by authorities (63%)
Data features	Financial ratios (52%)
Data imbalance	Match fraud firms with non-fraud firms (71%)
Data region	USA (38%) and Taiwan (13%)
Data size	min (27), mean (2 365), median (190), max (49 039)
Methods used	ANN (21%), logistic regression (18%) and SVM (13%)
Feature selection	Filter based approaches (69%)
Missing data treatment	Not specified or delete records (94%)
Performance measures	Classification accuracy (35%)
Learning approach	Supervised classification (97%)
Best FSF detection method	Varies across datasets

References

[1] M. Abdar, F. Pourpanah, S. Hussain, D. Rezazadegan, L. Liu, M. Ghavamzadeh, P. Fieguth, X. Cao, A. Khosravi, U.R. Acharya, et al., A review of uncertainty quantification in deep learning: techniques, applications and challenges, Information Fusion 76 (2021) 243–297.

[2] E. Abi Jaber, Lifting the Heston model, Quantitative Finance 19 (12) (2019) 1995–2013.

[3] H.M. Afshar, R. Oliveira, S. Cripps, Non-volume preserving Hamiltonian Monte Carlo and no-u-turnsamplers, in: International Conference on Artificial Intelligence and Statistics, PMLR, 2021, pp. 1675–1683.

[4] E. Aguilar, M. Brunet, Seasonal Patterns of Air Surface Temperature and Pressure Change in Different Regions of Antarctica, Springer Berlin Heidelberg, Berlin, Heidelberg, 2001, pp. 215–228.

[5] Y. Aït-Sahalia, C. Li, C.X. Li, Closed-form implied volatility surfaces for stochastic volatility models with jumps, Journal of Econometrics 222 (1) (2021) 364–392.

[6] E. Akhmatskaya, S. Reich, The targeted shadowing hybrid Monte Carlo (tshmc) method, in: New Algorithms for Macromolecular Simulation, Springer-Verlag, 2006, pp. 145–158.

[7] A. Alaa, M. Van Der Schaar, Frequentist uncertainty in recurrent neural networks via blockwise influence functions, in: International Conference on Machine Learning, PMLR, 2020, pp. 175–190.

[8] M. Alghalith, Pricing options under simultaneous stochastic volatility and jumps: a simple closed-form formula without numerical/computational methods, Physica A: Statistical Mechanics and its Applications 540 (2020) 123100.

[9] I. Amara, A.B. Amar, A. Jarboui, Detection of fraud in financial statements: French companies as a case study, International Journal of Academic Research in Accounting, Finance and Management Sciences 3 (3) (2013) 40–51.

[10] T. Andersen, T. Bollerslev, A. Hadi, ARCH and GARCH Models, John Wiley & Sons, 2014.

[11] C. Andrieu, J. Thoms, A tutorial on adaptive mcmc, Statistics and Computing 18 (4) (2008) 343–373.

[12] G. Tollo, A. Roli, A neural network approach for credit risk evaluation, The Quarterly Review of Economics and Finance 48 (4) (2008) 733–755.

[13] C. Arndt, R. Davies, S. Gabriel, L. Harris, K. Makrelov, B. Modise, S. Robinson, W. Simbanegavi, D. Van Seventer, L. Anderson, Impact of Covid-19 on the South African economy, in: Southern Africa-Towards Inclusive Economic Development Working Paper, 2020, p. 111.

[14] Y.F. Atchadé, An adaptive version for the Metropolis adjusted Langevin algorithm with a truncated drift, Methodology and Computing in Applied Probability 8 (2) (2006) 235–254.

[15] Auditor-General South Africa, Background to the three aspects we audit, https://www.agsa.co.za/portals/0/AGSA_Terminology.pdf, 2011. (Accessed 16 August 2020).

[16] Auditor-General South Africa, MFMA 2018–2019, https://www.agsa.co.za/Reporting/MFMAReports/MFMA2018-2019.aspx, 2020. (Accessed 16 August 2020).

[17] C. Badue, R. Guidolini, R.V. Carneiro, P. Azevedo, V.B. Cardoso, A. Forechi, L. Jesus, R. Berriel, T.M. Paixao, F. Mutz, et al., Self-driving cars: a survey, Expert Systems with Applications 165 (2021) 113816.

[18] Y. Bai, L. Yao, T. Wei, F. Tian, D.-Y. Jin, L. Chen, M. Wang, Presumed asymptomatic carrier transmission of Covid-19, Jama 323 (14) (2020) 1406–1407.

[19] N. Bakhvalov, The optimization of methods of solving boundary value problems with a boundary layer, U.S.S.R. Computational Mathematics and Mathematical Physics 9 (4) (1969) 139–166.

[20] V. Barthelmann, E. Novak, K. Ritter, High dimensional polynomial interpolation on sparse grids, Advances in Computational Mathematics 12 (4) (2000) 273–288.

[21] A.G. Baydin, B.A. Pearlmutter, A.A. Radul, J.M. Siskind, Automatic differentiation in machine learning: a survey, Journal of Machine Learning Research 18 (1) (2017) 5595–5637.

[22] Á. Berihuete, M. Sánchez-Sánchez, A. Suárez-Llorens, A Bayesian model of Covid-19 cases based on the Gompertz curve, Mathematics 9 (3) (2021) 228.

[23] M. Betancourt, A general metric for Riemannian manifold Hamiltonian Monte Carlo, in: International Conference on Geometric Science of Information, Springer, 2013, pp. 327–334.

[24] M. Betancourt, Generalizing the no-u-turn sampler to Riemannian manifolds, arXiv preprint arXiv: 1304.1920, 2013.

[25] M. Betancourt, A conceptual introduction to Hamiltonian Monte Carlo, arXiv preprint arXiv:1701. 02434, 2017.

[26] M. Betancourt, M. Girolami, Hamiltonian Monte Carlo for hierarchical models, Current Trends in Bayesian Methodology with Applications 79 (30) (2015) 2–4.

[27] C.M. Bishop, Pattern Recognition and Machine Learning (Information Science and Statistics), Springer-Verlag New York, Inc., Secaucus, NJ, USA, 2006.

[28] F. Black, M. Scholes, The pricing of options and corporate liabilities, Journal of Political Economy 81 (3) (1973) 637–654.

[29] J. Blackwood, L. Childs, An introduction to compartmental modeling for the budding infectious disease modeler, Letters in Biomathematics 5 (1) (2018) 195–221, https://doi.org/10.30707/LiB5. 1Blackwood.

[30] L. Bottou, Stochastic gradient descent tricks, in: Neural Networks: Tricks of the Trade, Springer, 2012, pp. 421–436.

[31] N. Bou-Rabee, A. Eberle, R. Zimmer, et al., Coupling and convergence for Hamiltonian Monte Carlo, The Annals of Applied Probability 30 (3) (2020) 1209–1250.

[32] I. Boulkaibet, L. Mthembu, T. Marwala, M. Friswell, S. Adhikari, Finite element model updating using the shadow hybrid Monte Carlo technique, Mechanical Systems and Signal Processing 52–53 (2015) 115–132.

[33] S.L. Boumediene, Detection and prediction of managerial fraud in the financial statements of Tunisian banks, Accounting & Taxation 6 (2) (2014) 1–10.

[34] A.P. Bradley, The use of the area under the ROC curve in the evaluation of machine learning algorithms, Pattern Recognition 30 (7) (1997) 1145–1159.

[35] F. Brauer, Compartmental models in epidemiology, in: Mathematical Epidemiology, Springer, 2008, pp. 19–79.

[36] F.-X. Briol, C.J. Oates, M. Girolami, M.A. Osborne, Frank-Wolfe Bayesian quadrature: probabilistic integration with theoretical guarantees, arXiv preprint arXiv:1506.02681, 2015.

[37] J.A. Brofos, R.R. Lederman, Magnetic manifold Hamiltonian Monte Carlo, arXiv preprint arXiv:2010. 07753, 2020.

[38] J.A. Brofos, R.R. Lederman, Non-canonical Hamiltonian Monte Carlo, arXiv preprint arXiv:2008. 08191, 2020.

[39] S. Brooks, A. Gelman, G. Jones, X.-L. Meng, Handbook of Markov Chain Monte Carlo, CRC Press, 2011.

[40] A. Buchholz, N. Chopin, P.E. Jacob, Adaptive tuning of Hamiltonian Monte Carlo within sequential Monte Carlo, Bayesian Analysis 1 (1) (2021) 1–27.

[41] H.-J. Bungartz, M. Griebel, Sparse grids, Acta Numerica 13 (2004) 147–269.

[42] C.M. Campos, J.M. Sanz-Serna, Extra chance generalized hybrid Monte Carlo, Journal of Computational Physics 281 (2015) 365–374.

[43] B. Carpenter, A. Gelman, M.D. Hoffman, D. Lee, B. Goodrich, M. Betancourt, M.A. Brubaker, J. Guo, P. Li, A. Riddell, Stan: a probabilistic programming language, Grantee Submission 76 (1) (2017) 1–32.

[44] G. Chandrashekar, F. Sahin, A survey on feature selection methods, Computers & Electrical Engineering 40 (1) (2014) 16–28.

[45] K.-C. Chen, Noncanonical Poisson brackets for elastic and micromorphic solids, International Journal of Solids and Structures 44 (24) (2007) 7715–7730.

[46] Q. Chen, K.A. Folly, Comparison of three methods for short-term wind power forecasting, in: 2018 International Joint Conference on Neural Networks (IJCNN), 2018, pp. 1–8.

[47] S. Chen, Detection of fraudulent financial statements using the hybrid data mining approach, SpringerPlus 5 (1) (2016) 1–16.

[48] T. Chen, E. Fox, C. Guestrin, Stochastic gradient Hamiltonian Monte Carlo, in: International Conference on Machine Learning, 2014, pp. 1683–1691.

[49] Y.-J. Chen, On fraud detection method for narrative annual reports, in: The Fourth International Conference on Informatics & Applications (ICIA2015), 2015, pp. 121–129.

[50] A.D. Cobb, A.G. Baydin, A. Markham, S.J. Roberts, Introducing an explicit symplectic integration scheme for Riemannian manifold Hamiltonian Monte Carlo, arXiv preprint arXiv:1910.06243, 2019.

[51] R. Cont, Empirical properties of asset returns: stylized facts and statistical issues, Quantitative Finance 1 (2001) 223–236.

[52] J. Cotterill, Steinhoff shareholders sue Deloitte for damages, https://www.ft.com/content/4f4d591a-6f0f-11e8-92d3-6c13e5c92914, 2018. (Accessed 15 November 2019).

[53] J. Cronje, Steinhoff's market cap a mere R20bn as shares drop another 30%, https://www.fin24.com/Companies/Retail/steinhoff-shares-drop-by-a-fifth-in-early-trade-20171220, 2017. (Accessed 15 November 2019).

[54] J. Dahlin, F. Lindsten, T.B. Schön, Particle Metropolis–Hastings using gradient and Hessian information, Statistics and Computing 25 (1) (2015) 81–92.

[55] L.O. Daniel, C. Sigauke, C. Chibaya, R. Mbuvha, Short-term wind speed forecasting using statistical and machine learning methods, Algorithms 13 (6) (2020) 132.

[56] C. de Villiers, D. Cerbone, W. Van Zijl, The South African government's response to Covid-19, Journal of Public Budgeting, Accounting & Financial Management (2020).

[57] J. Dehning, J. Zierenberg, F.P. Spitzner, M. Wibral, J.P. Neto, M. Wilczek, V. Priesemann, Inferring change points in the spread of Covid-19 reveals the effectiveness of interventions, Science 369 (6500) (2020).

[58] P.L. Delamater, E.J. Street, T.F. Leslie, Y.T. Yang, K.H. Jacobsen, Complexity of the basic reproduction number (r0), Emerging Infectious Diseases 25 (1) (2019) 1.

[59] E. Dong, H. Du, L. Gardner, An interactive web-based dashboard to track Covid-19 in real time, Lancet. Infectious Diseases 20 (5) (2020) 533–534.

[60] S. Duane, A.D. Kennedy, B.J. Pendleton, D. Roweth, Hybrid Monte Carlo, Physics Letters B 195 (2) (1987) 216–222.

[61] S. Duane, J.B. Kogut, The theory of hybrid stochastic algorithms, Nuclear Physics B 275 (3) (1986) 398–420.

[62] M.W. Dusenberry, D. Tran, E. Choi, J. Kemp, J. Nixon, G. Jerfel, K. Heller, A.M. Dai, Analyzing the role of model uncertainty for electronic health records, in: Proceedings of the ACM Conference on Health, Inference, and Learning, 2020, pp. 204–213.

[63] B. Ernst, B. Oakleaf, M.L. Ahlstrom, M. Lange, C. Moehrlen, B. Lange, U. Focken, K. Rohrig, Predicting the wind, IEEE Power and Energy Magazine 5 (6) (2007) 78–89.

[64] A. Eseye, J. Zhang, D. Zheng, D. Shiferaw, Short-term wind power forecasting using artificial neural networks for resource scheduling in microgrids, International Journal of Science and Engineering Applications 5 (2016) 144–151.

[65] A.T. Eseye, J. Zhang, D. Zheng, H. Ma, G. Jingfu, A double-stage hierarchical anfis model for short-term wind power prediction, in: 2017 IEEE 2nd International Conference on Big Data Analysis (ICBDA), 2017, pp. 546–551.

[66] A. Esteva, K. Chou, S. Yeung, N. Naik, A. Madani, A. Mottaghi, Y. Liu, E. Topol, J. Dean, R. Socher, Deep learning-enabled medical computer vision, npj Digital Medicine 4 (1) (2021) 1–9.

[67] K.M. Fanning, K.O. Cogger, Neural network detection of management fraud using published financial data, International Journal of Intelligent Systems in Accounting, Finance & Management 7 (1) (1998) 21–41.

[68] N.M. Ferguson, D. Laydon, G. Nedjati-Gilani, et al., Impact of non-pharmaceutical interventions (NPIs) to reduce COVID-19 mortality and healthcare demand, Imperial College London, London, March 16, 2020, Available online: https://www.imperial.ac.uk/media/imperial-college/medicine/sph/ide/gida-fellowships/Imperial-College-COVID19-NPI-modelling-16-03-2020.pdf.

[69] M.A. Fernández-Gámez, F. García-Lagos, J.R. Sánchez-Serrano, Integrating corporate governance and financial variables for the identification of qualified audit opinions with neural networks, Neural Computing and Applications 27 (5) (2015) 1427–1444.

[70] G.S. Fishman, B.D. Huang, Antithetic variates revisited, Communications of the ACM 26 (11) (1983) 964–971.

[71] A. Frigessi, J. Gasemyr, H. Rue, Antithetic coupling of two gibbs sampler chains, The Annals of Statistics (2000) 1128–1149.

[72] L. Fugon, J. Juban, G. Kariniotakis, Data mining for wind power forecasting, in: European Wind Energy Conference & Exhibition EWEC 2008. EWEC, 2008.

[73] C. Gaganis, Classification techniques for the identification of falsified financial statements: a comparative analysis, Intelligent Systems in Accounting, Finance & Management 16 (3) (2009) 207–229.

[74] Y. Gal, Uncertainty in Deep Learning, PhD thesis, University of Cambridge, 2016.

[75] Y. Gal, Z. Ghahramani, Dropout as a Bayesian approximation: representing model uncertainty in deep learning, in: International Conference on Machine Learning, PMLR, 2016, pp. 1050–1059.

[76] Y. Garcia-Chimeno, B. Garcia-Zapirain, M. Gomez-Beldarrain, B. Fernandez-Ruanova, J.C. Garcia-Monco, Automatic migraine classification via feature selection committee and machine learning techniques over imaging and questionnaire data, BMC Medical Informatics and Decision Making 17 (1) (2017) 38.

[77] A. Gelman, D.B. Rubin, Inference from iterative simulation using multiple sequences, Statistical Science 7 (4) (1992) 457–472.

[78] S. Ghosh, P. Birrell, D. De Angelis, Variational inference for nonlinear ordinary differential equations, in: International Conference on Artificial Intelligence and Statistics, PMLR, 2021, pp. 2719–2727.

[79] M. Girolami, B. Calderhead, Riemann manifold Langevin and Hamiltonian Monte Carlo methods, Journal of the Royal Statistical Society, Series B, Statistical Methodology 73 (2) (2011) 123–214.

[80] F.H. Glancy, S.B. Yadav, A computational model for financial reporting fraud detection, Decision Support Systems 50 (3) (2011) 595–601.

[81] P.W. Glynn, C.-h. Rhee, Exact estimation for Markov chain equilibrium expectations, Journal of Applied Probability 51 (A) (2014) 377–389.

[82] Google Finance, Google finance, https://www.google.com/finance/, 2021. (Accessed 15 August 2021).

[83] M. Graham, A. Storkey, Continuously tempered Hamiltonian Monte Carlo, in: Conference on Uncertainty in Artificial Intelligence, 2017.

[84] Z. Grundiene, The model of fraud detection in financial statements by means of financial ratios, Procedia – Social and Behavioral Sciences 213 (2015) 321–327.

[85] M. Gu, S. Sun, Neural Langevin dynamical sampling, IEEE Access 8 (2020) 31595–31605.

[86] T. Gunter, M.A. Osborne, R. Garnett, P. Hennig, S.J. Roberts, Sampling for inference in probabilistic models with fast Bayesian quadrature, in: Advances in Neural Information Processing Systems, 2014, pp. 2789–2797.

[87] R. Gupta, N.S. Gill, Financial statement fraud detection using text mining, International Journal of Advanced Computer Science and Applications 3 (12) (2012).

[88] H. Haario, E. Saksman, J. Tamminen, Adaptive proposal distribution for random walk Metropolis algorithm, Computational Statistics 14 (3) (1999) 375–395.

[89] A.N. Hahmann, C. Lennard, J. Badger, C.L. Vincent, M.C. Kelly, P.J. Volker, B. Argent, J. Refslund, Mesoscale modeling for the wind atlas of South Africa (wasa) project, DTU Wind Energy 50 (2014) 80.

[90] E. Hairer, Backward error analysis for multistep methods, Numerische Mathematik 84 (2) (1999) 199–232.

[91] E. Hairer, M. Hochbruck, A. Iserles, C. Lubich, Geometric numerical integration, Oberwolfach Reports 3 (1) (2006) 805–882.

[92] S. Hamori, M. Kawai, T. Kume, Y. Murakami, C. Watanabe, Ensemble learning or deep learning? Application to default risk analysis, Journal of Risk and Financial Management 11 (1) (2018) 12.

[93] L. Harmes, South Africa's Gini Coefficient: Causes, Consequences and Possible Responses, Gordon Institute of Business Sciences, Pretoria, 2013.

[94] T. Hastie, R. Tibshirani, J. Friedman, The Elements of Statistical Learning, Springer Series in Statistics, Springer New York Inc., New York, NY, USA, 2001.

[95] W.K. Hastings, Monte Carlo sampling methods using Markov chains and their applications, Biometrica 57 (1) (1970) 97–109.

[96] M. Haugh, Mcmc and Bayesian modeling, http://www.columbia.edu/~mh2078/MachineLearningORFE/MCMC_Bayes.pdf, 2017. (Accessed 15 September 2021).

[97] P.M. Healy, K.G. Palepu, The fall of Enron, The Journal of Economic Perspectives 17 (2) (2003) 3–26.

[98] C. Heide, F. Roosta, L. Hodgkinson, D. Kroese, Shadow manifold Hamiltonian Monte Carlo, in: International Conference on Artificial Intelligence and Statistics, PMLR, 2021, pp. 1477–1485.

[99] J. Heng, P.E. Jacob, Unbiased Hamiltonian Monte Carlo with couplings, Biometrika 106 (2) (2019) 287–302.

[100] S.L. Heston, A closed-form solution for options with stochastic volatility with applications to bond and currency options, The Review of Financial Studies 6 (2) (1993) 327–343.

[101] G.E. Hinton, D. Van Camp, Keeping the neural networks simple by minimizing the description length of the weights, in: Proceedings of the Sixth Annual Conference on Computational Learning Theory, ACM, 1993, pp. 5–13.

[102] M. Hoffman, A. Radul, P. Sountsov, An adaptive-mcmc scheme for setting trajectory lengths in Hamiltonian Monte Carlo, in: International Conference on Artificial Intelligence and Statistics, PMLR, 2021, pp. 3907–3915.

[103] M.D. Hoffman, D.M. Blei, C. Wang, J. Paisley, Stochastic variational inference, Journal of Machine Learning Research 14 (5) (2013).

[104] M.D. Hoffman, A. Gelman, The No-U-Turn sampler: adaptively setting path lengths in Hamiltonian Monte Carlo, Journal of Machine Learning Research 15 (1) (2014) 1593–1623.

[105] M.D. Hoffman, A. Gelman, The no-u-turn sampler: adaptively setting path lengths in Hamiltonian Monte Carlo, Journal of Machine Learning Research 15 (1) (2014) 1593–1623.

[106] A. Horowitz, Stochastic quantization in phase space, Physics Letters B 156 (1–2) (1985) 89–92.

[107] A.M. Horowitz, A generalized guided Monte Carlo algorithm, Physics Letters B 268 (2) (1991) 247–252.

[108] S.L. Humpherys, K.C. Moffitt, M.B. Burns, J.K. Burgoon, W.F. Felix, Identification of fraudulent financial statements using linguistic credibility analysis, Decision Support Systems 50 (3) (2011) 585–594.

[109] A.R. Ives, C. Bozzuto, Estimating and explaining the spread of Covid-19 at the county level in the USA, Communications Biology 4 (1) (2021) 1–9.

[110] J.A. Izaguirre, S.S. Hampton, Shadow hybrid Monte Carlo: an efficient propagator in phase space of macromolecules, Journal of Computational Physics 200 (2) (2004) 581–604.

[111] P.E. Jacob, J. O'Leary, Y.F. Atchadé, Unbiased Markov chain Monte Carlo with couplings, arXiv preprint arXiv:1708.03625, 2017.

[112] L.P. James, J.A. Salomon, C.O. Buckee, N.A. Menzies, The use and misuse of mathematical modeling for infectious disease policymaking: lessons for the Covid-19 pandemic, Medical Decision Making 41 (4) (2021) 379–385.

[113] V.E. Johnson, Studying convergence of Markov chain Monte Carlo algorithms using coupled sample paths, Journal of the American Statistical Association 91 (433) (1996) 154–166.

[114] V.E. Johnson, A coupling-regeneration scheme for diagnosing convergence in Markov chain Monte Carlo algorithms, Journal of the American Statistical Association 93 (441) (1998) 238–248.

[115] J.H. Jones, Notes on r0, California: Department of Anthropological Sciences 323 (2007) 1–19.

[116] T.R. Kiehl, B.K. Hoogs, C.A. LaComb, D. Senturk, Evolving multi-variate time-series patterns for the discrimination of fraudulent financial filings, in: Proc. of Genetic and Evolutionary Computation Conference, Citeseer, 2005.

[117] A.W. Kim, T. Nyengerai, E. Mendenhall, Evaluating the mental health impacts of the Covid-19 pandemic: perceived risk of Covid-19 infection and childhood trauma predict adult depressive symptoms in urban South Africa, Psychological Medicine (2020) 1–13.

[118] E. Kirkos, C. Spathis, Y. Manolopoulos, Data mining techniques for the detection of fraudulent financial statements, Expert Systems with Applications 32 (4) (2007) 995–1003.

[119] L. Kish, Survey sampling. HN29, K5, Tech. Rep. 4, Wiley, New York, NY, USA, 1965.

[120] A. Klimke, B. Wohlmuth, Algorithm 847: spinterp: piecewise multilinear hierarchical sparse grid interpolation in Matlab, ACM Transactions on Mathematical Software 31 (4) (2005) 561–579.

[121] S. Kotsiantis, E. Koumanakos, D. Tzelepis, V. Tampakas, Financial application of neural networks: two case studies in Greece, in: Artificial Neural Networks – ICANN 2006, Springer, Berlin Heidelberg, 2006, pp. 672–681.

[122] S.G. Kou, Jump-diffusion models for asset pricing in financial engineering, Handbooks in Operations Research and Management Science 15 (2007) 73–116.

[123] A.S. Kwekha-Rashid, H.N. Abduljabbar, B. Alhayani, Coronavirus disease (Covid-19) cases analysis using machine-learning applications, Applied Nanoscience (2021) 1–13.

[124] B. Lakshminarayanan, A. Pritzel, C. Blundell, Simple and scalable predictive uncertainty estimation using deep ensembles, in: Advances in Neural Information Processing Systems, 2017, pp. 6405–6416.

[125] Y. LeCun, Y. Bengio, G. Hinton, Deep learning, Nature 521 (7553) (2015) 436–444.

[126] D. Levy, M.D. Hoffman, J. Sohl-Dickstein, Generalizing Hamiltonian Monte Carlo with neural networks, arXiv preprint arXiv:1711.09268, 2017.

[127] J.W. Lin, M.I. Hwang, J.D. Becker, A fuzzy neural network for assessing the risk of fraudulent financial reporting, Managerial Auditing Journal 18 (8) (2003) 657–665.

[128] Z. Liu, Z. Zhang, Quantum-inspired Hamiltonian Monte Carlo for Bayesian sampling, arXiv preprint arXiv:1912.01937, 2019.

[129] M. López-Marcos, J. Sanz-Serna, R.D. Skeel, Explicit symplectic integrators using Hessian–vector products, SIAM Journal on Scientific Computing 18 (1) (1997) 223–238.

[130] J. Lourenco, R. Paton, M. Ghafari, M. Kraemer, C. Thompson, P. Simmonds, P. Klenerman, S. Gupta, Fundamental principles of epidemic spread highlight the immediate need for large-scale serological surveys to assess the stage of the Sars-cov-2 epidemic, MedRxiv (2020).

[131] Y. Lu, Y. Fan, J. Lv, W.S. Noble, Deeppink: reproducible feature selection in deep neural networks, in: Advances in Neural Information Processing Systems, 2018, pp. 8676–8686.

[132] J. Ma, V. Rokhlin, S. Wandzura, Generalized Gaussian quadrature rules for systems of arbitrary functions, SIAM Journal on Numerical Analysis 33 (3) (1996) 971–996.

[133] D.J. MacKay, Bayesian interpolation, Neural Computation 4 (3) (1992) 415–447.

[134] D.J. MacKay, A practical Bayesian framework for backpropagation networks, Neural Computation 4 (3) (1992) 448–472.

[135] D.J. MacKay, Probable networks and plausible predictions—a review of practical Bayesian methods for supervised neural networks, Network Computation in Neural Systems 6 (3) (1995) 469–505.

[136] A.M. Makarieva, V.G. Gorshkov, D. Sheil, A.D. Nobre, B.-L. Li, Where do winds come from? A new theory on how water vapor condensation influences atmospheric pressure and dynamics, Atmospheric Chemistry and Physics 13 (2) (2013) 1039–1056.

[137] B.B. Mandelbrot, The variation of certain speculative prices, in: Fractals and Scaling in Finance, Springer, 1997, pp. 371–418.

[138] T. Marwala, Economic Modeling Using Artificial Intelligence Methods, Springer-Verlag, London, 2013.

[139] T. Marwala, Flexibly-bounded rationality and marginalization of irrationality theories for decision making, arXiv preprint arXiv:1306.2025, 2013.

[140] R. Mbuvha, Bayesian neural networks for short term wind power forecasting, Master's thesis, KTH, School of Computer Science and Communication (CSC), 2017.

[141] R. Mbuvha, I. Boulkaibet, T. Marwala, Bayesian automatic relevance determination for feature selection in credit default modelling, in: International Conference on Artificial Neural Networks, Springer, 2019, pp. 420–425.

[142] R. Mbuvha, I. Boulkaibet, T. Marwala, F.B. de Lima Neto, A hybrid ga-pso adaptive neuro-fuzzy inference system for short-term wind power prediction, in: International Conference on Swarm Intelligence, Springer, 2018, pp. 498–506.

[143] R. Mbuvha, M. Jonsson, N. Ehn, P. Herman, Bayesian neural networks for one-hour ahead wind power forecasting, in: 2017 IEEE 6th International Conference on Renewable Energy Research and Applications (ICRERA), IEEE, 2017, pp. 591–596.

[144] R. Mbuvha, T. Marwala, Bayesian inference of Covid-19 spreading rates in South Africa, PLoS ONE 15 (8) (2020) e0237126.

[145] R. Mbuvha, W.T. Mongwe, T. Marwala, Separable shadow Hamiltonian hybrid Monte Carlo for Bayesian neural network inference in wind speed forecasting, Energy and AI (2021) 100108.

[146] F. Mehrdoust, A.R. Najafi, S. Fallah, O. Samimi, Mixed fractional Heston model and the pricing of American options, Journal of Computational and Applied Mathematics 330 (2018) 141–154.

[147] C. Merow, M.C. Urban, Seasonality and uncertainty in global Covid-19 growth rates, Proceedings of the National Academy of Sciences 117 (44) (2020) 27456–27464.

[148] U.K. Mertens, A. Voss, S. Radev, Abrox—a user-friendly python module for approximate Bayesian computation with a focus on model comparison, PLoS ONE 13 (3) (2018).

[149] R.C. Merton, Option pricing when underlying stock returns are discontinuous, Journal of Financial Economics 3 (1–2) (1976) 125–144.

[150] D. Michie, D.J. Spiegelhalter, C.C. Taylor, J. Campbell (Eds.), Machine Learning, Neural and Statistical Classification, Ellis, Horwood, USA, 1995.

[151] P.R. Miles, Pymcmcstat: a python package for Bayesian inference using delayed rejection adaptive Metropolis, Journal of Open Source Software 4 (38) (2019) 1417.

[152] A. Mobiny, P. Yuan, S.K. Moulik, N. Garg, C.C. Wu, H. Van Nguyen, Dropconnect is effective in modeling uncertainty of Bayesian deep networks, Scientific Reports 11 (1) (2021) 1–14.

[153] S.O. Moepya, S.S. Akhoury, F.V. Nelwamondo, Applying cost-sensitive classification for financial fraud detection under high class-imbalance, in: 2014 IEEE International Conference on Data Mining Workshop, IEEE, 2014, pp. 183–192.

[154] S.O. Moepya, S.S. Akhoury, F.V. Nelwamondo, B. Twala, The role of imputation in detecting fraudulent financial reporting, International Journal of Innovative Computing, Information and Control 12 (1) (2016) 333–356.

[155] W.T. Mongwe, Analysis of equity and interest rate returns in South Africa under the context of jump diffusion processes, Masters Thesis, University of Cape Town, 2015, Last accessed: 18 March 2021.

[156] W.T. Mongwe, Hybrid Monte Carlo methods in machine learning: stochastic volatility methods, shadow Hamiltonians, adaptive approaches and variance reduction techniques, PhD Thesis, 2022, Available: https://hdl.handle.net/10210/500098.

[157] W.T. Mongwe, K.M. Malan, The efficacy of financial ratios for fraud detection using self organising maps, in: 2020 IEEE Symposium Series on Computational Intelligence (SSCI), IEEE, 2020, pp. 1100–1106.

[158] W.T. Mongwe, K.M. Malan, A survey of automated financial statement fraud detection with relevance to the South African context, South African Computer Journal 32 (1) (2020).

[159] W.T. Mongwe, R. Mbuvha, T. Marwala, Adaptive magnetic Hamiltonian Monte Carlo, IEEE Access 9 (2021) 152993–153003.

[160] W.T. Mongwe, R. Mbuvha, T. Marwala, Adaptively setting the path length for separable shadow Hamiltonian hybrid Monte Carlo, IEEE Access 9 (2021) 138598–138607.

[161] W.T. Mongwe, R. Mbuvha, T. Marwala, Antithetic magnetic and shadow Hamiltonian Monte Carlo, IEEE Access 9 (2021) 49857–49867.

[162] W.T. Mongwe, R. Mbuvha, T. Marwala, Antithetic Riemannian manifold and quantum-inspired Hamiltonian Monte Carlo, arXiv preprint arXiv:2107.02070, 2021.

[163] W.T. Mongwe, R. Mbuvha, T. Marwala, Bayesian inference of local government audit outcomes, PLoS ONE (2021), https://10.1371/journal.pone.0261245.

[164] W.T. Mongwe, R. Mbuvha, T. Marwala, Locally scaled and stochastic volatility Metropolis-Hastings algorithms, Algorithms 14 (12) (2021).

[165] W.T. Mongwe, R. Mbuvha, T. Marwala, Magnetic Hamiltonian Monte Carlo with partial momentum refreshment, IEEE Access 9 (2021) 108009–108016.

[166] W.T. Mongwe, R. Mbuvha, T. Marwala, Quantum-inspired magnetic Hamiltonian Monte Carlo, PLoS ONE 16 (10) (2021) e0258277.

[167] W.T. Mongwe, R. Mbuvha, T. Marwala, Utilising partial momentum refreshment in separable shadow Hamiltonian hybrid Monte Carlo, IEEE Access 9 (2021) 151235–151244.

[168] W.T. Mongwe, R. Mbuvha, T. Marwala, Shadow magnetic Hamiltonian Monte Carlo, IEEE Access 10 (2022) 34340–34351, https://doi.org/10.1109/ACCESS.2022.3161443.

[169] W.T. Mongwe, T. Sidogi, R. Mbuvha, T. Marwala, Probabilistic inference of South African equity option prices under jump-diffusion processes, in: 2022 IEEE Symposium on Computational Intelligence for Financial Engineering and Economics (CIFEr), 2022, pp. 1–8.

[170] National Treasury Republic Of South Africa, MFMA circular no. 71, http://mfma.treasury.gov.za/Circulars/Pages/Circular71.aspx, 2014. (Accessed 16 August 2020).

[171] National Treasury Republic Of South Africa, Municipal finance data, https://municipaldata.treasury.gov.za/, 2019. (Accessed 16 August 2020).

[172] R.M. Neal, Bayesian learning via stochastic dynamics, in: Advances in Neural Information Processing Systems 5, Morgan Kaufmann Publishers Inc., San Francisco, CA, USA, 1993, pp. 475–482.

[173] R.M. Neal, Probabilistic inference using Markov chain Monte Carlo methods, Technical Report CRG-TR-93-1, University of Toronto, Department of Computer Science, 1993.

[174] R.M. Neal, Slice sampling, The Annals of Statistics 31 (3) (2003) 705–767.

[175] R.M. Neal, Bayesian Learning for Neural Networks, vol. 118, Springer Science & Business Media, 2012.

[176] R.M. Neal, Circularly-coupled Markov chain sampling, arXiv preprint arXiv:1711.04399, 2017.

[177] R.M. Neal, Non-reversibly updating a uniform [0, 1] value for Metropolis accept/reject decisions, arXiv preprint arXiv:2001.11950, 2020.

[178] R.M. Neal, et al., Mcmc using Hamiltonian dynamics, Handbook of Markov Chain Monte Carlo 2 (11) (2011) 2.

[179] S. Nguse, D. Wassenaar, Mental health and Covid-19 in South Africa, South African Journal of Psychology (2021), 00812463211001543.

[180] S.H. Nia, Financial ratios between fraudulent and non-fraudulent firms: evidence from Tehran stock exchange, Journal of Accounting and Taxation 7 (3) (2015) 38–44.

[181] J. O'Donnel, Who's to blame for wirecard? Germany passes the buck, https://www.reuters.com/article/us-wirecard-accounts-responsibility/whos-to-blame-for-wirecard-germany-passes-the-buck-idUSKBN24320O, 2020. (Accessed 18 August 2020).

[182] P. Omid, N. pour Hossein, A. Zeinab, Identifying qualified audit opinions by artificial neural networks, African Journal of Business Management 6 (44) (2012) 11077–11087.

[183] M. Osborne, R. Garnett, Z. Ghahramani, D.K. Duvenaud, S.J. Roberts, C.E. Rasmussen, Active learning of model evidence using Bayesian quadrature, in: Advances in Neural Information Processing Systems, 2012, pp. 46–54.

[184] P.D. O'Neill, G.O. Roberts, Bayesian inference for partially observed stochastic epidemics, Journal of the Royal Statistical Society. Series A. Statistics in Society 162 (1) (1999) 121–129.

[185] A.Ç. Pehlivanlı, B. Aşıkgil, G. Gülay, Indicator selection with committee decision of filter methods for stock market price trend in ise, Applied Soft Computing 49 (2016) 792–800.

[186] J. Perols, Financial statement fraud detection: an analysis of statistical and machine learning algorithms, Auditing: A Journal of Practice & Theory 30 (2) (2011) 19–50.

[187] J.L. Perols, B.A. Lougee, The relation between earnings management and financial statement fraud, Advances in Accounting 27 (1) (2011) 39–53.

[188] O.S. Persons, Using financial statement data to identify factors associated with fraudulent financial reporting, Journal of Applied Business Research (JABR) 11 (3) (2011) 38.

[189] D. Piponi, M.D. Hoffman, P. Sountsov, Hamiltonian Monte Carlo swindles, in: Proceedings of the Twenty Third International Conference on Artificial Intelligence and Statistics, 2020.

[190] C.W. Potter, M. Negnevitsky, Very short-term wind forecasting for Tasmanian power generation, IEEE Transactions on Power Systems 21 (2) (2006) 965–972.

[191] S.J. Press, A compound events model for security prices, Journal of Business 40 (3) (1967) 317–335.

[192] T. Radivojević, E. Akhmatskaya, Mix & match Hamiltonian Monte Carlo, arXiv preprint arXiv:1706.04032, 2017.

[193] Q.I. Rahman, G. Schmeisser, Characterization of the speed of convergence of the trapezoidal rule, Numerische Mathematik 57 (1) (1990) 123–138.

[194] E. Raimúndez, E. Dudkin, J. Vanhoefer, E. Alamoudi, S. Merkt, L. Fuhrmann, F. Bai, J. Hasenauer, Covid-19 outbreak in Wuhan demonstrates the limitations of publicly available case numbers for epidemiological modeling, Epidemics 34 (2021) 100439.

[195] T.V.N. Rao, A. Gaddam, M. Kurni, K. Saritha, Reliance on artificial intelligence machine learning and deep learning in the era of industry 4. 0., Smart Healthcare System Design: Security and Privacy Aspects (2021) 281.

[196] S. Ravuri, K. Lenc, M. Willson, D. Kangin, R. Lam, P. Mirowski, M. Fitzsimons, M. Athanassiadou, S. Kashem, S. Madge, R. Prudden, A. Mandhane, A. Clark, A. Brock, K. Simonyan, R. Hadsell, N. Robinson, E. Clancy, A. Arribas, S. Mohamed, Skilful precipitation nowcasting using deep generative models of radar, Nature 597 (7878) (2021) 672–677.

[197] C. Robert, G. Casella, A Short History of MCMC: Subjective Recollections from Incomplete Data, Chapman and Hall/CRC, 2011.

[198] G.O. Roberts, J.S. Rosenthal, et al., Optimal scaling for various Metropolis-Hastings algorithms, Statistical Science 16 (4) (2001) 351–367.

[199] G.O. Roberts, O. Stramer, Langevin diffusions and Metropolis-Hastings algorithms, Methodology and Computing in Applied Probability 4 (4) (2002) 337–357.

[200] L.C.G. Rogers, Arbitrage with fractional Brownian motion, Mathematical Finance 7 (1) (1997) 95–105.

[201] J.S. Rosenthal, Faithful couplings of Markov chains: now equals forever, Advances in Applied Mathematics 18 (3) (1997) 372–381.

[202] V. Roy, Convergence diagnostics for Markov chain Monte Carlo, Annual Review of Statistics and Its Application 7 (2020) 387–412.

[203] F. Ruiz, M. Titsias, A contrastive divergence for combining variational inference and mcmc, in: International Conference on Machine Learning, PMLR, 2019, pp. 5537–5545.

[204] C. Safta, J. Ray, K. Sargsyan, Characterization of partially observed epidemics through Bayesian inference: application to Covid-19, Computational Mechanics 66 (5) (2020) 1109–1129.

[205] T. Salimans, D. Kingma, M. Welling, Markov chain Monte Carlo and variational inference: bridging the gap, in: International Conference on Machine Learning, PMLR, 2015, pp. 1218–1226.

[206] S. Sibisi, Regularization and Inverse Problems, Springer Netherlands, Dordrecht, 1989, pp. 389–396.

[207] G. Sideratos, N. Hatziargyriou, Using radial basis neural networks to estimate wind power production, in: 2007 IEEE Power Engineering Society General Meeting, 2007, pp. 1–7.

[208] S. Silal, J. Pulliam, G. Meyer-Rath, B. Nichols, L. Jamieson, Z. Kimmie, H. Moultrie, Estimating cases for COVID-19 in South Africa Long-term national projections, Retrieved from https:// www.heroza.org/publications/estimating-cases-for-covid-19-in-southafrica-long-term-national-projections-report-update-6-may-2020/, 2020.

[209] R.D. Skeel, D.J. Hardy, Practical construction of modified Hamiltonians, SIAM Journal on Scientific Computing 23 (4) (2001) 1172–1188.

[210] J. Sohl-Dickstein, M. Mudigonda, M. DeWeese, Hamiltonian Monte Carlo without detailed balance, in: International Conference on Machine Learning, PMLR, 2014, pp. 719–726.

[211] X.-P. Song, Z.-H. Hu, J.-G. Du, Z.-H. Sheng, Application of machine learning methods to risk assessment of financial statement fraud: evidence from China, Journal of Forecasting 33 (8) (2014) 611–626.

[212] C.R. Sweet, S.S. Hampton, R.D. Skeel, J.A. Izaguirre, A separable shadow Hamiltonian hybrid Monte Carlo method, Journal of Chemical Physics 131 (17) (2009) 174106.

[213] N. Tripuraneni, M. Rowland, Z. Ghahramani, R. Turner, Magnetic Hamiltonian Monte Carlo, in: International Conference on Machine Learning, PMLR, 2017, pp. 3453–3461.

[214] R.-H. Tsaih, W.-Y. Lin, S.-Y. Huang, Exploring fraudulent financial reporting with GHSOM, in: Intelligence and Security Informatics, Springer, Berlin Heidelberg, 2009, pp. 31–41.

[215] UNFCCC, Historic Paris agreement on climate change, United Nations Framework Convention on Climate Change (UNFCCC) (2015).

[216] A.W. Van der Stoep, L.A. Grzelak, C.W. Oosterlee, The Heston stochastic-local volatility model: efficient Monte Carlo simulation, International Journal of Theoretical and Applied Finance 17 (07) (2014) 1450045.

[217] K. Vanslette, A. Al Alsheikh, K. Youcef-Toumi, Why simple quadrature is just as good as Monte Carlo, Monte Carlo Methods and Applications 26 (1) (2020) 1–16.

[218] D. Vats, J.M. Flegal, G.L. Jones, Multivariate output analysis for Markov chain Monte Carlo, Biometrika 106 (2) (2019) 321–337.

[219] M. Veraar, The stochastic Fubini theorem revisited, Stochastics An International Journal of Probability and Stochastic Processes 84 (4) (2012) 543–551.

[220] J. Vogrinc, W.S. Kendall, Counterexamples for optimal scaling of Metropolis–Hastings chains with rough target densities, The Annals of Applied Probability 31 (2) (2021) 972–1019.

[221] K. Wang, Z. Lu, X. Wang, H. Li, H. Li, D. Lin, Y. Cai, X. Feng, Y. Song, Z. Feng, et al., Current trends and future prediction of novel coronavirus disease (Covid-19) epidemic in China: a dynamical modeling analysis, Mathematical Biosciences and Engineering 17 (4) (2020) 3052–3061.

[222] Y. Wang, D.M. Blei, Frequentist consistency of variational Bayes, Journal of the American Statistical Association 114 (527) (2019) 1147–1161.

[223] Z. Wang, N. de Freitas, Predictive adaptation of hybrid Monte Carlo with Bayesian parametric bandits, in: NIPS Deep Learning and Unsupervised Feature Learning Workshop, vol. 30, 2011.

[224] Z. Wang, S. Mohamed, N. Freitas, Adaptive Hamiltonian and Riemann manifold Monte Carlo, in: International Conference on Machine Learning, PMLR, 2013, pp. 1462–1470.

[225] R. Wehrens, L.M.C. Buydens, Self- and super-organizing maps in R: the Kohonen package, Journal of Statistical Software 21 (5) (2007) 1–19.

[226] K. Xu, H. Ge, W. Tebbutt, M. Tarek, M. Trapp, Z. Ghahramani, Advancedhmc.jl: a robust, modular and efficient implementation of advanced hmc algorithms, in: Symposium on Advances in Approximate Bayesian Inference, PMLR, 2020, pp. 1–10.

[227] H.-C. Yang, Y. Xue, Y. Pan, Q. Liu, G. Hu, Time fused coefficient sir model with application to Covid-19 epidemic in the United States, Journal of Applied Statistics (2021) 1–15.

[228] J. Yang, G.O. Roberts, J.S. Rosenthal, Optimal scaling of random-walk Metropolis algorithms on general target distributions, Stochastic Processes and Their Applications 130 (10) (2020) 6094–6132.

[229] I.-C. Yeh, Modeling of strength of high-performance concrete using artificial neural networks, Cement and Concrete Research 28 (12) (1998) 1797–1808.

[230] J.H. Zar, Spearman rank correlation, Encyclopedia of Biostatistics 7 (2005).

[231] C. Zenger, W. Hackbusch, Sparse grids, in: Proceedings of the Research Workshop of the Israel Science Foundation on Multiscale Phenomenon, Modelling and Computation, 1991, p. 86.

[232] C. Zhang, B. Shahbaba, H. Zhao, Precomputing strategy for Hamiltonian Monte Carlo method based on regularity in parameter space, Computational Statistics 32 (1) (2017) 253–279.

[233] S. Zhao, Q. Lin, J. Ran, S.S. Musa, G. Yang, W. Wang, Y. Lou, D. Gao, L. Yang, D. He, et al., Preliminary estimation of the basic reproduction number of novel coronavirus (2019-ncov) in China, from 2019 to 2020: a data-driven analysis in the early phase of the outbreak, International Journal of Infectious Diseases 92 (2020) 214–217.

Index

A

A-HMC algorithm, 5
A-MHMC algorithm, 101
A-S2HMC algorithm, 101
Adaptive
  algorithm, 88, 98
    MHMC, 100
  method
    MHMC, 93, 98
    S2HMC, 84
  MHMC, 93
  scheme, 86, 90
    MCMC, 94
Adaptive Magnetic Hamiltonian Monte Carlo,
    93, 95, 100
Adaptive Neuro-Fuzzy Inference System
    (ANFIS), 109
Adaptive separable shadow hybrid
    Hamiltonian Monte Carlo algorithm, 85
Adjusted SIR model, 129
Airfoil dataset, 35
Alert levels, 137
Algorithm
  A-HMC, 5, 25
  A-MHMC, 101
  A-S2HMC, 101
  adaptive, 88, 98
    MHMC, 100
    separable shadow hybrid Hamiltonian
      Monte Carlo, 85
  Antithetic Magnetic Hamiltonian Monte
    Carlo, 102
  Antithetic Separable Shadow Hamiltonian
    Hybrid Monte Carlo, 103
  for iteratively doubling the trajectory length,
    24
  Hamiltonian Monte Carlo, 14

Locally Scaled Metropolis-Hastings Markov
    Chain Monte Carlo, 51
magnetic Hamiltonian Monte Carlo, 17
  with partial momentum refreshment, 64
Markov Chain Monte Carlo, 2
Metropolis adjusted Langevin, 2, 10, 52
Metropolis-Hastings, 2, 8, 9, 11
No-U-Turn Sampler, 21
  with Primal-Dual Averaging, 23
NUTS, 28, 161
parameter tuning, 38
partial momentum retention, 63
proposed, 92
  adaptive shadow, 83
Quantum-Inspired Hamiltonian Monte
    Carlo, 17
Quantum-Inspired Magnetic Hamiltonian
    Monte Carlo, 27, 54
S2HMC, 5
Separable Shadow Hamiltonian Hybrid
    Monte Carlo, 21, 112
  with partial momentum refreshment, 65
Shadow Magnetic, 75
  Hamiltonian Monte Carlo, 76
Stochastic Volatility Metropolis-Hastings, 51
vanilla Metropolis-Hastings, 51
Antithetic Hamiltonian Monte Carlo (A-HMC),
    5, 24
algorithm, 25
Antithetic Magnetic Hamiltonian Monte Carlo
    (A-MHMC), 101
algorithm, 102
Antithetic samplers, 101
Antithetic Separable Shadow Hamiltonian
    Hybrid Monte Carlo (A-S2HMC), 101
algorithm, 103

Approach
   Bayesian, 1, 28, 140, 150, 158
   Gibbs sampling, 153
ARD, 152
   committees, 112, 121, 169
   hyperparameters, 111
Area Under the Receiver Operating Curve
      (AUC), 37
Artificial neural networks (ANN), 109
Auditor General of South Africa (AG-SA), 149
Australian credit dataset, 35, 56, 57, 66, 68, 77,
      88
Automatic Relevance Determination (ARD),
      28, 110

B
Background, 73, 91, 109, 123, 139, 149
Baker-Campbell-Hausdorff (BCH), 74
Banana shaped distribution, 31, 87
Basic reproduction ratio, 123
Bayesian
   approach, 1, 28, 140, 150, 158
   framework, 1, 2, 27, 122, 123, 126, 138, 140,
         161, 162
      optimisation, 94
   logistic regression, 33, 44, 51, 92, 96, 100, 152
      datasets, 34
   quadrature, 6, 7
Bayesian Logistic Regression (BLR), 31
Bayesian Neural Network (BNN), 16, 33, 110
   datasets, 35
   re-training, 121
Benchmark datasets, 31, 33, 44, 96, 106, 108
Benchmark problems, 31
Bitcoin dataset, 34, 98
BLR dataset, 35, 89

C
Classification datasets, 33, 92
Compartment models for Covid-19, 125
Concrete dataset, 35
Conservation of energy, 13
Convergence analysis, 37
Covid-19, 125

D
Data description, 141, 150
Dataset, 35
   airfoil, 35
   Australian credit, 35, 56, 57, 66, 68, 77, 88
   Bayesian Neural Network, 35
   benchmark, 31, 33, 44, 96, 106, 108
   Bitcoin, 34, 98
   BLR, 35, 89
   classification, 33, 92
   concrete, 35
   German credit, 35, 57, 66, 70, 106
   Heart, 34, 70, 73, 77
   jump-diffusion process, 34
   logistic regression, 47, 96–98
   Pima Indian diabetes, 34
   power, 35
   Protein, 73, 77
   regression, 33, 35, 116, 120
   S&P 500, 34
   USDZAR, 34, 44, 98
   WASA meteorological, 114
Deep learning, 1
Density
   Neal's funnel, 32, 87
   shadow, 19, 84
   stationary target, 8
Derivatives from non-canonical Poisson
      brackets, 165
Description
   data, 141, 150
   experiment, 102, 142, 150
Deterministic quadrature methods, 6
Discretisation step size, 14, 110
Distribution
   Banana shaped, 31, 87
   equilibrium, 2, 8
   funnel, 32
   Gaussian, 2, 8, 32, 41, 58, 141
      multivariate, 31, 44, 51, 56, 60, 66, 73, 77,
            84, 86, 87, 89, 92, 95, 96
      prior, 33
   joint, 56
   marginal, 25, 153
   Poisson, 32, 139

posterior, 1–3, 8, 11, 31, 41, 42, 56, 91, 110,
        125, 126, 130, 131, 140
prior, 130
probability, 6, 16, 17
proposal, 8, 9, 41, 50
stationary, 7–9, 11, 159
target, 2, 39, 41–43, 53, 57, 58, 63, 66, 77, 82,
        84, 86, 96, 110, 140, 159, 160, 162
    posterior, 7, 10, 12, 22, 63, 94, 106, 142
Dynamics, 13, 16
    HMC, 19
    Langevin, 10, 140
    MHMC, 15, 74, 92

E
Effective Sample Size (ESS), 24, 36
Efficacy of restrictions, 137
Equilibrium, 8
    distribution, 2, 8
Euler-Maruyama integration scheme, 10
Experiment, 95
    description, 102, 142, 150

F
Financial ratio, 151
Financial Statement Fraud (FSF), 38
Five-level lockdown, 123
Forecasting, 28, 109, 122, 125, 161
FSF detection, 173
Funnel
    distribution, 32
    Neal's, 43, 44, 51, 84, 86

G
Gaussian
    distribution, 2, 8, 32, 41, 58, 141
        prior, 33
        proposal, 2
    targets, 70
German credit dataset, 35, 57, 66, 70, 106
Gibbs sampling, 25, 101, 112, 122
    approach, 153
    scheme, 14, 63, 153
Gross Domestic Product (GDP), 124

H
Hamiltonian
    shadow, 4, 5, 18, 19, 63, 66, 70, 73–75, 77, 83,
        84, 101, 105, 110, 118, 119, 160, 162
    vector field, 19, 74
Hamiltonian Monte Carlo (HMC), 2, 3, 11, 54,
        94
    algorithm, 14
    dynamics, 19
    Magnetic, 54, 100
    Quantum-Inspired Magnetic, 3, 42, 43, 54
Hamiltonian Monte Carlo With Partial
        Momentum Refreshment (PHMC), 28
Heart dataset, 34, 70, 73, 77

I
Infection data, 128
Integrator
    function, 92
    leapfrog, 13, 18, 19, 84, 92, 160

J
Jittered S2HMC (JS2HMC), 84
Johannesburg Stock Exchange (JSE), 149
Joint distribution, 56
Jump-diffusion model, 139
Jump-Diffusion Process (JDP), 31
    datasets, 34

L
Langevin dynamics, 10, 140
Leapfrog integration scheme, 13, 18, 19, 23, 85,
        105
Leapfrog integrator, 13, 18, 19, 84, 92, 160
Locally Scaled Metropolis-Hastings (LSMH),
        27, 41
Locally Scaled Metropolis-Hastings Markov
        Chain Monte Carlo algorithm, 51
Lockdown
    alert
        level 0, 131
        level 1, 136
        level 2, 135
        level 3, 135
        level 4, 135

level 5, 132
levels, 123, 124, 127, 128, 131, 136, 161
revised, 127, 128
five-level, 123
Logistic regression
Bayesian, 33, 44, 51, 92, 96, 100, 152
datasets, 47, 96–98
Bayesian, 34

M
Machine learning, 1, 162
methods, 109, 159
models, 1
Magnetic Hamiltonian Monte Carlo (MHMC),
4, 14
algorithm, 17
Magnetic Hamiltonian Monte Carlo With
Partial Momentum Refreshment
(PMHMC), 27
algorithm, 64
Marginal distribution, 25, 153
Markov chain, 2, 5, 7, 8, 24, 36, 76, 108
Markov Chain Monte Carlo (MCMC), 2, 6
algorithm, 2
estimators, 160
methods, 110
Mean Absolute Error (MAE), 38
Mean Square Error (MSE), 38, 117
Merton jump diffusion option pricing model,
140
Merton jump-diffusion process model, 32
Method, 128
adaptive MHMC, 93, 98
adaptive S2HMC, 84
deterministic quadrature, 6
machine learning, 109, 159
MCMC, 110
Monte Carlo, 5, 7, 63
NUTS, 91
shadow Hamiltonian, 4, 5, 77, 84, 160
SVMH, 42
Metropolis Adjusted Langevin Algorithm
(MALA), 2, 10, 52
Metropolis-Hastings (MH) algorithm, 2, 8, 9,
11

MHMC, 74, 91
adaptive, 93
dynamics, 15, 74, 92
Mix & Match Hamiltonian Monte Carlo, 110
Model
adjusted SIR, 129
jump-diffusion, 139
machine learning, 1
Merton jump diffusion option pricing, 140
Merton jump-diffusion process, 32
Momentum refreshment parameter, 66, 77
Monte Carlo, 6, 7, 9
estimate, 7
Hamiltonian, 11, 54, 94
Magnetic, 54, 100
Quantum-Inspired Magnetic, 3, 42, 43, 54
method, 5, 7, 63
Multilayer Perceptron (MLP), 33
Multivariate Gaussian distribution, 31, 44, 51,
56, 60, 66, 73, 77, 84, 86, 87, 89, 92, 95, 96

N
Neal's funnel, 43, 44, 51, 84, 86
density, 32, 87
No-U-Turn Sampler (NUTS), 3, 130
algorithm, 21
with Primal-Dual Averaging algorithm, 23
Numerical Weather Predictions (NWP), 109
NUTS algorithm, 28, 161
NUTS method, 91

P
Parameter
inference, 130
momentum refreshment, 66, 77
sampling, 110
trajectory length, 3, 4, 21, 91, 93, 104, 140
vol-of-vol, 57
Partial momentum
refreshment, 5
retention algorithms, 63
update, 5, 63, 70
Performance, 86
evaluation, 116
measure, 21, 37, 38

metrics, 35, 38, 43, 65, 102, 141
   predictive, 37
   sampling, 117
Pima Indian diabetes dataset, 34
Poisson distribution, 32, 139
Posterior
   distribution, 1–3, 8, 11, 31, 41, 42, 56, 91, 110,
      125, 126, 130, 131, 140
   targets, 2, 10, 11, 38, 41, 140, 141
   variances, 111, 113, 121, 167
Power dataset, 35
Predictive performance, 37
   with ARD, 120
Prior distributions, 130
Probability distribution, 6, 16, 17
Proposal distribution, 8, 9, 41, 50
   Gaussian, 2
Proposed adaptive shadow algorithm, 83
Proposed algorithm, 92
Protein dataset, 73, 77

Q

Quantum-Inspired Hamiltonian Monte Carlo
      (QIHMC), 3, 16, 42, 43
   algorithm, 17
Quantum-Inspired Magnetic Hamiltonian
      Monte Carlo (QIMHMC), 27
   algorithm, 54

R

Radial Basis Function (RBF), 109
Random
   sampling, 7
   trajectory length, 85, 89, 90
   walk Metropolis, 8
Re-training BNNs, 121
Receiver Operating Curve (ROC), 37
Recovery rate, 137
Regression, 118
   datasets, 33, 35, 116, 120
Reversibility, 13
Revised lockdown alert, 127, 128
Riemannian Manifold Hamiltonian Monte
      Carlo (RMHMC), 3
Root MSE (RMSE), 117

S

S2HMC, 164
   algorithm, 5
S&P 500 dataset, 34
Sampler
   antithetic, 101
   No-U-Turn, 130
Sampling
   behaviour, 10, 27, 63, 158, 159
   efficiency, 14, 15
   Gibbs, 25, 101, 112, 122
   parameters, 110
   performance, 117
   problem, 2
   process, 14, 63, 126, 162
   random, 7
   time, 153
Scheme
   adaptive, 86, 90
      MCMC, 94
   Euler-Maruyama integration, 10
   Gibbs sampling, 14, 63, 153
   leapfrog integration, 13, 18, 19, 23, 85, 105
Separable shadow Hamiltonian, 163
Separable Shadow Hamiltonian Hybrid Monte
      Carlo (S2HMC), 5, 18
   algorithm, 21, 112
Separable Shadow Hamiltonian Hybrid Monte
      Carlo With Partial Momentum
      Refreshment (PS2HMC), 27
   algorithm, 65
Severe Acute Respiratory Syndrome
      Coronavirus 2 (SARS-CoV-2), 123
Shadow
   density, 19, 84
   Hamiltonian, 4, 5, 18, 19, 63, 66, 70, 73–75,
      77, 83, 84, 101, 105, 110, 118, 119, 160,
      162
Shadow Hamiltonian Monte Carlo (SHMC), 19
Shadow Magnetic algorithm, 75
Shadow Magnetic Hamiltonian Monte Carlo
      (SMHMC), 28
   algorithm, 76
Smooth Hamiltonian function, 18
Sparse grids, 6

Stationary distribution, 7–9, 11, 159
Stationary target density, 8
Stochastic volatility, 32, 52, 139
Stochastic Volatility Metropolis-Hastings
    (SVMH), 27, 41, 51
  algorithm, 51
  method, 42
Susceptible Infected Recovered (SIR), 28, 125

T
Target
  distribution, 2, 39, 41–43, 53, 57, 58, 63, 66,
      77, 82, 84, 86, 96, 110, 140, 159, 160, 162
  Gaussian, 70
  posterior, 2, 10, 11, 38, 41, 140, 141
    distributions, 7, 10, 12, 22, 63, 94, 106, 142
Targeted Shadow Hybrid Monte Carlo, 110

Trajectory length
    parameters, 3, 4, 21, 91, 93, 104, 140
    random, 85, 89, 90

U
USDZAR dataset, 34, 44, 98

V
Vanilla Metropolis-Hastings algorithm, 51
Vol-of-vol parameter, 57
Volume preservation, 13

W
WASA meteorological datasets, 114
Wind Atlas for South Africa (WASA), 114
Wind power, 115
Wind speed, 115

Printed in the United States
by Baker & Taylor Publisher Services